# BIOECOLOGY
## OF
# THRIPS

*Andrethrips floydi.*Copyright Trustees of The British
Museum (Natural History).

# BIOECOLOGY

## OF

# THRIPS

**T. N. Ananthakrishnan**
Entomology Research Institute
Loyola College, Madras 600 034, India

## Indira Publishing House

*Publisher and Distributor of Books and Journals in Biological Sciences*
**P.O. BOX 37256, OAK PARK, MICHIGAN 48237-0256, U.S.A.**
**(313) 661-2529**

First Printing: 1984

Published by:
Indira Publishing House
P.O.Box 37256, Oak Park
Michigan 48237-0256, U.S.A.

Printed in U.S.A.
ISBN 0-930337-00-X

To

Aparna and Ashwini

# PREFACE

Thrips as a group have gained increasing importance over the years with their tendency to inflict significant damage to agricultural and horticultural crops through their numerical strength, their uncanny ability to occupy a variety of niches, as well as their ever-expanding host range resulting in polyphagous habits. Besides, their vector potential in causing bacterial, fungal, and viral diseases of plants has also been recognized. Such aspects as thrips and agroecosystems, reproduction strategies, host-prey/predator interaction, ecology of mycophagous and cecidcolous thrips, as well as thrips-host plant interactions appear essential parameters for providing an integrated picture of the bioecological aspects of thrips through consideration of a holistic approach to such studies.

In presenting this integrated picture of the bioecological aspects of thrips species inhabiting diverse habitats in various parts of the world, special attention has been paid to such aspects as (1) Thrips communities, (2) Thrips and agroecosystems, (3) Reproductive strategies and life cycles, (4) Ecology of gall thrips and Cryptophilous species inhabiting dead tree complex and litter, (5) Thrips and natural control agents and (6) Thrips and host plant interactions.

The significance of thrips communities comprising co-existing interdependent populations has been incorporated on the basis of information on wide range of habitats comprising leaf, flower, bark and litter and gall communities, particularly in terms of species associations, succession as well as regulation of populations. The diversity of resources available in a community naturally determines the variety of opportunities for ecological diversification within it. The role of thrips in agroecosystems has been emphasized in relation to cropping systems such as involved in cereal, pulses, oilseeds and plantation crops, wherein the abundance, the pattern of distribution of various host plants involving the crops as well as their alternate weed hosts in space and time, have been highlighted. As such the chapter on agroecosystems presents a picture of dynamism involving the crop plant and weeds as well as thrips infesting them.

Information on the ecology of gall inhabiting thrips as well as of mycophagous thrips serves to complete the ecological gamut in terms of the habitat diversity enjoyed by thrips. The multifacted approach to our understanding of the boecological aspects of thrips also necessarily involves their co-evolution with plants, their ability to act as pollinators as well as on the extent of host specificity enjoyed by the different species. These aspects have been considered rather exhaustively in the Chapter on Thrips-host plant interactions. Consideration has been given to the fact that the relationship between food plants, thrips populations, competition and coexistence appear to be essential parameters in the organization of communities. The role of mono-, oligo- and polyphagy in thrips has been discussed particularly in view of polyphagy having

ecological implications, as it tends to prevent over-exploitation of preferred plant species, enabling a more even feeding pressure on available
resources. An assessment of thrips-host plant interactions has been made
in the light of such aspects as stage of development of host and time of
attack, source of infestation and build-up of thrips populations, host
plant strategies and regulation of thrips populations and host plant
resources in terms of gall formation and co-evolution of thrips and their
host plant families.

This work was undertaken during the tenure of the Nehru Fellowship
awarded to me by the Jawaharlal Nehru Foundation, New Delhi. In addition
to facilities made available by the Foundation, several other organiza-
tions also provided assistance in completing this work. These include
visits to several institutions in the United States during the summer of
1981; British Council Bursary to visit the British Museum of Natural
History, London; the Rothamstead Experimental Station, Harpenden; the
Overseas Pest Research Centre; and the Commonwealth Institute of Entomology, London. I wish to express my deep sense of appreciation of the
gesture on the part of Nehru Foundation which enabled me to finalize most
of my work.

In enabling me to examine material, to undertake field work, hold
discussions, as well as for making available a host of literature on
thrips and Insect-plant relations, my most sincere thanks are due to:
Dr. Trevor Lewis of the Rothamstead Experimental Station, Harpenden;
Dr. Lawrence Mound of the British Museum of Natural History, London;
Dr. N.C. Pant, Director of the Commonwealth Institute of Entomology,
London; Dr. R.F. Chapman of the Overseas Pest Research Centre, London;
Dr. Michael Irwin of the Illinois Natural History Survey, Urbana;
Dr. Lewis J. Stannard formerly of the Illinois Natural History Survey;
Prof. Frank Young of the University of Indiana, Bloomington; Prof. James
Howell and Miss Ramona Beshear of the University of Georgia, Agricultural
Experimental Station, Experiment; Prof. William L. Peters of the Florida;
A & M University, Tallahassee; and Prof. J.D. Shorthouse of the
University of Sudbury, Canada.

The assistance rendered by my students in this Institute in several
ways, deserve particular mention. My special thanks are also due to Mr.
Mohan Daniel for his help in the preparation of the Appendices and to
Prof. E.T. Haridass for his help in photography. For reading through the
manuscripts and for helpful discussions, I wish to extend my sincere
appreciation to Dr. A. Raman of this Institute. The services of the
artist, Mr. S. Mahadevan, of Dr. G. Suresh for preparing the index and of
Mr. G. Sampath for typing the manuscripts are gratefully acknowledged.
Last but not least, I wish to record my indebtedness to the authorities
of the Loyola College whose sustained interest in my work all these years
has been a source of encouragement.

Entomology Research Institute
Loyola College, Madras.                T.N. ANANTHAKRISHNAN

CONTENTS

# INTRODUCTION

Thrips are comparatively small-sized insects of considerable economic importance, often referred to as 'fringe wings', 'bladder feet',
'thunder flies', and 'storm flies'. They are mostly phytophagous, mycophagous or predacious, extending over a wide range of habitats mostly in
the tropical, subtropical and temperate regions, and speedily exploit
suitable niches resulting in their increased damage potential. What they
lack in size, they easily make up by their numbers and by their aggregate
feeding, cause severe damage to young leaves, buds, blossoms, fruits and
seeds. Many polyphagous species often build up reservoirs in weed hosts
from where they periodically migrate to crop plants. Species like *Thrips
hawaiiensis*, *Thrips tabaci*, *Scirtothrips dorsalis*, *Frankliniella schultzei*, *Megalurothrips distalis*, *Heliothrips haemorrhoidalis*, *Selenothrips
rubrocinctus*, to mention but a few, have been recorded on numerous host
plants both in this country and abroad, many of these not constituting
hosts in the real sense of the term. *Taeniothrips atratus*, for instance
in England, has been recorded on more than 500 hosts, though breeding
actually takes place only on very few host plants. Many species of
*Thrips*, *Taeniothrips*, *Frankliniella*, *Sericothrips*, *Caliothrips*, *Haplothrips* are polyphagous distributed in various parts of the world. The
scale of air-borne dispersal being considerable, fluctuations in populations or numerical abundance within a given habitat often results from
immigration and migration, as well as through subsequent breeding and
mortality.

Because of the fringed nature of the wings, thrips are included
under the order Thysanoptera (*thysanos*-fringe) possessing a peculiar
asymmetrical 'punch and suck' mouth parts with vestigial right mandible,
and protrusible bladder at the apex of the tarsi of legs. Two principal
groups or suborders are recognized: (a) the Terebrantia with wings lying
parallel to each other, bearing veins, crossveins and setae on veins,
generally with an ovipositor (absent in *Uzelothrips* Hood, and reduced in
merothripids) and with only a single pupal stage, and (b) the Tubulifera
with wings overlapping, not bearing cross veins, without an ovipositor
and with two pupal stages. It is beyond the scope of this work to de-
scribe morphological and taxonomic details, as many monographic works on
these aspects are available, some of the more recent contributions being
those of Priesner (1949, 1960, 1964), Stannard (1957, 1968), Ananthakrishnan (1969, 1974), Mound et al. (1976), and Schleiphake (1979).
However, to stress the degree of structural diversity within the group, a
passing mention is made in the next chapter of some notable instances of
their structural complexity in order to appreciate the trends of adaptive
specialization, which provide a basic understanding for biosystematic and
bioecological investigations.

## SYSTEMATIC POSITION AND PHYLOGENETIC TRENDS

Thysanoptera are believed to have evolved from litter-dwelling pso-
copteroid ancestors sometime in the lower Permian and to constitute the

sister group of Hemiptera (Heming, 1979). Earlier, Stannard (1957, 1968) indicated their forming a distinct part of the Hemiptera-Corrodentia unit. However Heming's (1979) work on the embryogenesis of *Haplothrips verbasci* clearly reveals their closeness to the Psocoptera-Phthiraptera and Homoptera complex as regards segregation of the germ cells and the direct development of the gonads. The similarity of the antennal sense cones of some thrips, aphids and philotarsid Psocoptera, the absence of ocelli in the larvae and in the reduction of the malpighian tubules to four, the homology of the maxillary stylets of thrips with the chisel-like lacinia of Corrodentia, as well as the great similarity in the wing venation of Terebrentia and Zoraptera and Psocoptera were stressed by Stannard (1957, 1968). From the evolutionary point of view, Heming (1971) considers that the thysanopteran pretarsus most closely resembles that of the nymphal cercopids and cicadids, the only difference being that the arolium is protrusible in larval thrips and not in cercopid nymphs. Because larval thrips lack tarsomeres, the ungues of each leg articulate with the distal end of the tibia, and Heming hypothesizes that the prototype thysanopteran was a plantigrade insect with a pretarsal mechanism consisting of two clawlike ungues, a median arolium, and a two-segmented tarsus. An excellent discussion on the evolutionary considerations of thysanopteran praetarsus is provided by Heming (1971).

Grinfel'd (1959) suggests a correlation of development of the right mandible with a corresponding reduction on the left, so that the single mandible serves as a more efficient tool for piercing pollen. From this he infers that the early Thysanoptera may have evolved into a distinct order in the pollen feeding niche. He postulates that the evolution of thrips fauna occurred through pollen feeding and till the angiosperms evolved successfully in the mid-Cretaceous and that thrips could have fed only on the pollen and spores of gymnosperms. Fossil material has not offered specific evidence of the early trends in the evolution of the group, and though *Permothrips longipennis* was considered for quite some time as the earliest known fossil, its status as a thysanopteran was rejected by Sharov (1972) and replaced by his genus *Karaotothrips*, whose position as a member of the Thysanoptera was subsequently doubted by Mound *et al.*, (1980). Studies on the mandibular ontogeny by Heming (1980) have shown that as the left mandible became progressively adapted for punching, its base narrowed and its primary articulations with the head capsules were lost so that it bacame more flexibly joined to the head so that it could protract and retract. Investigations on the differentiation of the mandibles in embryos of *Haplothrips verbasci* and in some Hemiptera seem to provide evidence to the fact that Thysanoptera and Hemiptera are sister groups. It is further presumed that both the groups have evolved from a common stem having small, paired mandibles, short lacinial stylets, a weakly developed cibarial pump, and prominent maxillary and labial palpi (Heming 1980). In view of the right mandible degenerating before it began to differentiate into a stylet-forming organ, its evolutionary loss probably occurred after splitting of the Thysanopteran and Hemipteran lines presumably as an adaptation to mycophagy in the leaf-litter habitat, in which Thysanoptera are believed to have originated (Heming, 1980; Mound and O'Neill, 1974). Taking an over-all picture, the placement of Thysanoptera before the Hemiptera in the phylogentic sequence appears reasonable in view of the retention of maxillary and labial palps and the possession of simplified maxillary stylets.

# CLASSIFICATORY TRENDS

Following the early attempts at classification of the group by
Bagnall (1912), Hood (1915), Karny (1921, 1922), as discussed in the ana-
lysed version on the landmarks in the classification of the group
(Ananthakrishnan 1969, 1979), Priesner (1949) proposed a system involving
four super families under the Terebrantia (Aeolothripoidea, Melan-
thripoidea, Heterothripidea, and Thripoidea), the family Thripidae
including the subfamilies Thripinae and Heliothripinae. The Tubulifera
included the only family Phlaeothripidae, with the subfamilies Phlaeothripinae, Hyidiothripinae, Megathripinae, Pygothripinae, and Urothripinae. Stannard (1957) recognized only the Phlaeothripinae and the Megathripinae, although Priesner (1960) also added the Urothripinae as the
third subfamily. Hood (1955) erected the family Uzelothripidae to include the unique genus *Uzelothrips*. For reasons of priority Wilson
(1975) retained the family name Panchaetothripinae over the Heliothripinae, and Mound (1974) similarly used Idolothripinae in preference
to Megathripinae. In an incisive discussion on the phylogenetic relationships between the families of recent Thysanoptera Mound *et al.*,
(1980) proposed a classification involving the rearrangement of the
generally accepted Heterothripidae into three distinct families:
Heterothripidae, Adiheterothripidae and Fauriellidae, and retained Uzelothripidae as a distinct family. The basic features of this classification are indicated in Table 1 (after Mound *et al.*, 1980).

TABLE 1. An outline classification of Thysanoptera (After Mound *et
al.*, 1980).

    Order:
THYSANOPTERA
    Suborder:
TEREBRANTIA
    Family:
UZELOTHRIPIDAE - Antennae 7 - segmented, thin. Fore wings without
    cross veins marginal cilia from sockets ovipositor absent.
MEROTHRIPIDAE - Antennae 9 - segmented, moniliform, without style; 3
    and 4 with tympanum-like sensory areas. Ovipositor very weak,
    degenerate.
AEOLOTHRIPIDAE - Forewings broad and rounded at apex bearing longi-
    tudinal veins and cross veins. Antennae 9 segmented, 3 and 4
    with elongated sensory areas. Ovipositor always curved upwards.
FAURIELLIDAE - Sensory areas on 3 and 4 not continuous.
HETEROTHRIPIDAE - Sensory areas on 3 and 4 segments of antennae in
    the form of simple, or convolute bands.
ADIHETEROTHRIPIDAE - Antennal segments 3 and 4 each with the broadly
    based conical trichome.
THRIPIDAE - Ovipositor well developed, always curved downwards.
    Antennae 6-9 segmented, style 1-3 segmented, fore wings more
    pointed, mostly with distinct veins and setae on veins.
    Subfamily:
THRIPINAE - Dorsum of body not polygonally reticulate, atmost with
    transverse striae. Terminal antennal segments short and thick.
PANCHAETOTHRIPINAE - Dorsum of body deeply polygonally reticulate.
    Terminal antennal segments long, thin and needle-like.

Suborder:
TUBULIFERA
Family:
PHLAEOTHRIPIDAE
Subfamily:
PHLAEOTHRIPINAE - Maxillary stylets uniformly thin.
Subfamily:
IDOLOTHRIPINAE - Maxillary stylets thickened, band-like.

Mound and Palmer (1982) have since, proposed a detailed classi‐
fication of the spore feeding Idolothripinae.

## EVOLUTIONARY TRENDS WITHIN THE GROUP

Within the family Aeolothripidae, primitive traits are reflected in
the broad wings bearing veins and cross-veins, the nine-segmented antennae without sense cones, and the laterally located gonopods. Though it
is generally presumed that the Merothripidae, Heterothripidae, and Thripidae evolved from this primitive *Aeolothrips*-like ancestor, it may be
pointed out that *Erotidothrips* has an almost similar wing, though not as
broad, but species of *Merothrips* have very narrow wings as in Thripidae.
From this it may also be presumed that the wings of both Aeolothripidae
and Thripidae could have developed from a wing similar to that of *Erotidothrips* (Mound and O'Neill, 1974). Although some of the merothripids,
ex., *Damerothrips*, *Erotidothrips*, and *Praemerothrips* and the Heterothripidae retained the nine-segmented antennae and flat, membranous sensoria
as in some aeolothripids, progressive evolutionary trends are indicated
in the loss of some wing veins and development of glandular areas on the
abdominal sternites of males. The upwardly directed ovipositor and
cocoon-breaking spurs are typical of aeolothripids, whereas the downward-
ly curved ovipositor and narrow wings are characteristics of Thripidae.
Mound and O'Neill (1974) have suggested that the chaetotaxy of the
seventh sternite of Aeolothripidae and Thripidae could be derived from
the Merothripidae by the progressive fusion of the seventh and eighth
sternites. The primitiveness of this trait in the Merothripidae as compared to that in the Aeolothripidae suggests that the earliest Thysanopteran lacked a large ovipositor. However, the absence of a functional
ovipositor is not typical of merothripids alone, but also of the Uzelothripidae and Phlaeothripidae. Adaptive radiation in the Tubulifera is
well evident with many phlaeothripines invading a wide variety of niches
and showing phytophagous, cecidicolous, mycophagous as well as predatory
habits. In view of their gradual establishment in the saprophytic fungal
zone, the Phlaeothripidae feeding on fungal spores radiated into a number
of phyletic lines, and by Oligocene they appear to have emerged as a
full-fledged family (Stannard, 1957). It is from adopting a mostly cryptophilous existence that many of the structural differences between the
two suborders arose.

An assessment of the phylogenetic relationship within the Phlaeothripidae is considerably difficult, particularly because no other group
presents such a diverse variety of structural modifications as in Tubulifera, which also comprise so many closely intergrading genera that it is
often difficult to fix the transitional species. In the Cryptothripini,
for instance, the individual genera intergrade considerably and one of
the best examples is the *Nesothrips* complex involving a host of such

genera (Mound, 1974). Similarly, many genera such as *Adelothrips*, *Poly-phemothrips* and *Apelaunothrips* are intermediates between the Phlaeothrip-inae and Idolothripinae, and do not fit in the established definition of the two subfamilies. The broad maxillary stylets, a specialization for spore feeding, have appeared in more than one phyletic line of Thysan-optera (Mound, 1974) and genera such as *Adelothrips*, *Polyphemothrips*, and *Empresmothrips* could have evolved from a *Hoplothrips*-like ancestor among the Phlaeothripinae. However, the spore-feeding group Idolothripinae, although by itself is holophyletic, probably evolved within Phlaeothrip-inae (Mound and Palmer, 1982).

Whether the Phlaeothripidae are independently derived from the Pro-tothysanoptera or constitute a sister-group of the Thripidae is an open question (Mound *et al.*,1980), but the phylogenetic relationships between Panchaetothripinae and Phlaeothripinae cannot be ignored.

### GEOGRAPHIC DISTRIBUTION

Several species of thrips enjoy a wide distribution, being mostly transported from continent to continent through human agency. Polyphag-ous species of economic importance known to enjoy such a wide distribu-tion are *Frankliniella schultzei*, *Thrips tabaci*, *Heliothrips haemorrhoid-alis*, and *Selenothrips rubrocinctus*. Viewed from a wider perspective, some species as *Limothrips cerealium*, *Haplothrips tritici* and the like have a comparatively restricted distribution, while species like *Scirto-thrips aurantii*, *Scirtothrips citri*, *Taeniothrips laricivorus*, *Sciothrips cardamomi* are totally restricted to small pockets in West Africa, Calif-ornia, Europe and Southern India respectively. Several mycophagous spe-cies are typical of tropical areas being more abundant in the Oriental, and parts of the Neotropical regions. The fauna of the Indian region comprises several elements derived from diverse sources such as Ethiopian and Indo-Chinese, Malaysian, as well as autochthonous ones (Ananthakrishnan, 1981a) and species from extreme North bordering the Himalayan regions have Palaearctic affinities. Sometimes colour forms exist particularly in the vector species such as *Frankliniella schultzei* and *Thrips tabaci* which are widely distributed. For instance, *Frankliniella schultzei* has its dark form distributed mainly south of the Equator, while its pale forms occur mainly north of the Equator. Both colour forms seem basically allopatric in distribution. India, Philippines, New Guinea and Northern Australia and in the Sudan-Uganda-Kenya belt, mixed colonies of both colour forms are often found on the same host plants (Sakimura, 1969).

Abundance of endemic species is very characteristic of the Oriental, Neotropical and Ethiopian regions, and a large number of species known from the European part of the USSR are distributed throughout the Holarc-tic region (Dyadechko,1977). The Nearctic and Palaearctic regions are characterised by more recent elements. It is interesting that the major-ity of the endemic thrips fauna of Central Asia form part of the bio-coenoses of arid regions, a part of which is related to the fauna of North African origin and a small part to the Oriental fauna. The Central Asian region (Uzbekistan, Kazhakastan, Turkmenia, etc.) according to Dyadechko(1977), is a powerful centre of formation of thrips fauna of arid areas and there is a very rapid formation of new species and subspe-cies. Southern Europe or the Mediterranean region appears to be the primary reserve of Steppe fauna, Eastern Europe and Siberia having species spread from Western Europe.

The Australian fauna is of particular interest from the view point of spore feeding thrips not being isolated from the surrounding areas, and several species are known from New Guinea and Queensland. But in those phlaeothripine species feeding on native Australian plants like *Casuarina, Geijera,* and phyllodinous *Acacia* species, there is strict endemicity and none of the 25 genera of phlaeothripids from these three plant genera have so far been recorded from outside Australia (Mound, 1974). A more detailed critical assessment of the zoogeography of thrips is bound to produce valuable information on the origin and evolution of the group.

* * * * *

## DIVERSITY SPECTRUM AND DAMAGE POTENTIAL

Thysanoptera are well-associated with different types of plant for-
mations, and are known to be very susceptible to environmental changes.
The main body of the Terebrantia continued to live in the leaf and flower
niches, whereas the Tubulifera became adapted to both phytophagous as
well as mycophagous habitats, and quite a number of species became associated with plant galls. The widespread nature of the fungal feeding
habitat has had a considerably strong impact on the biology of thrips,
their dispersal patterns, and resultant speciation. The fluctuations in
the habitat combined with internal environmental factors have positively
stimulated the evolution of structurally diverse series of forms, very
characteristic of Thysanoptera in general, and the Tubulifera in particular. The spectrum of diversity involving both the general structure
as well as adaptive trends in relation to their habitats are discussed
briefly in this chapter.

Thrips offer a wide range of structural diversities, many being
brightly coloured, some bicolorous or tricolorous, others with a variety
of shades form pale yellowish white to very dark and blackish forms with
considerable red to crimson subhypodermal pigment, often, more conspi-
cuous in larvae. The cuticle of many species is beautifully sculptured,
mostly with raised polygonal reticulations or transverse striae (Plate
2). In size they may range from very minute forms (*Uzelothrips*,
*Merothrips*, *Leucothrips*, *Asprothrips*, *Ascirtothrips*, *Enneothrips*,
*Halmathrips* among Terebrantia; *Smicrothrips*, *Hyidiothrips*, *Nanothrips*,
*Sophiothrips* among Tubulifera, all less than 1 mm in length) to moderately large-sized species belonging to the genera (*Bactridothrips*,
*Tiarothrips*, *Mecynothrips*, *Kleothrips*, *Elaphrothrips* etc., (10-14 mm).
Incidentally, the largest terebrantian species so far recorded is
*Psectrothrips delostomae*, while *Arachisothrips* presents the most unthysa-
nopterous appearance with greatly inflated and reticulated forewings
looking like those of a tingid. Some are bizarre looking, and hence of
interest, involving such genera as *Veerabahuthrips*, *Carcinothrips*,
*Androthrips*, *Hartwigia*, *Rhinoceps*, *Leptogastrothrips*, *Franklinothrips* to
mention the more striking ones. In *Andrethrips floydi* the entire body
is armed with many long, barbed setae placed on elongate tubercles
(*Plate 1*); *Hartwigia* has a head greatly swollen dorsally, almost rounded
and with very short prothorax; *Carcinothrips* has forelegs so grotesquely
modified as to look like the claws of a crab; *Franklinothrips* has a
rounded head partially retracted within the prothorax. Countless
examples are available to show the great diversity of form in thrips
which have contributed to the continued interest in the study of this
group the world over. An unusual phenomenon relates to the unbelievably
fantastic patterns of diversity within many species of Tubulifera making
species-recognition a difficult task, unless done by a competent worker on
the basis of a large series of individuals from diverse populations.

The shape of the head is equally diverse, ranging from a small rec-
tangle in dendrothripids, to several times longer than wide as in several

8

Idolothripines, such as *Megalothrips*, *Aesthesiothrips*, some *Polyphe-mothrips*, *Mecynothrips* etc. In some species as *Tiarothrips subramanii* there is a very long head process, much longer than the head, in the extreme males; *Rhinoceps* has the head produced between antennae, into a prominent, laterally flattened horn as long as the combined lengths of the first two or three antennal segments; *Kaleidothrips* has two prominent horns about the insertion of antennae. The eyes may be well-developed or reduced to 3 or 4 ommatidia as in some apterous species of *Allothrips*. More infrequently they may be large and ventrally prolonged as in *Lep-togastrothrips*, large and confluent as in *Macrophthalmothrips*, laterally bulging prominent structures as in *Exophthalmothrips*, or with very little interocular space as in *Holopothrips* etc. The mouth cone

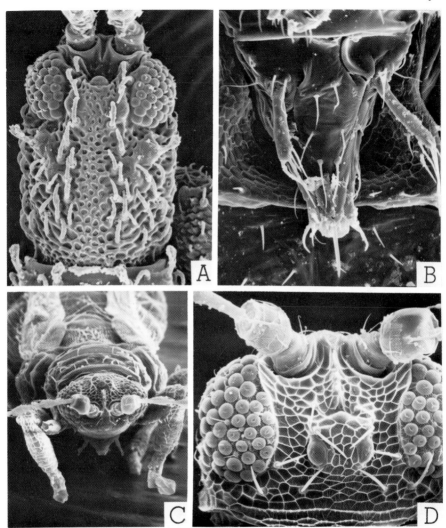

Plate 2. SEM photograph to show- A: Head of *Thilakothrips babuli* female; B: Mouth cone of *Thilakothrips babuli* showing maxillary and labial palps, mandible and sensory setae; C: Frontal view showing feeding posture of a Panchaetothripine; D: Dorsal surface of head showing reticulation and ommatidia. C,D Copyright, Trustees of the British Museum (Natural History).

with parts adapted for punching and sucking may vary from a very short and broad type (*Antillothrips*, *Bamboosiella* and *Matilethrips*) to very long, broadly rounded or narrowly pointed (*Rhamphothrips*, *Rhinothripiella*, *Perissothrips*, *Sedulothrips*, *Poecilothrips*, *Bunothrips*) ones; very rarely as in *Calamothrips* it is extremely narrow and elongated. The maxillary stylets are always confined to the mouthcone in the Terebran-

10

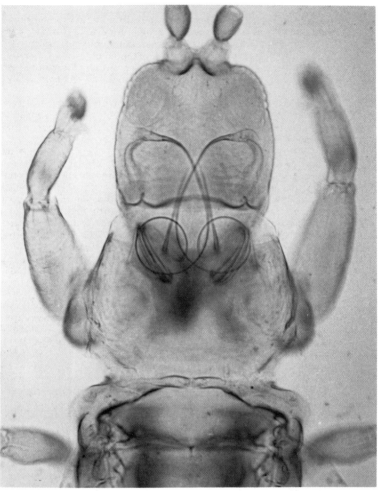

Plate 3. Casuarina feeding species showing long,coiled maxillary
stylets, Copyright Trustees of the British Museum (Natural History).

tia, even when the mouthcone is much elongate. In the Tubulifera they
may be short and confined to the mouthcone (*Bamboosiella*, *Antillothrips*)
or elongate and very deeply retractile within the head, and long and
highly convolute as in some of the *Casuarina*-feeding species of
*Adrothrips*, *Heligmothrips*, etc. (Plate 3). The antennae are mostly 7, 8
or 9 segmented, rarely 4-6 segmented or even lesser as in some urothripids. In form, the segments range from very short, stocky, globose
structures (*Allothrips*) to very long, narrow ones as in *Franklinothrips*
and *Meiothrips*. The sensory apparatus on antennal segments, particularly
on 3 and 4, may be in the form of transverse, band-like, pale areas
(*Merothrips*) or more elongated, narrow or convolute (aeolothripids, or
as continuous porous bands (heterothripids), or as emergent trichomes,

forked or simple as in thripids and panchaetothripines, and always simple in the Tubulifera. *Taeniothrips aethiops* has very long forked sense cones in the males; very long sense cones also occur in *Aesthesiothrips*, *Eupathithrips*, while *Ecacanthothrips* has often a circlet of sense cones on segment 3; *Zactinothrips elegans* has peculiar antennal sensoria on 3rd and 4th segments, with numerous minute elliptical or clubbed setae.

The forelegs particularly in the males of mycophagous species show profound diversity resulting in the development of bizarre forms with strikingly enlarged parts, with varying degrees of expression of armature, from forms with very weak unarmed forelegs (gynaecoids) to those with an unimaginably grotesque (oedymerous) nature. The wings may be very narrow and parallel-sided as in urothripids, or broad and parallel-sided (aeolothripids), or expanded distally (*Mymarothrips*), or twisted (*Stictothrips*) or more elaborately developed, pea-nut shaped, bulged and balloon-like as in *Arachisothrips*. Totally wingless forms are known in very few genera as *Leptogastrothrips*, *Emprosthiothrips* etc. The apex of the abdomen in some panchaetothripines as *Dinurothrips* and *Panchaeto-thrips* is typically tube-like. Though the term Tubulifera indicates that the last segment is often drawn into a tube, it may be broad and swollen (*Pygothrips*) or very narrow and much elongate as in *Leeuwenia*, *Holurothrips* and others, as also urothripids or extremely short as in some species of *Apterygothrips* (Plates 4A & 4B).

Added to these structural complexities, thrips are endowed with remarkable reproductive strategies involving uni-, and multivoltine species, parthenogenetic (thelytokous, arrhenotokous and amphitokous) as well as sexually reproducing species. Instances of ovoviviparity in species of *Bactridothrips*, *Elaphrothrips*, *Tiarothrips subramanii*, etc. appear to be adaptations for shortening the life cycles to enable the young to complete the cycle before the food is exhausted, (Bournier 1957, 1966; Ananthakrishnan and Viswanathan, 1973; Lewis, 1973 ; Ananthakrishnan *et al*, 1983). Adaptive aspects of reproduction are also evident in *Thilakothrips babuli*, the *Acacia*-gall thrips which completes its life cycle more quickly within inflorescence galls than in their normal rosette leaf galls (Varadarasan and Ananthakrishnan 1981a). Most Terebrantia lay eggs singly within plant tissues, the Tubulifera laying eggs on any suitable substratum, singly or in small clusters. Some species of *Chirothrips* lay eggs partly embedded in the leaf tissue. Gregarious species lay hundreds of eggs in flat clusters. Adaptive radiation is well evident in thrips (Ananthakrishnan, 1979a) and the subsocial behaviour is being increasingly recognized in many mycophagous, idolothripine Tubulifera, showing tendencies towards subsocial behaviour.

## FOOD AND FEEDING HABITS AND DAMAGE POTENTIAL

While the majority of thrips species are phytophagous and mycophagous, predatory species feeding on thrips, mites, coccids and psocids are not uncommon, indicating some potential for their use as biocontrol agents (Ananthakrishnan, 1976). Some species occur within the galleries of termite mounds along with the grass seeds (Jacot-Guillarmod, 1964). Phytophagous species which may be phyllophilous (leaf-inhabiting), anthophilous (flower-inhabiting) and cecidicolous (gall-inhabiting) are generally associated mostly with angiosperms. Very rarely thrips are subaquatic like *Organothrips bianchii*, the tarothrips, infesting

Plate 4A. Thrips with a swollen tube.

cultivated and wild *Colocasia esculenta* plants growing in stagnant water
and living in the slime collecting in the crevices at the bases of the
thick, fleshy, overlapping stalks, a few centimetres above the water
level (Sakimura and Krauss, 1944, 1945; Lewis, 1973; Titschack, 1969).
Another such species is *Iridothrips mariae* living in the axils of reeds
and which can move along subaquatic parts (Pelikan 1961; Dyadechko,
1977).

Records of the incidence of thrips on bryophytes, pteridophytes and
gymnosperms also exist. Moss and lichen inhabiting species are rare,
*Lissothrips muscorum* being the well-known species, the other occasional
intruders recorded being from the genus *Bournierothrips* inhabiting moss
in West Africa and *Aptinothrips stylifer* on dry lichen and heath.
Fern-infesting species though limited, are comparatively more in number,
some of the well known species being *Monilothrips kempi*, *Indusiothrips
seshadrii* and *Scirtothrips pteridicola*. Several mycophagous species are
known to live on fungus-infested, dry or decaying vegetation, dead wood,
bark, leaf litter, drying grass tussocks, feeding on fungal spores or

Plate 4B. *Leeuwenia* showing a very long and narrow tube.

hyphae and their breakdown products mostly of Ascomycetes and
Coelomycetes, and rarely of Hyphomycetes. Species infesting dead wood
are associated with early stages of fungal attack, before the wood
becomes soft, waterlogged and ant-infested (Mound, 1974). While the
majority of mycophagous Tubulifera inhabit a variety of niches,
(Ananthakrishnan 1973; Mound 1974, 1976), some terebrantian species like
*Euphysothrips minozzi* feeding on spores of wheat rust *Puccinia graminis*,

14

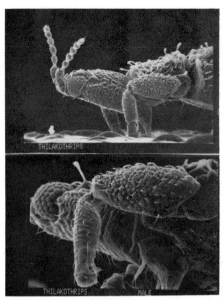

Plate 5. SEM of *Thilakothrips babuli*- Side view to show feeding posture.

*Megaphysothrips subramanii* on the coffee leaf rust *Hamileia vastatrix*, *Chaetanaphothrips signipennis* on the banana leaf rust and *C.orchidii* on the red rust of bananas, are known to play a vector role. *Thrips tabaci* are known to carry powdery mildews. Spores of *Alternaria, Aspergillus, Drechslera, Torula, Anthostomella, Melanographium, Pestalotia, Lasiodiplodium*, to mention but a few, are carried by several species of sporophagous Tubulifera. Instances of transmission of bacterial and viral pathogens are also known, *Thrips tabaci* and *Frankliniella schultzei* being the recognized vectors of the tomato-spotted wilt virus (Ananthakrishnan 1973, 1980b; Mound 1973; Sakimura 1964) and *Scirtothrips dorsalis*, the chilli-thrips observed recently as a vector of the bud necrosis virus of groundnut (Ghanekar *et al.*, 1978). Thrips are also frequently associated with structural abnormalities referred to as 'galls', of active plant tissues caused by the secretion and injection of salivary substances while feeding. Several gall-inhabiting thrips are known mostly from the tropics, these galls occurring mostly on the leaf blade and axillary and terminal buds, the younger plants and juvenile plant tissues being more susceptible to gall-formation.

For a better understanding of the ability of thrips to exploit diverse niches for feeding and breeding, an idea of their feeding habits would appear important. When the mouth cone is short as in most Terebrantia and some Tubulifera, there is hardly any penetration of stylets and so the feeding is often of the shallow-type, resulting in the rupture of only the epidermal and a few superficial mesophyll cells. Species with longer mouth cones as in the Tubulifera have the penetrative mode of feeding, extending deeper into the leaf tissues, but rarely reaching the vascular tissues. (Plate 5) The musculature of the head as

Plate 6. Damage to onions by *Thrips tabaci*.

well as those around the pharynx by their contractile and pumping action
aid in the ingestion of cell sap. The maxillary stylets have a 'tongue
and groove' system on either side and fit into each other along their
length. The two grooved maxillary stylets form a tube through which the
liquid contents are sucked up (Mound, 1971a). The degree of infestation
of phytophagous species often depends on microclimatic conditions,
physiological age, the degree of protection available, water stress,
quality of food as well as intra-, and interspecific competition (Lewis,
1973). Environmental stress resulting in the weakening of the plant
makes it susceptible to infection. Most species concentrate their
feeding activities to restricted regions on the plants, but some like
*Thrips tabaci* infest the bulbs, leaves and flowers of onion and the
entire vegetative parts of the cotton plant. (Plate 6) The age of the
leaves is often important and though very young leaves are susceptible,
species like *Retithrips syriacus*, *Caliothrips indicus* etc., infest their
principal host plants only after they have reached a certain stage of
growth and have become mature. Galls are inititated in plants during
early stages of plant/organ development mostly at a time when the tissues

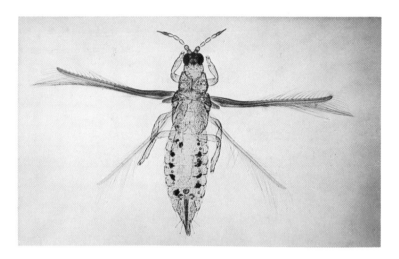

Plate 7. *Indusiothrips seshadrii (Top)*, *Panchaetothrips indicus*, (Bottom).

are not fully differentiated. Sometimes definite patterns of distribution of thrips are observed as in the case of *Selenothrips rubrocinctus* which are localised along the basal midrib and primary veins or in the distal intervenal areas of the lamina or in the immediate vicinity of injured tissues (Fennah, 1965) and many other species like *Caliothrips indicus* show a vertical stratification on the host plants. While thrips occur mostly on the lower surfaces of leaves, particularly where there is shade, they also move on to the upper surface when unshaded or exposed and they occur on both sides, displaying often a correlation between the stomatal frequency and infestation factor (Ananthakrishnan, 1955). Many thrips infesting cereals occupy different positions on the plant during different times of the day, often seeking

Plate 8. *Rhipiphorothrips cruentatus* showing damage to rose leaves (left) and cashew leaves (right).

shelter in the leaf sheaths and panicles. Details pertaining to aspects of thrips-host plant relations and choice of specific niches are discussed in a later chapter.

In terms of feeding of thrips on various plant parts, it may be said in general that, while leaf feeding species often move about, those confined to sheaths of plants tend to be confined to their immediate niches. Species like *Limothrips cerealium* cause considerable damage to other plants (*Hordeum vulgare*) when the ears are still confined to their leaf sheaths. *Stenchaetothrips indicus* within sugarcane sheaths, *Anaphothrips sudanensis* within the leaf sheaths of *Pennisetum*, *Eleusine* and *Zea mays*, *Sorghothrips jonnaphilus* within *Sorghum* leaf sheaths, are well-known Indian species. *Haplothrips apicalis* is also a typical

Plate 9. - 1. Castor leaf showing damage by *Retithrips syriacus*
2. Female, 3. Pupae, 4. Male.

grass-sheath inhabitant confined to *Cynodon dactylon*. While species
inhabiting open leaf habitats are many, such species like
*Stenchaetothrips biformis*, and *S.bambusae* occur within rolled leaves of
paddy seedlings and bamboo spindles respectively. Species infesting pine
cones and needles, like *Taeniothrips laricivorus* in Europe, *Oxythrips
kochummani* and *Apterygothrips pini* in India and species feeding on
*Casuarina* referred to earlier are also of interest.

Among several species infesting leaves of economically important
plants causing recognizable damage are the soyabean thrips, *Sericothrips
variabilis* and *Frankliniella tritici* in the United States, the
chilli-thrips *Scirtothrips dorsalis* long known to inflict extensive
damage to chilli crops in India, the coffee thrips *Scirtothrips bispinosus*
in India and *Diarthrothrips coffeae* in Africa; leaves of the cotton plant
in India, Africa and the United States are severly infested by
*Scirtothrips dorsalis*, *Thrips tabaci*, *Frankliniella tritici*, *F.fusca* to
mention the major species. Peanut 'pouts' are caused by *Frankliniella
fusca* in the United States resulting in the inhibited development of the
peanut plants in the very early stages (Poos, 1941). The flax thrips of
Europe, *Thrips angusticeps* and *Thrips linarius* breed on *Linum* sp., the
former species in its brachypterous condition hibernating in the soil and
destroying young flax plants. Feeding by the larvae of the macropterous
generation of *T.angusticeps* as well as *T.linarius* result in spotted

19

Plate 10 Cardamom fruits showing different stages of attack by *Sciothrips cardamomi*.

leaves, swollen terminal shoots and retarded growth (Frannsen & Mantel
1961, 1962, 1965). The well-known panchaetothripine species
Panchaetothrips indicus infesting the leaves of turmeric,
Rhipiphorothrips cruentatus abounding on the leaves of grapevine, rose,
almond, cashew etc., Retithrips syriacus on the leaves of rose, castor
and cassava, Selenothrips rubrocinctus on cocoa, cashew and mango leaves,
Helionothrips kadaliphilus on banana and colocasia leaves, Caliothrips
indicus on the leaves of groundnut are notable examples of phyllophilous
species with considerable damage potential (Plates 8 and 9).

Anthophilous or flower infesting species feed on pollen and floral
parts including the stamens, pistil and nectaries. The more common
flower feeders in India are Thrips hawaiiensis, Megalurothrips distalis,
Frankliniella schultzei, Haplothrips ganglbaueri, Microcephalothrips
abdominalis, Thrips flavus, Haplothrips tardus and Taeniothrips simplex.
Many species of Thrips, Taeniothrips, Frankliniella and Haplothrips are
well established flower inhabitants in Europe and America. Frankliniella
parvula and F.musaeperda are reported to severly damage banana flowers
and inflorescences of Compositae and Amarantacae, while Taeniothrips
simplex is confined to liliaceous plants. Thrips feed on sepals, petals,
anthers, stigma, ovary, fruits and seeds, and ripe grains. Species of
Chirothrips like C.mexicanus, C.manicatus, C.hamatus, C.pallidicornis,
C.falsus are well known seed-feeding species (Doull, 1956; Lewis 1973;
Ananthakrishnan and Thirumalai, 1977). Adults of Limothrips cerealium
often get lodged in the crease of grains causing scars in wheat, as also
L.denticornis in barley, and Stenothrips graminum in oats in the United
Kingdom, Europe and the United States of America. L.denticornis
introduced from Europe into the United States of America is known to
cause the typical 'goose neck'-like stalk in these seeds, with reduction
in plump kernels, (Post & Colberg, 1958), while the oat thrips
Anaphothrips obscurus causes sterility in oats, the basal parts of
coleoptiles withering due to severe attacks. Haplothrips tritici, the
wheat thrips, inflicts serious injuries to young leaves and ears of wheat
all over Europe, while Haplothrips ganglbaueri, the rice thrips causes
chaffiness of grains in India. Young earheads of Sorghum, Pennisetum and
Zea mays in India are infested by Chirothrips mexicanus, Exothrips
hemavarna, Florithrips traegardhi etc.

The larvae of Kakothrips robustus, the pea thrips of Europe do more
damage than the adults to the pods, flower buds and terminal shoots
effecting a 20% reduction in seed yield. When small, the pods become
sticky, under-sized, curled and covered by silvery brown areas and turn
blackish through fungal attacks (Frannsen, 1960). Tender panicle stalks
of cardamom subject to attack by heavy populations of Sciothrips
cardamomi, become stunted resulting in shrivelled and aromaless pods
(Plate 10). Odontothrips confusus and Thrips flavus cause sterility of
lucerne flowers by feeding on keel petals, and the flowers are damaged
with the stamens trapped inside the shrivelled keel petals. Scirtothrips
aurantii is responsible for 'russety marking', 'thrips marking' or
'tear-staining' resulting in shrinking and malformation of fruits in the
United States of America and Africa. Several terebrantian species are
known to cause serious damage to fruit crops and some like the pear
thrips Taeniothrips inconsequens, Frankliniella tritici etc., prevent
fruit formation in prunes, apple blossom, cherries, apricots, peaches
etc.; distorted, scarred and cracked fruits result from feeding on

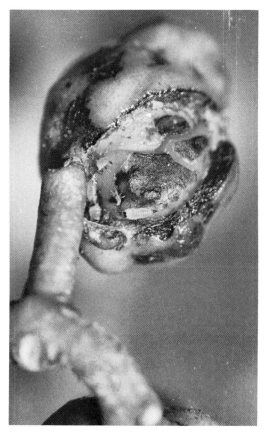

Plate 11. A damaged fruit of *Syzygium jambolanum* showing the immature stages of *Mallothrips indicus*.

blossoms or on young fruits. Serious infestations of *Mallothrips indicus* on *Syzygium jambolanum* are also known (Plate 11).

It is not proposed here to provide an exhaustive account of thrips as crop pests, in view of the more detailed accounts provided by Ananthakrishnan (1971, 1973) and Lewis (1973). However, it has to be recognized that most of the pest species ranging around a few hundred species belong to the Terebrantia. While some species are typically monophagous, many others are oligophagous and many crops support numerous species ranging from a few to as many as 23 species on a single host plant. Very few species attack the same crop in widely separated parts of the world, the best examples being *Thrips tabaci* on onions, *Caliothrips sudanensis* and *Caliothrips impurus* on cotton, *Taeniothrips simplex* on gladiolus, *Selenothrips rubrocinctus* on Cashew, and *Heliothrips haemorrhoidalis* to mention a few. In view of the more efficient systems of communication and transport, the spread of thrips to great distances has been quicker so that many exotic species get introduced in different countries of the world. An exhaustive list of the economically important species of the thrips of the world is provided in Apendix I.

* * * * *

## THRIPS COMMUNITIES

Enumeration of the number of species as well as of populations of individuals of different insects inclusive of thrips inhabiting diverse habitats enables an assessment of the degree of diversity in different communities (Whittaker, 1962, 1967; Lewis, 1973; Futuyma, 1973; Poole, 1974; Price, 1975; Pianka, 1978). The effective number of species present either in a community or a portion of a community or over a broad geographic area, constitutes species diversity (Hill, 1973). Plant and animal communities comprise a functional system of interacting species forming a collection of individual-dispersed species (Poole, 1974), each with different degrees of tolerance to physical and other factors. The distribution and commonness of each species of thrips as of other insects, in general, is different from the distribution and abundance of any other species. Thrips populations are not limited to one plant community, but may spread to many and no two distribution patterns are alike, so that it is often difficult to precisely define associations in a community. The pattern of distribution of such species of thrips inhabiting Compositae as *Microcephalothrips abdominalis*, *Frankliniella schultzei*, *Haplothrips tardus*, *Haplothrips gowdeyi* etc., varies with the succession of the weed-hosts. *Microcephalothrips abdominalis* is dominant in *Wedelia chinensis* from May to November and with the decline of the flowering season of *Wedelia*, *Synedrella nodiflora* starts blooming, followed by *Ageratum conizoides* so that the continuous availability of host-plants prevents the decline of thrips populations, but the patterns of distribution of thrips varies with the host. Diversity tends to lead to stability under stable physical factors and species diversity increases from simple communities of early succession to richer communities of late succession. This is also evident in the diversity of mycophagous thrips in a mature tropical forest such as the Western Ghats. Stability is difficult when only a few species exist and as suggested by MacArthur (1955), complexity of food web 'buffers the community' against change and leads to stability. Paine (1966) suggests that diversity is related to the number of predators in the system and their efficiency in preventing single species from monopolising limited resources.

While species diversity and complexity of association among species are essential for the stability of a community, an understanding of the components of diversity would be useful in assessing community diversity. Basically they involve (a) the number of species and their relative importance (b) intra-, and interhabitat diversity (c) Diversity of resources, average utilisation and overlap (Pianka, 1978). The actual number of species and their relative importance are measured by their relative abundance. While the number of species in a sample is easy to determine, a natural community is an open system without a fixed number of species and hence the term 'species richness' is often used. The total number of species is variously referred to as 'species richness or species diversity', while their relative importance is judged by equitability and evenness. The distribution of individuals among species involves evenness, while richness is measured in terms of the number of species of samples  generally of constant size.  Direct counts of species numbers in samples have been equally considered the most effective richness measure.  Diversity is therefore dependent not only on the number of species in a collection, but also on the relative abundance of each species.  A community with all its species of about equal population density is more diverse than any other community of the same number of species, but with some species common and others rare.

Regarding intra- and interhabitat diversity and diversity in relation to utilization of resources, it may be indicated that those with a greater number of effective habitats support more species as in the case of the tropical forest ecosystem, provided a larger area is sampled, so that the 'turn over' in species composition from region to region within an area is greater in those with more effective habitats.  This has been defined as 'between habitat diversity' (MacArthur, 1965; Pianka, 1978), to distinguish from diversity of species found together within only a given habitat (within habitat diversity), such as a bamboo clump or leaf litter localized in a given area.  It is interesting that 30 species of Glyptothripini alone were collected in a single, comparatively large area of a forest in Southern Brazil less than 50 km in diameter (Mound, 1977). Whittaker (1965) refers to these as  α and β diversity, indicating that the total diversity in a heterogeneous area includes both between-habitat and within-habitat components.  There is always a certain degree of overlapping or intergrading of habitats with one another and this is very

Plate 12. Larvae and adults of *Mallothrips indicus* swarming on the bark of *Syzygium jambolanum*.

characteristic of ecotones such as those found bordering the forest habitat with that of grasslands.

The great mobility of thrips within-, and between- habitats is exemplified by *Isoneurothrips australis* on a single gum tree (*Eucalyptus calycogona*) in Southern Australia (Laughlin, 1970; Lewis, 1973). The movement of thrips to and from the tree reflected the cycle of flower production. Immigration of thrips to the tree from elsewhere was massive and an almost equal number was accounted for this local emergence from the ground. It is still an enigma as to how the population on the whole tree is regulated, and as Lewis (1973) indicates, perhaps most of the emerging adults flew away from the tree before settling to feed and reproduce, due to their inability to tolerate overcrowding. A similar instance of a massive invasion relates to *Mallothrips indicus* on *Syzygium jambolanum* where the entire tree trunk, branches and leaves had severe infestation to the extent that populations of individuals over flowed on to the pavement below (Plates 12 & 13).

Plate 13. Larvae and adults of *Mallothrips indicus* swarming on the bark of *Syzygium jambolanum* (a portion of the bark enlarged).

The diversity of resources available in a community determines the variety of opportunities for ecological diversification within it. Communities with restricted resources as in comparatively smaller niches will naturally support fewer species than those with greater variety of resources. However as the degree of utilization of available resources by an average species increases, the number of species that can coexist within a community decreases. A community with greater overlap will support more species than one with less overlap simply because more species use each of the resources. This is very true of thrips infesting crops in cultivated lands particularly along their marginal zones where wild vegetation exists. Diversity also depends on the extent of saturation of species as well as the niche dimensions.

It is possible to measure the rate of increase in the number of species to the increase in sample size. Of the more commonly used measures of diversity is the William's index of diversity ($\alpha$) (1944) obtained from $S = \alpha \log_e (1 + \frac{N}{\alpha})$ where S is the number of species, N is the number of individuals, provided sampling is random and frequency of species distribution conforms to a logarithmic series (Lewis, 1973). The greater the value of $\alpha$, the more the diversity and richer the community; larger the sampling period, greater the diversity, because species appearing in different seasons would be involved. Samples taken at different times of the day show varying values because species are active at different times of the day. The same is the case with indices for collection in the same area in spring, summer and late summer (1.2, 2.6, and 2.4) (Lewis, 1973). Diversity of thrips communities in tropical forest habitats appear greater than the richest temperate grasslands. Lewis (1973) indicates that as a result of water trap catches for a few common flower-dwelling species, 18,900 individuals involving 33 species, gave an overall index of 4.2. Tree and bark-dwelling species with 8300 specimens and 22 species gave a value of $\alpha$ as 2.8. In closed communities such as within galls, the indices vary from very low values 0.78 to 2.17. Analysis of data pertaining to ten species recorded within galls of *Acacia harpophylla* (Mound, 1973) with 216 individuals gave a value of 2.17, while lower values were obtained for *A.aneura*, *A.pendula*, and *A.oswaldi* with 1.06, 1.09, and 0.78 respectively. Indices of diversity in rich natural or seminatural habitats with over 30 species vary from 4.5 to 8.5, though higher values have been indicated for subtropical and tropical rain forests. It must also be indicated that though different communities may have similar indices of diversity the species composition may be different, mostly caused by differences in the plant species present. These results are comparable with those obtained from different communities such as (a) a single flower community as in *Ruellia tuberosa* involving six species with a total number of 821 and 1078 individuals during the years 1972 and 1973, and with an index of 0.879 and 0.838, (b) a dense thrips community from dense Bamboo clusters obtained from Palghat (Kerala, India) with 14 species and 787 individuals, the diversity index being 2.42, (3) a forest floor community in Tenmalai ranges of Western Ghats (Kerala, India) comprising 27 species with an index of 6.6. Some of the forests in Eastern Ghats of Southern India, with 32 species gave a value of 9.0.

Among other indices is the Shannon-Weaver index which assumes that a random sample is taken from an infinitely large population and that all

the species in the community poplulation are represented in the sample.
This index, however, is not dependent on sample size. Some species
groups association require a similar set of environmental factors for
their reproduction and survival and are not spatially discrete, because
many species overlap in their distribution. The degree of similarity
between samples has to be guaged with samples belonging to the same association and expressed by Sorenson's Similarity Quotient (QS), also
used by Kontakkannen in his studies on leaf hoppers (1950).

$$QS = \frac{2\ C\ x\ 100}{ab}$$

where $a$ is the number of species in sample $B$ and $C$ is the number of species common to both samples. When communities have a QS less than 50%
they are arbitrarily considered to be distinct, but the margins of these
communities cannot be identified. It must also be noted there that an
insect population is not limited to one plant community, but may spread
over many, and this is very true of the several oligophagus species of
thrips.

It was mentioned earlier that both species diversity and complexity
of associations are essential for species stability. Restricted diet
such as in one prey and one predatory system lowers stability, while a 4
or 5 species system will involve different pathways so that stability
will increase as links increase. A large number of species each with a
fairly restricted diet or a smaller number of species, each consuming a
wide variety of species will increase stability. In other words the
modes of nutrition or partitioning of available resources among individuals within ecological communities is a major determining factor in the
diversity of coexisting species. *Schedothrips orientalis* occurring
within galls of *Ventilago maderasapatana*, is an interesting example of
predator/prey interaction in a thrips community. Involved in this
interaction are predatory bugs, predatory thrips, some arachnids like
pseudoscorpions and spiders as well as a larval parasite.

## NATURE OF THRIPS COMMUNITIES

1. *Phyllophilous communities* - We may recognise four principal communities, (i) the grassland, (ii) crop, and (iii) forest, which are open
communities, and (iv) plant galls which form closed communities. While
these primary habitats harbour their own representative communities of
thrips, there exist several microhabitats as well, very often influenced
by local differences in microclimate as evident in the inflorescence of
angiosperms, within grass sheaths, cracks and tissues of dead wood, under
fallen leaves, etc. Similarly differences in thrips communities exist in
arid and semi-arid areas as well as in valleys and at higher altitudes,
the overall causes of diversity being the diversity in plant communities
which are largely determined by the physical environment including the
soil induced differences in microclimate. Oettingen (1942) has indicated
that the richness of the grassland fauna is affected by microclimate produced by soil and floral diversity. Changing the botanical composition
with fertilizers also eventually changes the nature and composition of
thrips communities. For a proper visualization of community structure
especially in cereal crops, consideration of the total environment
involving crops, grasses and other wild vegetation comprising numerous
weed species appears to be a basic necessity. Thrips communities in such
crops like rice, wheat, *Sorghum* etc., result from the segregation of a

few local species associated with related plants and their adaptation to
the crop, which often presents very similar, but vastly improved condition for existence (Uvarov, 1964). Besides continually migrating to
the crops, these weeds still continue to serve as reservoirs of thrips
communities enabling replenishment of species whenever populations go
down due to artificial control methods. Regarding the communities of
thrips in grassland/weed and cultivated fields, the generalization indicated by Bey Bienko (1961), Uvarov (1964) appears practical, and could be
visualized as (a) that there are more than twice as many species in the
grassland/weeds as there are in wheat/rice/sorghum fields, (b) that the
density of population in a cereal field is almost double that of the
grassland. (c) that the number of dominant and constant species in the
grassland is twice that of the cereal fields, (d) that there is a greater
specific variety on the population of grasslands and a better numerical
balance between its species, while in the cereal fields a few species
became dominant, and (e) that most of the dominant species in cereal
fields are major pests. The dominance of these pests in cereal fields
appears to be due to the substantial decrease in the numbers of predators
and parasites particularly in newly cultivated fields.

Bey-Bienko (1961) observed only 1.07 *Haplothrips tritici* in an $m^2$ of
grassland, while in the wheat field, they were of the order of $300.40/m^2$.
On the other hand, Tansky (1961) showed the presence of an average of
4994 individuals/$m^2$ of wheat *Haplothrips tritici* forming 89-99% indicating
its adaptation to the wheat plants where natural enemies were far fewer
than in uncultivated grasses. Recent studies on the population of thrips
infesting graminaceous and cyperaceous weeds in paddy, sorghum, ragi
fields around Madras (Ananthakrishnan & Thangavelu, 1976; Ananthakrishnan
& Kandaswamy, 1977; Ananthakrishnan & Thirumalai, 1977, 1978) have
identified an almost similar picture, the dominant species in paddy being
*Haplothrips ganglbaueri*, *Florithrips traegardhi* in *Sorghum* and
*Chirothrips mexicanus* and *Exothrips hemavarna* in *Pennisetum*.

The close relationship between such weeds as *Echinochloa crusgalli*,
*E.colona*, *Cyperus iri*, *C.rotundus* and *C.difformis* and paddy as well as
*Chloris barbata* in *Sorghum* and maize fields has been discussed by
Ananthakrishnan and Thirumalai (1977, 1978), and will be elaborated in
the Chapter on Thrips and agroecosystems. The thrips community in the
same crop may have a different composition, ecological succession and
dominant species in various parts of the world, in view of widely varying
environmental conditions. As indicated by Lewis (1973), the wheat crop
is the best example to illustrate this. *Haplothrips tritici* is the
dominant species in Eastern and Southern Europe, *L.cerealium*, *Frankliniella tenuicornis*, and *Haplothrips aculeatus* in Scandinavian countries,
where the population of the different species depends on whether the crop
is a winter or autumn cereal. In India *Anaphothrips sudanensis* is the
wheat thrips, while it is *Prosopothrips cognatus* which occurs in some
parts of the United States. Species of *Chirothrips* forming well-
established communities on different types of grasses in various parts of
the world, causing profound seed damage are *Chirothrips mexicanus* and
*C.flavus* on Bermuda grass in Arizona, *C.manicatus* and *C.hamatus* on
timothy grass in Sweden, *C.mexicanus* and *Exothrips hemavarna* in India.
Changes in the patterns of community structure in thrips are often
noticed and examination of the composition of grass species and their

TABLE 1. Numerical relationships of Thrips communities in cultivated crops.

| | | | in 50 Panicles | | | | 1/8 m² of soil grass sods | Tender cob of corn (50) |
|---|---|---|---|---|---|---|---|---|
| Species | Oats June | Rye June | Wheat | | | Meadow Grass | | |
| | | | A May | B June | C June | | | |
| Aeolothrips intermedius | – | 29 | – | – | – | – | – | 76 |
| Anaphothrips obscurus | – | 42 | 21 | – | – | – | – | – |
| Anaphothrips secticornis | – | – | – | – | – | – | – | 1 |
| Aptinothrips elegans | – | – | – | – | – | 18 | 2 | – |
| Aptinothrips rufus | – | 3 | 2 | – | 42 | – | 31 | – |
| Aptinothrips stylifer | 1 | – | – | – | – | – | 6 | – |
| Belothrips acuminatus | – | – | – | – | – | – | – | – |
| Chirothrips aculeatus | – | – | 17 | – | – | – | – | – |
| Chirothrips hamatus | 1 | – | – | – | – | – | – | 1 |
| Chirothrips manicatus | 67 | 18 | – | – | – | 719 | 62 | – |
| Chirothrips pallidicornis | – | – | – | – | – | – | – | *1* |
| Frankliniella tenuicornis | 46 | – | 41 | 309 | 75 | 11 | – | 46 |
| Haplothrips aculeatus | 12 | 493 | 118 | – | 32 | 9 | 27 | 212 |
| Haplothrips tritici | – | 1 | 442 | 1175 | 921 | – | – | – |
| Limothrips cerealium | – | 7 | – | – | – | – | – | – |
| Limothrips denticornis | 42 | 67 | 158 | 7 | 73 | – | – | 4 |
| Limothrips schmutzi | – | – | – | – | – | – | – | – |
| Rhipidothrips gratiosus | 24 | – | – | – | – | – | – | – |
| Stenothrips graminum | 317 | – | – | – | – | – | – | – |

(modified from Dyadechko, 1977)

thrips inhabitants in 10 m$^2$ area from different localities would illustrate this. Results will naturally indicate that changes in composition of thrips communities result from changes of host plant composition, essentially due to indirect effects on the host by weather conditions. Thrips communities in graminaceous crops being regarded as an integral part of the grassland communities of the area even during the non-cropping season, an idea of composition, and/population dynamics species in the latter would appear essential in view of their maintaining a population reserve. Dyadechko (1977) has shown the numerical relationship of thrips communities in cultivated crops, oats, wheat and grasses in USSR summarized as in Table 1. Oettingen (1942) records 90

TABLE 2 - Thrips Composition in Grassland Communities
(only major species included)

| Germany (Van Oettingen, 1942) | India (Ananthakrishnan & Sen 1980) |
|---|---|
| Aeolothrips fasciatus | Allelothrips pandyani |
| Anaphothrips obscurus | Allelothrips sudanensis |
| Aptinothrips rufus | Antillothrips graminellus |
| Aptinothrips stylifer | Antillothrips malabaricus |
| Chirothrips hamatus | Apterygothrips pellucidus |
| Chirothrips manicatus | Bolacidothrips graminis |
| Frankliniella intonsa | Caliothrips graminicola |
| Frankliniella tenuicornis | Caliothrips impurus |
| Haplothrips acanthoscelis | Caliothrips luckmani |
| Haplothrips aculeatus | Caliothrips striatopterus |
| Limothrips denticornis | Caprithrips orientalis |
| Stenothrips graminum | Chirothrips maximi |

| England (Pitkin, 1976) | |
|---|---|
| | Chirothrips meridionalis |
| | Chirothrips mexicanus |
| | Danothrips setifer |
| | Ernothrips lobatus |
| Aeolothrips albocinctus | Euphysothrips minozzi |
| Anaphothrips obscurus | Exothrips anolis |
| Apterothrips secticornis | Exothrips hemavarna |
| Aptinothrips elegans | Haplothrips apicalis |
| Aptinothrips karnyi | Haplothrips bagnalli |
| Aptinothrips rufus | Haplothrips clarisetis |
| Aptinothrips stylifer | Haplothrips ganglbaueri |
| Bolacothrips jordani | Haplothrips gowdeyi |
| Cephalothrips monilicornis | Haplothrips talpa |
| Chirothrips aculeatus | Melanthrips affluens |
| Chirothrips hamatus | Melanthrips baileyi |
| Chirothrips manicatus | Melanthrips indicus |
| Chirothrips molestus | Neolimothrips brachycephalus |
| Frankliniella tenuicornis | Phibalothrips peringueyi |
| Haplothrips aculeatus | Podothrips graminum |
| Limothrips cerealium | Podothrips moultoni |
| Limothrips denticornis | Podothrips placitus |
| Limothrips schultzei | Podothrips scitulus |
| Rhaphidothrips longistylosus | Praepodothrips nigrocephalus |
| Stenchaetothrips dispar | Segnothrips trivandrensis |
| Stenchaetothrips graminum | |

species from grassland habitats in North Germany and 26% fed solely on Poaceae. Ananthakrishnan and Sen (1980) list about 83 species of which about 40 species are known to feed exclusively on Poaceae (49%) while 10% occurs in dried grass clumps feeding on fungi. A general picture of thrips composition indicating some of the major species in grassland communities in India, England and Germany is given in Table 2. A distinct change in species composition is evident particularly in view of the obvious differences in grass composition. Thrips communities therefore show diversity in relation to plant species.

The distribution patterns of phytophagous thrips on the leaves of many crop plants appear to be essential elements in an understanding of the behaviour of thrips communities. For instance, studies on soybean thrips in Urbana, indicated that three major species *Sericothrips variabilis, Frankliniella fusca* and *Frankliniella tritici* accounted for more than half of the arthropod species (Irwin et al., 1979). *Sericothrips variabilis* and *Frankliniella tritici* were unevenly distributed on the soybean plants. All stages of *F.tritici* were concentrated in terminal buds and blossoms. (Fig. 2) Adults of *S.variabilis* were found most commonly on the uppermost, fully-expanded trifoliate or the trifoliate immediately below it. Larvae of *S.variabilis* were generally concentrated on from 3rd to 6th trifoliates below the terminal bud. (Fig. 2) An almost similar pattern has been observed in a thrips community living on the castor plant *Ricinus communis* around Madras, involving 7

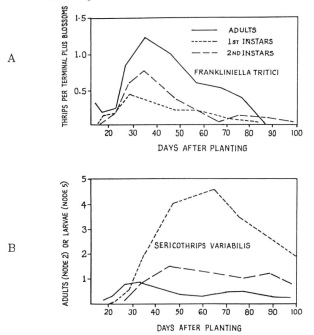

Fig.1. Seasonal distribution of *Frankliniella tritici* (A) and *Sericothrips variabilis* (B) in a Soyabean field, Illinois (after Irwin 1976).

32

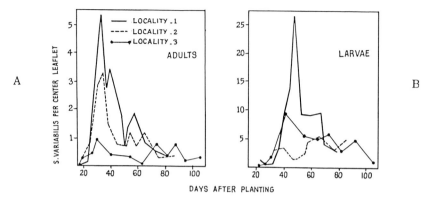

Fig.2. Seasonal abundance of *Sericothrips variabilis*. A–Mean numbers of adults from central leaflet of upper most expanded trifoliate. B–Mean numbers of First and Second instars per centre leaflet of 3,4 and 6 trifoliate below the terminal (Irwin *et al.* 1979)


species, *Retithrips syriacus, Scirtothrips dorsalis, Zaniothrips ricini, Toxothrips ricinus, Astrothrips tumiceps, Ayyaria chaetophora* and *Rhipiphorothrips cruentatus* indicative of site restriction on the host-plant, with a characteristic pattern of vertical distribution. *Toxothrips ricinus* and *Scirtothrips dorsalis* are restricted only to the buds and tender leaves of the first and second nodal leaves respectively while the leaves from fourth to seventh nodes show a mixed population of the other species (Fig. 3).


 *2. Anthophilous communities* – Aggregations of heavy thrips populations are generally met with in the flowers and inflorescences of several plants, some invariably not being the host for the larvae, the aggregating behaviour being perhaps to ensure that the sexes are brought together for mating (Morison, 1957; Lewis, 1973). Interesting information on both individual species occurring within flowers as well as on species complexes have enabled a better understanding of the distribution patterns, population dynamics and the species succession. While *Thrips imaginis* and *Isoneurothrips australis* from Australia and *Megalurothrips sjostedti* in Africa provide ideal instances of the dynamics of single species, multiple species complexes occur in *Cyperus papyrus* in Africa, in lucerne in Europe and India, in *Glyricidia maculata* and *Ruellia tuberosa* and several members of Compositae from India, to mention a few well-known instances.

Anthophilous thrips communities involving a single species showing abundant fluctuations as in *Thrips imaginis* infest roses in Australia, where populations were observed to be large in November, declining rapidly with the advance of summer and continuing to decline through winter, until the trend got reversed with the onset of spring (Andrewartha, 1971). Adults and larvae live on a wide variety of weeds and garden plants. The number of flowers in an area fluctuates regularly with seasons, long and dry summers producing very few flowers, with pro-

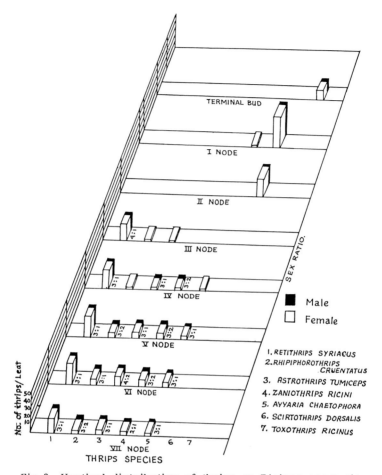

Fig.3. Vertical distribution of thrips on *Ricinus communis*.

fuse flowering in spring decreasing in winter, so that seasonal changes
in the access to food appear related to changes in the abundance of
thrips communities. The need for anthophilous thrips to disperse in view
of the limited duration of the flowers in inflorescences appear important. Variation in thrips activity was evident everyday, with the movements in and out of the flowers, more thrips moving out into the surrounding fields where they were breeding, and subsequently finding their
way into newly opened rose buds. As a result of partial regression studies it was found that the independent influence of temperature was
highly significant, and that on an average the number of thrips in
flowers on any one day increased by 5% for every one degree rise in the
daily maximum atmospheric temperature. Prior to the onset of flowering,
infestation commenced with flying adult populations from alternate host
plants, followed by their rapid rate of reproduction enabling population
build-up.

Two very good examples of this spurt in thrips activity are also illustrated by the work of Taylor (1969, 1974) on cowpea flowers infested by *Megalurothrips sjostedti* in Nigeria, and of Laughlin (1970) on the gum tree thrips, *Isoneurothrips australis* in Australia. Studies on population of thrips on the early and late crops of cowpea showed that infestation was initiated by immigrant populations from a large number of alternate host plants species, mostly belonging to Fabaceae (Papilionaceae), in the pre-flowering stage. Population build-up to a peak occurred within 12-34 days and was influenced by the rate of flower production, variety and season, with a positive correlation between total population of thrips and cumulative number of flowers (Taylor 1974). Studies on the growth and decline of numbers of adults, eggs and larvae of *Isoneurothrips australis* revealed that soon after feeding, maturing and oviposition by the adult females, the developing full-grown second larva drops off the gum tree and enters the soil; on emergence from the soil, the adult returns to the flower. Invasion of flowers by adults was from outside, of the order of about 2000 thrips each day, the arrival rate being often higher. It is evident that the number of thrips arriving, duration of stay and numbers leaving could be influenced by the number of flowers on the tree.

In his studies on the abundance and flower preference of thrips in Japan, Kudo (1971) indicated the presence of a more or less definite structure and phenology of thrips assemblage with a limited number of dominant species such as *Chirothrips manicatus*, *Frankliniella intonsa*,

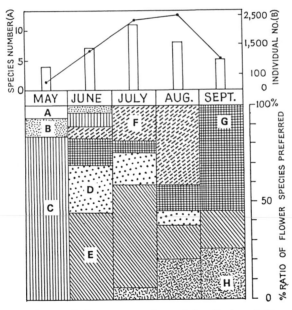

Fig.4. Phenology of flowers preferred by thrips (after Kudo, 1971): A - *Viola glypoceras*, B - *Arabis japonica*, C - European dandelion, D - White clover, E - Red clover, F - *Rosa rugosa*, G - *Lathyrus maritimus*, H - *Vicia* spp.

*Haplothrips niger* and *Haplothrips chinensis*, each with a characteristic flower preference, either wide as in *Frankliniella intonsa* or narrow and specialized to legumes as in *H.niger* and *Megalurothrips distalis*. Of a total number of 5473 individuals sampled, the most predominant were *H.niger* and *H.chinensis* forming 35% of the total followed by *Frankliniella intonsa* and all the three species constituted 95% of the total individuals (Fig. 4). Similar studies on the ecological succession of thrips species on *Ruellia tuberosa* in Madras revealed the relative duration of different thrips species within the flowers so as to recognize them as primary, secondary and tertiary inhabitants. *Haplothrips gowdeyi*

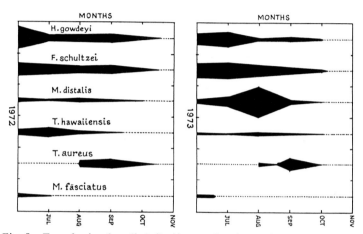

Fig.5. Trends in the distribution and succession of thrips within flowers of *Ruellia tuberosa*.

and *Frankliniella schultzei* being the first to appear within the flowers and occurring as they do throughout the flowering season, are the primary species. *Megalurothrips distalis* and *Thrips hawaiiensis* representing the secondary species occur comparatively in fewer numbers than the primary species. These secondary species also occur throughout the period of study, but display considerable irregularity in their population trends. Equally characteristic of the secondary species is their belated appearance within the flowers after a severe environmental stress. The tertiary species represented by *T. aureus* and *Micothrips fasciatus* occurring in lesser numbers than the primary or secondary are present only for a short period and appear highly host-specific. All these species never occur together in a single collection in view of their graded periodicities and of the tertiary species only one is found to occur at a time (Viswanathan & Ananthakrishnan, 1976). (Fig. 5)

Thrips community studies within inflorescences of Compositae reveal the seasonal incidence of host plants as well as thrips inhabiting them. Flowering in *Wedelia chinensis*, *Synedrella nodiflora* and *Ageratum conyzoides* is seasonal from restricted May–November, November–January and December–March respectively, whereas *Tridax procumbens* and *Vernonia cineria* flower throughout the year. Species-packing was observed in *T.procumbens* and *W.chinensis* with all the four species, viz., *Haplothrips tardus*, *H.gowdeyi*, *Frankliniella schultzei* and *Microcephalothrips abdominalis* within a single in florescence. *Micothrips fasciatus* and *H.ganglbaueri* occurred only as occasional visitors. Considering the dominance of populations of the invading species in a flower, *M.abdominalis* seemed to show preference for *Wedelia*, *Synedrella* and *Ageratum*, *Haplothrips tardus* only for *Tridax*, and *H.gowdeyi* for *Vernonia* (Ananthakrishnan *et al.*, 1981, 1981a).

TABLE 3. Showing the diversity of genera of leaf-litter thrips from Peninsular India, the New World and Australia (only well represented genera included).

| India | New World | Australia |
|---|---|---|
| *Allothrips* | *Adelothrips* | *Carientothrips* |
| *Antillothrips* | *Adraneothrips* | *Dactylothrips* |
| *Apelaunothrips* | *Anactinothrips* | *Dunaitothrips* |
| *Azaelothrips* | *Erkosothrips* | *Empresmothrips* |
| *Bactrothrips* | *Eschatothrips* | *Emprosthiothrips* |
| *Baenothrips* | *Eurythrips* | *Kleothrips* |
| *Elaphrothrips* | *Glyptothrips* | *Phaulothrips* |
| *Hoplothrips* | *Holopothrips* | *Pelinothrips* |
| *Karnyothrips* | *Mystrothrips* | *Scotothrips* |
| *Leptogastrothrips* | *Nanothrips* | (mostly from Eucalyptus |
| *Loyolia* | *Neurothrips* | litter) |
| *Meiothrips* | *Orthrothrips* | |
| *Mecynothrips* | *Phthirothrips* | |
| *Mystrothrips* | *Polyphemothrips* | |
| *Plectrothrips* | *Sophiothrips* | |
| *Phylladothrips* | *Sophikothrips* | |
| *Pyrgothrips* | *Terthrothrips* | |
| *Stigmothrips* | *Tylothrips* | |
| *Strepterothrips* | *Williamsiella* | |
| *Xylapothrips* | *Zeugmatothrips* | |

**3. Bark and litter communities** - Litter comprising dry and decaying fallen leaves, branches and twigs as well as bark of dead, fallen tree trunks or of some living trees harbour complex communities of insects including thrips. Diverse fungi become established in these habitats providing sufficient opportunities for feeding on the mycelia and spores. Accordingly thrips feeding on fungal hyphae or their breakdown products are termed mycetophagous, involving some of the members of the Phlaeothripinae, while the sporophagous species, feeding on the spores of fungi involve the Idolothripinae. An increase in plant species diversity particularly in the tropics is followed by animal species diversity, so that spatial heterogenity and complexity of the physical environment appear essential criteria in species diversity. This is typical of mature forest ecosystems such as that of the Western Ghats. In these forests, the leaf litter of the forest floor is formed by a wide variety of trees like *Messua*, *Dipterocarpus*, *Ternstromoeia*, *Pterocarpus*, *Barringtonia*, *Kigelia*, etc. constituting a specific microhabitat comprising the saprophytic fungal zone, which is inhabited by diverse mycophagous species. In more temperate conditions, such as in Europe there is a

restriction in the composition of the mycophagous species in view of the
limited diversity of forest trees which are mostly of the category of
pine, firs, larches, spruce, balsam fir etc. Some of the more common
thrips species inhabiting such areas in Europe are *Hoplothrips pedicularius*, *H.semicaceus*, *H.propinquus*, *H.pini*, *H.griseus*, *Acanthothrips
nodicornis*, *Phlaeothrips minor*, *P.coriaceus*, *P.albovittatus*, *Cryptothrips
latus*, *C.angustus*, *Megathrips lativentris* etc. The composition of
mycophagous communities in a tropical forest is much greater with several
species of *Ecacanthothrips*, *Polyphemothrips*, *Strepterothrips*, several
*Urothripids*, *Elaphrothrips*, *Bactrothrips*, *Machatothrips*, *Nesothrips*, to
mention a few. The occurrence of litter thrips communities has been well
established through studies on mycophagous species (Ananthakrishnan,
1977; Mound, 1972, 74, 76, 77). Being an extensive and semi-permanent
habitat, leaf litter harbours very characteristic communities which are
known to involve diverse species as in the New World leaf litter where in
a forest area of less than 50 kms diameter, up to 50 species were
recorded (Mound, 1977). A similar picture has been obtained in some
areas of the Western Ghats in India prior to deforestation of certain
areas. Not only does the species composition differ very much in the two
areas, but also the numerical abundance (Table 3). A more detailed
discussion on mycophagous species is included in a subsequent chapter.

\* \* \* \* \*

## REPRODUCTIVE STRATEGIES AND LIFE CYCLES

Adaptations towards realising the maximum progeny survival are well
known in insects. Among the factors contributing to 'effective designs
for reproductive survival', the more important ones appear to be the ability of the fairly closely related species to live for different periods
of time, and be endowed with varying fecundity involving also the production of one or more generations during the life time of a single individual (Price, 1975). The number of progeny produced is subject to considerable variation between species and within species, based mostly on
the environmental and nutritional attributes. High fecundity ensures
population survival and natural selection favours adjustment of egg production so as to result in the long run in a balance between fecundity
and mortality. Viewed from this angle, thrips are endowed with efficient
reproductive mechanisms facilitating build up of populations. Though
sexual reproduction is more common, parthenogenesis is equally well
known, involving both thelytoky and arrhenotoky. While ovipary is the
normal rule, instances of ovoviviparity and viviparity are typical of
*Tiarothrips,* some species of *Elaphrothrips, Bactrothrips (=Caudothrips)*
etc.

The females of thrips are generally darker and larger than the males
in Terebrantia, the terminal abdominal segments and genitalia being
characteristic of the two sexes, being more bluntly rounded in the males.
Emphasised abdominal spines on the eighth segment are characteristic of
males of species of several genera of the Thripinae and Panchaetothripinae. Females of Tubulifera have a short median rod, the fustis, lying
ventrally anterior to the base of the tube. The male genital opening is
placed between the eighth and ninth segments in the Terebrantia, and between ninth and tenth abdominal segments in the Tubulifera. Females of
Terebrantia possess a saw-like ovipositor, comprising two chitinous
values whose edges bear saw-like teeth and the valves enclose between
them the egg channel. An ovipositor is absent in the Tubulifera, as also
in the primitive terebrantian family Uzelothripidae, reduced in the
Merothripidae, turned upwards in the Aeolothripidae, and downwards in the
Thripidae. The external male genitalia show considerable diversity and
have been used as a tool for the confirmation of species identification.
The parameres are short, confined to the base in the Tubulifera, while
they are lateral, almost as long as the aedeagus in the Tubulifera, borne
at the apex of a baloon-like vesicle, the *epiphallus,* which in the
Terebrantia may be variously armed with denticles.

Antennal dimorphism and emphasised abdominal setae, horns or
feather-like appendages in the males of Terebrantia are not infrequent.
In addition, *Exothrips, Plesiothrips, Rhopalandrothrips,* and *Sorghothrips*
show very characteristic antennal dimorphism in the males. Males of
*Exothrips* have the first segment of the antennae very stout, and the
fourth segment strongly curved and persistently asymmetrical. In *Rhopa-*
*landrothrips* the sixth segment of the antennae of males is highly
enlarged and setose, almost as in *Sorghothrips* where the sixth segment of

40

the antennae of the male is rod-shaped, long and cylindrical with numerous whorls of long setae. In many species of *Haplothrips* the antennal
segments of the male are generally more slender than in the females. The
forelegs in the Tubulifera are generally simple in females, but in the
males they tend to show extensive modifications from simple unarmed to
excessively enlarged and strongly-armed conditions, the armature often
being in the form of strongly chitinised teeth on the forefemora, foretibia and foretarsi, invariably followed by an enlargment of the prothorax
and sometimes bearing additional appendages as in some species of *Mecynothrips, Nesothrips* and *Dinothrips*. The opposite condition is seen in
species like *Machatothrips*, wherein the forefemora and prothorax of females are enlarged and bear teeth and other prominances. (Ananthakrishnan,
1973).

## SEX INDICES

Koppa (1969) introduces the term 'sex-index' which is expressed as
the percentage of females in relation to the total number of species.
Sex-index indicates the ability of the species having flightless males to
breed or reproduce on different host-plants. Calculation of the mean
sex-indices of the two species *Limothrips denticornis* and *Frankliniella
tenuicornis* showed that in *L.denticornis* the sex-index appears to be the
lowest on winter rye (72) and barley (82) on which this species reproduce
vigorously. The sex-indices of this species in winter wheat, spring
wheat and oats were 92, 93 and 90 respectively. On the other hand, the
sex-index of *F.tenuicornis* is relatively low on the other species of
cereals, being of the order of 77, 79, 82, 76, and 77, in winter rye,
winter wheat, spring wheat, barley and oats respectively (Koppa, 1969)
(Fig. 6, 7).

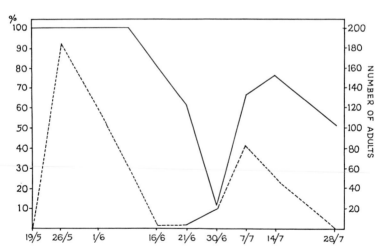

Fig.6. *Limothrips denticornis*, sex index ( — ) and the number of
specimens (....) on winter rye (after Koppa, 1969).

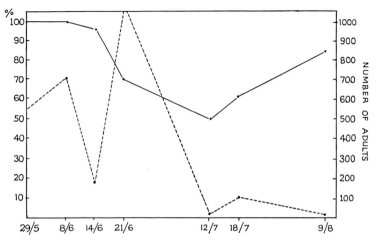

Fig.7. *Franklinella tenuicornis*, sex index ( — ) and number of species (....)in winter rye (after Koppa, 1969).

## REPRODUCTIVE ORGANS AND THEIR POST-EMBRYONIC DEVELOPMENT

The internal reproductive organs of the female consists of a pair of panoistic ovaires, each comprising four ovarioles (sometimes even two or five) grouped on either side of the abdomen, the ovarioles in each group opening posteriorly into a lateral oviduct on each side which unite to form a common median oviduct leading to the vagina (Sharga, 1933 & Priesner, 1959). Lewis (1959, 1973) has correlated the size of the ovaries with the approximate age of the females, recognizing stages such as undifferentiated, early maturing, late maturing, laying and senile ovaries. The apices of the ovarioles coalesce in the region of the germarium and are connected to the salivary gland by terminal filaments. Five regions are recognisable in mature ovarioles (Haga, 1975):- (i) the terminal filament, (ii) the germarium, (iii) developing square-shaped oocytes oriented linearly, (iv) follicular epithelium developing around oocytes which become longer than wide, and (v) fully developed oocytes with well developed follicular epithelium. Haga (1975) also describes the 'Bournier Apparatus' present on the dorsal wall of vagina consisting of a median cuticle, stalk, pouch sheath, to hold the male genitalia and accept sperm bundles and as an outlet of the spermathecal duct. Cary (1902) described five ovarioles on each side in *Anaphothrips striatus* while Sharga (1933) recorded in *Aptinothrips rufus* nine ovarioles altogether lying in groups of five and four ovarian tubes. In *Lygothrips jambuvasi*, a gall inhabiting thrips in *Anogeissus* sp., each ovary is composed of two ovarioles and the lateral oviduct is 2-3 times longer as compared with the lateral oviduct of other gallthrips. In *Tiarothrips subramanii* the long and wide lateral oviduct as well as the enlarged median common oviduct serve to retain the mature and partially developed eggs (Fig. 8).

Muller (1927), Melis (1934), Davies (1961, 1969) and Heming (1970a) have made histological investigations on the internal changes taking

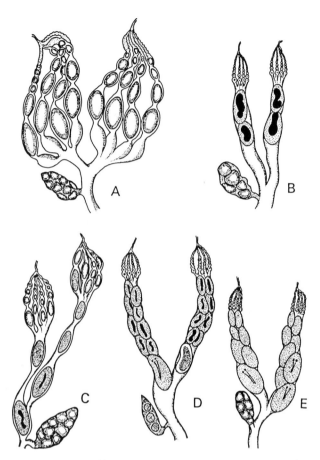

Fig.8. Ovarian types in *Tiarothrips subramanii*: A. Oviparous ovary,
B. partial ovoviviparous ovary with enlarged lateral oviduct (early
stage), C. Partial ovoviviparous ovary (late stage), D. complete
ovoviviparous ovary with fully developed embryos at the distal end of the
lateral oviduct, E. Viviparous ovary.

place during post-embryonic development of the ovary. Taking *Neoheegeria
varbasci* as detailed by Heming (1971a), in the prepupal stage the first
indication of the approaching division of each ovarian rudiment into four
ovarioles is evident in the cells of median ligament. These cells are
arranged in eight rows, each row eventually becoming a terminal filament
of one ovariole. In the prepupal stage the ovarian rudiment appears as
two flattened structures with a long thin oviduct. Each of them begins
to divide into four ovarioles only during the first pupal stage, the four
ovarioles are completely separated from each other and coalesce at their
apices to have a common germarium. In *Androthrips flavipes* all the four
ovarioles coalesce to form a common germarium, whereas in gall forming
Hoplothripini like *Arrhenothrips ramakrishnae*, the four ovarioles of each

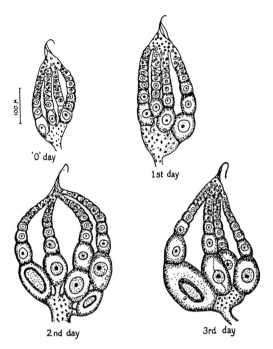

'0' day

1st day

2nd day

3rd day

Fig.9. Post-embryonic development of the ovary in *Androthrips flavipes*.

ovary fuse in pairs at their apices (Figs. 9, 10). It is only in freshly emerged adults that the terminal filaments of the ovarioles are attached to the salivary glands.

The rate of development of the ovarioles and individual oocytes shows a distinct correlation with that of preoviposition period in different species. In *Arrhenothrips ramakrishnae* and *Crotonothrips dantahasta* where the preoviposition period is as long as eight days, there occurs a gradual growth in the individual ovarioles and oocytes from the second pupa to the second day adult and a steep rise from the third day up to oviposition. Ovariole development in *S. chedothrips* appears gradual up to the fourth day, with the length and width increasing from the fifth day onwards. Growth of ovarioles and basal oocyte is gradual from the second pupa till oviposition in *Gynaikothrips flaviantennatus*, *Teuchothrips longus*, and *Thilakothrips babuli* and the preoviposition period is comparatively short. In the predatory *Androthrips flavipes* the development of ovarioles and individual oocytes presents a unique pattern; they grow well from the second pupa onwards up to the third day adult at which stage they being to oviposit (Varadarasan and Ananthakrishnan, 1981).

The anlagen of the two testes is seen in the first stage larva situated dorsally in the abdominal segments 5 and 6, each rudiment being

44

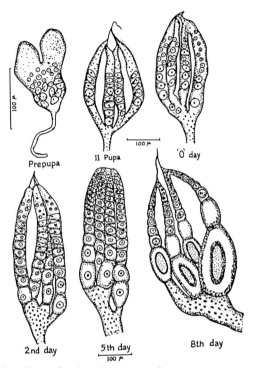

Fig.10. Post-embryonic development of the ovary in *Arrhenothrips ramakrishnae*.

bordered by a thin primary epithelial sheath. In the second instar larvae the rudiments are larger and the primary epithelial sheath of each
rudiment is produced cephald as a delicate terminal filament. In the
first pupa, the testicular rudiments are usually slightly longer and
mostly more slender than most of the prepupa; longitudinally arranged
sperm bundles or spermatophores are also evident. In pupa II, the testes
become more and more slender, and in the adults the testes are smaller
than in the previous instars. The pigments of the testis begin to appear
in the middle of the first pupal stage due to flattened chromatophores
adhering to the epithelial cells. The first pair of accessory glands
develops early in the first pupa and the second pair subsequently. Both
these pairs increase considerably in length and the proximal length of
the accessory gland and of the vasa deferentia unite in the eighth
segment of the abdomen with the anterior end of the ejaculatory duct
(Heming, 1970a).

## MATING

Individuals of the two sexes appear to be ready for mating 2-3 days
after the last pupal moult, a single male being known to fertilize a
number of females. Lewis (1973) provides sufficient information on the
mating process and duration of mating in some species, as also of the

unusual form of mating of males with the female prepupae in *Limothrips denticornis*. In *Chirothrips mexicanus*, the apterous males always emerge before the females, the latter being in the pupal stage. The males enter the glumes of grass spikelets, and mate with female pupae which have only ovaries. Oviposition, however, starts only after four to five days after adult emergence (Ananthakrishnan & Daniel, 1981). In larger idolothripines like *Tiarothrips subramanii*, the mating period ranges from 15 to 20 minutes and from 25 to 30 minutes in *Elaphrothrips procer*. Considerable behavioural diversity is evident in polymorphic males, where the normal and gynaecoid individuals mate easily with the females, which avoid mating with the more grotesque oedymerous males. In *Ecacanthothrips tibialis* the females exhibit an upward deflexion of the abdominal apex to receive the gynaecoid male, and such a behaviour is lacking in the oedymerous males, there being a strong, initial avoiding tendency on the part of the females, though reproductive incompatibility never occurs (Viswanathan & Ananthakrishnan, 1973).

Gynandromorphs and intersexes though rare, have nevertheless been recorded. *Oxythrips flavus* shows a good range from an apparently functional female complete with ovarioles, fully developed ovipositor, no sternal glandular areas, but with one thorn-like seta on ninth abdominal segment, to a male with a complete testes, sternal glandular areas, thorn-like setae on tenth segment, but with only incompletely developed genital parameres (Mound, 1970). *Thrips fuscipennis*, also a reported gynandromorph, shows the third to seventh abdominal sternites with a typical male glandular area on the left side. The abdominal apex is of particular interest in view of the presence of an apparently normal ovipositor valve on the right side and a well-developed male paramere on the left (Mound, 1970).

## VIVIPARITY

Though very few examples of viviparity are known in Thysanoptera, they are sufficient to show that this method of reproduction also exists. Viviparity was first demonstrated by John (1922) in *Megathrips lativentris* and later Hood (1934, 1936, 1938, 1939) recorded several instances in many species of *Diceratothrips* and *Anactinothrips*. It would appear that species of idolothripines such as of *Elaphrothrips* and *Tiarothrips* reproduce by oviparity and ovoviviparity as well as by viviparity. Both partial and complete ovoviviparity are evident in *Tiarothrips subramanii* and *Elaphrothrips procer*. In the case of partial ovoviviparity, oocytes develop in the lateral oviduct up to germ band formation and subsequent egg laying and hatching occurr within one to two days of egg laying. In complete ovoviviparity, the oocytes develop within the lateral oviduct up to a fairly advanced stage of development as evident by the development of eyespots, maxillary stylets etc., the eggs hatching within a few hours after laying. In viviparous females, the fully developed nymphs are retained within the common oviduct, the thin chorion surrounding the nymph ruptures, and they emerge alive, as in *Tiarothrips*, *Dinothrips*, *Elaphrothrips*, *Meiothrips*, *Bactrothrips* etc.

## PARTHENOGENESIS

The incidence of parthenogenesis in Thysanoptera was first reported by Heeger (1852) in *Parthenothrips dracaenae* and subsequently by Jordan

(1888), Uzel (1895), Shull (1917), McGill (1927), Sakimura (1932), Bailey (1933), and many others too. Shull (1917) reared all male progeny from virgin females of *Neoheegeria verbasci*, while Davidson and Bald (1931) achieved similar results with *Frankliniella schultzei*. *Frankliniella fusca* is also known to be arrhenotokous (Livingstone, 1931, Newsom *et al.*, 1953). Reyne (1921) recorded 378 females to 1 male in the cacao thrips *Selenothrips rubrocinctus* and subsequently recorded the percentage of males to be 0.14% out of 29177 thrips counted in cacao and 2.33% of 3520 individuals counted in cashew in Trinidad. McGill (1927) recorded the male, female sex ratio of *Thrips tabaci* as 1 : 3000, while Sakimura (1932) found no males in 85 progenies from the unmated females of *Thrips tabaci*, and of the 5000 specimens collected from various seasons, only five males were found. Bailey (1933) indicated that *Caliothrips fasciatus*, *Frankliniella tritici* and *Neoheegeria verbasci* normally reproduced sexually, but the females also reproduced parthenogenetically, the unfertilized females always giving rise to males. In *Rhipiphorothrips cruentatus* the occurrence of parthenogenesis was recorded by Rahman and Bharadwaj (1937) indicating the predominance of females in the beginning of the season. Watson (1941) raised twenty generations of *Taeniothrips simplex* in Florida and only males developed from unfertilised eggs, while Putman (1942) showed that parthenogenesis occurred in *Haplothrips niger* when a female was reared through six generations without the appearance of a male. Bournier (1956) observed that parthenogenetically developing eggs give rise to both the sexes (amphitoky) as in *Heliothrips haemorrhoidalis*, *Parthenothrips dracaenae* and *Aptinothrips rufus* or exclusively to males (Arrhenotoky). Morison (1957) recorded only one male and 50 females in *Aptinothrips rufus* and indicated that only one male has so far been recorded in *Heliothrips haemorrhoidalis*. Other species where very few males are known are *Hercinothrips bicinctus*, *Helionothrips errans*, *Chaetanophothrips orchidii*, and *Taeniothrips simplex*. *C.orchidii*, an extremely thermophilic species, originating from the north coast of South America and introduced along with its natural host plants into Europe, and subsequently spread to Asia, has been known to reproduce parthenogenetically all the year round, a single female laying 80-100 eggs (Pelikan, 1954). The females in general live much longer than males and hence there is often an overlapping of generations as could be observed in species like *Thrips tabaci*, *C.orchidii*, and *Caliothrips indicus*, to mention a few instances. Three generations of parthenogenetically reproducing individuals of *Caliothrips indicus*, for instance, gave the female, male ratio as 0:42, 0:56 and 0:48 respectively, while in sexually reproducing individuals the ratio was 19:12, 21:16 and 21:13 respectively (Ananthakrishnan, unpublished data). Similar instances are evident in *Chirothrips mexicanus*, the parthenogenetic generation showing a ratio of female:male 1:5 (Ananthakrishnan & Thirumalai, 1977). Parthenogenesis is affected by environment or seasonal changes, and usually occurs in many species introduced from areas of hot or warm climate to areas of colder climate, particularly where they are bred in glass-houses (Morison, 1957).

*Frankliniella occidentalis* is a typical example of localized unisexual polymorphism in which females exhibit three distinct colour forms – dark, intermediate and light forms, and males unicolorous (Bryan and Smith, 1956) (Fig. 11). Oviposition normally begins 72 hours after emergence and continues intermittently throughout almost all adulthood. Normal parthenogenesis common among thrips may be classified into obliga-

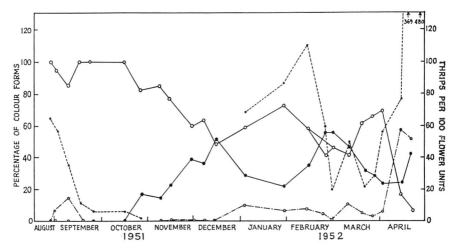

Fig.11. Percentage of colour forms in *Frankliniella occidentalis* (After Bryan Smith, 1956).

tory and facultative. Within the obligatory category, constant, cyclical and paedogenetic parthenogenetic patterns may be distinguished. Constant facultative parthenogenesis normally occurs in thrips, and the eggs in the same parent may be either fertilized or develop parthenogenetically. Both female and male progeny may be produced by a single female, and when males, they are of parthenogenetic origin. This type of reproduction is always facultative and arrhenotokous (Suomalainen, 1960; Bryan & Smith, 1956). Males produced by unfertilized females and both sexes by fertilized females is a feature equally common in *Microcephalothrips abdominalis*. Facultative arrhenotoky where eggs may or may not be fertilized is characteristic of species like *Chirothrips mexicanus, Caliothrips indicus*, etc. Risler and Kempter (1961) confirmed that arrhenotokous males in *Haplothrips statices* are haploid. Thelytoky resulting from unfertilized eggs giving rise to females, occurs in some Thysanoptera where males are extremely rare as in *Heliothrips haemorrhoidalis* and *Taeniothrips simplex*. Thelytoky is considered advantageous in that the female spends all the time in feeding and reproduction, with no time or energy being lost in mate finding. The reproductive potential is also much greater, since the whole population is made of females, with the only disadvantage that no genetic recombination occurs at mating. The long-term effect of thelytoky therefore involves lack of adaptation to environmental changes (Chapman, 1969).

Examining a few specific cases of parthenogenesis and sexual reproduction, we find that species such as *Anaphothrips sudanensis* breed throughout the year through parthenogenesis and sexual reproduction. Each female lays 24-67 eggs, with an average of 44/individual, the maximum laid per day being 4, the eggs being laid parallel to the leaf veins in the vicinity of the leaf sheath area and tender foliage. The parthenogenetic female lays more eggs, as many as 67 (Patel & Patel, 1953). Population of thrips in ten tillers from different plants in the field varies from 58-70 individuals inclusive of larvae. Peaks of abundance coincided with the lowest temperture of the growing season; when the

average temperature was 70°F and when 15 tillers were used, the population varied from 22-124. Ananthakrishnan and Jagadish (1968) have indicated that parthenogenetic females have a longer oviposition period
increased longevity, as shown in the Table 4.

TABLE 4. Oviposition records of *Anaphothrips sudanensis*.

| Average temp. | Type of repro- duction | Pre-ovi position period | Oviposi- tion period | Post-ovi position period | No. of eggs per day | Total eggs laid | Adult fe- male longe- vity |
|---|---|---|---|---|---|---|---|
| | | | January - February | | | | |
| 25-25°C | Sexual | 2-3 days | 6-8 days | 6-8 | 3-6 | 20-47 | 16-21 |
| 25-28°C | Partheno- genetic | 3-4 days | 9-10 days | 6-9 | 4-8 | 41-56 | 18-23 |
| | | | July - August | | | | |
| 33-36°C | Sexual | 1-2 days | 4-5 days | 4-5 | 5-13 | 25-32 | 11-14 |
| 33-36°C | Partheno- genetic | 2-3 | 5-6 | 6-7 | 9-13 | 54-65 | 13-16 days |

In the predatory species *Scolothrips sexmaculatus*, 15 unmated females produced 10.12 male progeny daily, but no female progeny. After
exposure to males, the same females produced 0.33 males and 7.48 female
progeny daily. This is a facultatively arrhenotokous species not having
a prolonged previposition period. For example, 15 control females
emerging in the presence of adult males produced 1.7 male progeny and 5.1
female progeny during the first 24 hours after eclosion (Gilstrap & Oatman, 1976).

In *Chirothrips mexicanus* both sexual and parthenogenetic modes of
reproduction occur, oviposition starting 4-5 days after emergence, the
rate of oviposition being 3-4 eggs/day and a total of 29-41/females. The
ovary of parthenogenetically reproducing individuals showed 4-6 mature
eggs at a time. Arrhenotokous parthenogenesis is the principal mode of
reproduction throughout its life span, producing only males. As such
males comprise the major portion of the population throughout the year,
excepting in January and July (Ananthakrishnan & Thirumalai, 1977, 1978),
when the sex ratio is 2:1 or 1:1, while in other months it is 1:5.

In *Haplothrips niger*, the red clover thrips, in the United States of
America and Canada, reproduction is parthenogenetic, virgin females
laying fertile eggs in all cases, no males occurring in the field or in
the laboratory experiments. A female laid 1-10 eggs each day for 3 or
more days. In a life span of 16-38 days, a female laid 3-55 eggs at 25°C
(Loan & Holdaway, 1955).

## ENVIRONMENTAL INFLUENCE ON REPRODUCTION

Environmental factors such as temperature, light, crowding etc., have their own impact on reproduction through variation in the production of macropterous or brachypterous or apterous individuals of a species, or through suppression of the production of males, or through inducing individuals as adults, larvae, and pupae, or rarely even as eggs to undergo overwintering. The proportion of macropterous to brachypterous individuals is also known to increase as a result of crowded conditions on the host-plant during development. Kamm (1972) has shown the effect of photoperiod on form and reproduction in *Anaphothrips obscurus*. Larvae exposed to short day regimes had underdeveloped ovaries in contrast to the well-developed ovaries in some adult forms from long day exposures. Substantially more macropterous individuals are produced under long days than under short days. Kamm (1972) observed that under 16 hr PP and 8 SP, *Anaphothrips obscurus* produced more macropterous adults than at 10 PP and 14 SP. Short days induced and maintained reproductive diapause, and long days rapidly terminated diapause. Hood (1940) also believed that immature thrips may respond to environmental stimuli to produce different morphs. The influence of photoperiod in nature on diapause maintenance presumably changes in winter so that temperature becomes a factor regulating resumption of development in spring (Kamm, 1972). Population growth is undoubtedly controlled by temperature, as the rate of reproduction increases very much at temperatures exceeding 25°C. Effect of temperature and photoperiod during the termination of diapause of overwintering females of *A.obscurus* collected from the field, on the subsequent rate of reproduction and morph determination is indicated in Table 5 (Kamm, 1972).

TABLE 5. Effect of temperature and photoperiod on diapausing females of *Anaphothrips obscurus* (after Kamm, 1972).

| Photo-period | Temp | No. progeny of overwintering adults | | | |
|---|---|---|---|---|---|
| | | Brachypterous adults | Macropterous adults | Larvae | Total |
| 10P:14S | 15°C | 269 | 0 | 194 | 463 |
| 10P:14S | 24°C:18°C | 524 | 12 | 211 | 747 |
| 16P:8S | 24°C:18°C | 446 | 136 | 417 | 1029 |

## OVERWINTERING

Overwintering is a common phenomenon mostly in non-tropical situations and is usually the case in many species occurring in Europe or Canada or most parts of the United States of America. Most of the phytophagous thrips have several generations a year, with an average generation time of 3-4 weeks. They pass winter as adult females under plant debris or under bark. The barley thrips in the United States of America, *Limothrips denticornis*, overwinters in forest litter, sod, birds' nests, leaf mould and insect galls and up to 360/sq.feet. in sods of grass (Post, 1957; Post & Colberg, 1958). Some species hibernate in specific

niches, while others migrate from the cereal fields in autumn to winter
shelter, mainly from the grass in the forest edge-zone or to winter
cereals. Thrips are able to hibernate in various stages of development
(Koppa, 1969). One and the same species may hibernate in several different situations wherein there is strong negative phototaxis and
positive thigmotaxis. *Anaphothrips obscurus* hibernates in winter cereals
and lives wedged in the shoot sheaths (77 species/m$^2$) or in grassy road-
side verges and grass; these are regarded as typical hibernation sites.
This species hibernates in both brachypterous and macropterous conditions
(Oettingen, 1942; Bailey, 1948; Koppa, 1969) and Weitmeier (1956) reports
its hibernation as second instar larvae. Among thrips living on cereal
plants, species like *Limothrips denticornis* and *Frankliniella tenuicornis*
very commonly hibernate in cereal stubbles and males do not generally
hibernate, since the first males do not appear until the new generation
appears (Koppa, 1969). Both females and males of *Haplothrips aculeatus*
hibernate (Wetzel, 1963; Franssen and Mantel, 1956, 1965). This is also
the case with *Chirothrips manicatus*, while in *Aptinothrips rufus* and
*A.stylifer*, the second stage larvae hibernate (Koppa, 1969) in fairly
humid forest edge zones where grasses and mosses grow. Those which live
in cereals hibernate mostly as imagines, and that too, as females
(Wetzel, 1963). Oettingen (1942) reported *Anaphothrips obscurus* hibernating as macropterous and brachypterous imagines, while Weitmeir (1956)
observed this phenomenon in the second instar larvae. In biotopes containing cultivated and wild grasses, the brachypterous forms of *A.obs-
curus* appeared to be the more common hibernating form (Koppa, 1969), 98%
of the hibernating population being brachypterous. Many species like
*Frankliniella moultoni*, *Thrips tabaci*, *Caliothrips fasciatus* have been
reported hibernating under vinebark in vineyards. One of the finest
examples of thrips overwintering in hedge bottoms, grass litter and bark
is that of *Limothrips cerealium* aggregating in numbers up to about sixty
in crevices of bark of Austrian pine and other trees, the numbers found
in different types of bark appearing to be largely dependent on the
number of habitable crevices available, which increase with the age of
the tree (Lewis and Navas, 1962). While very few overwintering individuals die during winter, emergence from overwintering sites is not
without mortality because of local pressure, temperature and relative
humidity. *L.cerealium* formed 93–98% of the population overwintering in
bark of different species of pine and *Aptinothrips rufus* 71–78% of thrips
overwintering in hedgebottoms and grass litter in England (Lewis, 1962).
Extreme cold and moderate temperature influence overwintering and laboratory cultures of *Limothrips cerealium* indicated that this species overwin-
tered for 18 days at -5°C, 50 days between -1°C and +1°C, and 60 days at
20°C. *L.cerealium* acclamatizes itself fast to temperature fluctuations
from +31°C to -7°C (Schleiphake, 1979). *Anaphothrips secticornis* hibernates as adults and eggs are hatched after snow melts in Sweden. The
hibernating period of adults is known to be 9–10 months (Kjellsen, 1975).

Many species hibernate in the soil and *Drepanothrips reuteri* is
reported to spend the winter in soil chiefly as adults (Bailey, 1942).
In the carnation thrips, *Taeniothrips dianthi* in Europe, full-grown larvae creep slowly into the soil between the roots of the carnations and
hibernation takes place in the soil. Adults are also known to hibernate
in the soil in September/October, emerging in April (Pelikan, 1954).
Second instar larvae of *Odontothrips loti* descend only to a level of
20-25 mm, where they select a suitable cavity among the soil particles

and the chamber is subsequently reinforced by fastening the surrounding soil particles together with a sparse cob-web like tissue spun from the anus (Obertel, 1963). *Thrips linarius* breeding only on flax has only one generation a year, the winged adults hibernating in the soil and leaving it either in the next spring or remain to hibernate once more (Franssen & Mantel, 1962). Table 6 indicates the depths at which *Thrips linarius* and *Stenothrips graminum* hibernate in the soil.

TABLE 6. Number of *Thrips linarium* hibernation in soil at various depths.

| Depth in cms | *Thrips linarius* | *Stenothrips graminum* |
|---|---|---|
| 20-30 | 35 | 3 |
| 30-40 | 226 | 15 |
| 40-50 | 48 | 18 |
| 50-60 | 37 | 5 |
| 60-70 | 6 | 2 |
| 70-80 | 0 | 0 |
| 80-90 | 0 | 0 |
| Total from 20-90 cms | 352 | 43 |

(After Franssen & Mantel, 1962)

Only females of the larch thrips *Taeniothrips laricivorus* in Denmark have been known to hibernate in the shoots of spruce trees (*Picea* sp.). After considerable efforts to locate the overwintering thrips, Tite (1956) discovered the hibernating larch thrips on spruce and also found that the larch intermingled with spruce seemed to be more attacked by thrips than the larch located at a distance from spruce. Two hibernating sites were noticed namely (1) between bud-scales beneath stout, flat needles surrounding terminal buds on shoots, and (2) in the crevices of shoots (Zenther-Moller, 1965; Maksymov, 1976).

## DIAPAUSE IN GALL-THRIPS

An interesting instance of diapause has been observed in *Acacia* gall-thrips, *Thilakothrips babuli*, which unlike the populations of most gall-thrips, occur almost throughout the year. Galls on *Acacia leucophloea* are highly seasonal with galls on the axillary buds (rosette galls) for about 45 days (May and June) and on the inflorescence (floret galls) for about twenty days (September) with 1-2 peaks in each niche. When the rosette gall matures and begins to dry, thrips population also dwindles, leaving behind very few apterous females. These adults remain within the dry galls and undergo diapause for about two months. When *Acacia* sprouts flower buds, the apterous adults leave the diapausing site and migrate to the flowers to form floret galls where the poly-morphic forms are established. The number of apterous females appearing

52

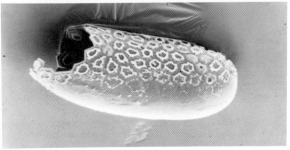

Plate 14. Stereoscan photographs of the egg of a Tubuliferan.
Copyright, Trustees of the British Museum (Natural History).

in the rosette gall and inflorescence gall differs significantly, with
more of apterous females in the inflorescence galls. These apterous
females again undergo diapause for seven months at the bases of thorns
and in dried rosette galls.

Crotonothrips dantahasta and Teuchothrips longus occurring within
the galls of Memecylon edule and Pavetta hispidula respectively were
observed for a period of seven months in sufficient numbers and their
absence for five months coincides well with the absence of young leaf-
formation in the hosts. The stragglers found during this period have
plenty of fat bodies in them and appear to be in a stage of 'akinesis' or
temporary diapause. Pruning of Pavetta hispidula during May when no
young leaves are normally seen, produced enough young leaves which became
infested by Teuchothrips longus. With such appearance of young leaves
this insect breaks its temporary diapause or akinesis caused by the non-
availability of food, and not any other abiotic factor, that influences
the gall thrips to undergo diapause (Varadarasan and Ananthakrishnan,
1981).

Plate 15. Eggs of some Tubulifera - *Elaphrothrips denticollis* (Top), *Priesneriana kabandha* (Middle), *Tiarothrips subramanii* (Bottom), *T.subramanii* laying eggs (Inset).

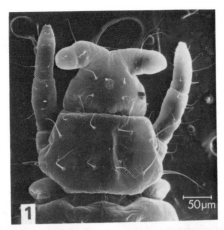

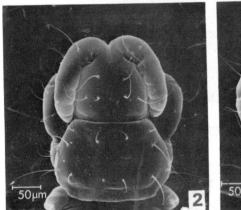

Plate 16. SEM picture of the pre-pupa, pupa I and pupa II of *Haplothrips verbasci* (Courtesy B. S. Heming).

## LIFE-CYCLES

Phytophagous species of both the Terebrantia and Tubulifera have an almost uniform life-history under normal situations, but the rate of development certainly differs with varying temperatures, being slower at lower temperatures and faster at moderately high temperatures. Lewis (1973) provides a good discussion on the relationship between temperature and rate of development. In general, the shortest time taken to complete post-embryonic development is about 10 days in contrast to 20-22 months taken by species which have a prolonged diapause. A general account of the process of mating has been indicated earlier and during this process which generally lasts for 10-20 minutes, the male climbs on the back of the female and places the venter of the abdomen alongside with that of the female. The male then twists the posterior end of the abdomen under that of the female, so that the ventral surface of the two are towards each other. In the phlaeothripids, the female then elevates the tube,

Plate 17. Pupae of *Thrips tabaci* from the soil.

leaving the sexual opening free. The phallus of the male is then elevated on to the common oviduct by hydrostatic pressure. Variations do occur, as for instance in *Bactrothrips* where the abdomen faces end to end, with the male abdomen strongly twisted, or as in aeolothripids the entire phallus is inserted within the vagina of female. Oviposition commences within one to three days, the adult females of Terebrantia inserting their eggs with thin colourless shells devoid of sculpture, inside the tender tissue of plant by their sac-like ovipositor. Oviposition is stimulated or retarded by temperature and light. During oviposition, there is an expansion of the eight and ninth segments of the abdomen and with a slight undulatory movement eggs are laid. The normal egg-laying capacity is 25-50, but the range could be 25-200. *Thrips imaginis* and *Heliothrips haemorrhoidalis* are known to oviposit steadily throughout their lives and though in general the rate of oviposition varies with temperature, it has also been known that in some species younger females oviposit faster than older ones. The eggs are laid singly as in Terebrantia or mostly in clusters as in the Tubulifera. They are more or less oval to bean-shaped in thripids and are almost cylindrical, longer than wide, more or less rounded at one end, and flattened at the other as in aeolothripids. A porous, cup-like aeropyle is present at the anterior end and a single posteroventrally placed micropyle as in *Haplothrips verbasci* are characteristic of the eggs (Heming, 1979). In view of the absence of the ovipositor in Tubulifera, the eggs are directly laid on the surface of the substrata like bark, leaf sheaths, within galls, culms of grasses etc. The eggs are often glued together and lie in groups and the egg-laying sequence varies with species (Plate 15). Because of the exposed nature of the eggs in

Tubulifera, egg mortality is greater due to natural causes and predator activity. The Terebrantia on the other hand are protected by the plant tissue from heat and from predators. But there is a distinct disadvantage, because the first stage nymphs in addition to bursting the chorion, have also to pierce their way through the epidermis, unlike the first stage numphs of Tubulifera. Considerable mortality of nymphs occurs during eclosion in Terebrantia. A full-grown embryo is seen through the chorion and at the beginning of eclosion the egg shell is ruptured, the rupture running transversely along the hexagonal reticulation in the apical third of the egg, but sometimes it runs longitudinally, or irregularly (Plate 14). The larval head appears from the rupture of the egg shell, very soon followed by the whole of the antennae of the new larva, followed by the rest of the body. It takes about 9 minutes from the beginning of hatching for a new larva to emerge (Haga, 1974). Different species of Terebrantia and Tubulifera vary considerably in their fecundity and may range from 2–5 in *Stigmothrips limpidus*, and 192–252 in *Thrips imaginis* and 93–103 in *Zaniothrips ricini*. Table 7 gives a comparative idea of the fecundity rates of different species of thrips.

TABLE 7. Fecundity rates in some thrips species with varying habits.

| Thrips species | Fecundity rate | Habit |
|---|---|---|
| *Androthrips flavipes* | 13–37 | Predator |
| *Arrhenothrips ramakrishnae* | 17–66 | Cecidogenous |
| *Bactridothrips brevitubus* | 10–40 | Sporophagous |
| *Caliothrips fasciatus* | 66 | Phytophagous |
| *Crotonothrips dantahasta* | 12–28 | Cecidogenous |
| *Ecacanthothrips tibialis* | 70–90 | Mycetophagous |
| *Elaphrothrips procer* | 3–10 | Sporophagous |
| *Gynaikothrips flaviantennatus* | 12–57 | Cecidogenous |
| *Haplothrips niger* | 3–55 | Predator |
| *Heliothrips haemorrhoidalis* | 25–47 | Phytophagous |
| *Liothrips oleae* | 250 | Phytophagous |
| *Liothrips vaneckeei* | 51 | Phytophagous |
| *Neosmerinthothrips indicus* | 25–30 | Sporophagous |
| *Retithrips syriacus* | 56–64 | Phytophagous |
| *Schedothrips orientalis* | 17–48 | Cecidogenous |
| *Sciothrips cardamomi* | 4–28 | Phytophagous |
| *Scirtothrips dorsalis* | 52–58 | Phytophagous |
| *Selenothrips rubrocinctus* | 32–40 | Phytophagous |
| *Tiarothrips subramanii* | 25–33 | Sporophagous |
| *Thilakothrips babuli* | 25–34 | Cecidogenous |
| *Thrips imaginis* | 80 | Phytophagous |

The fecundity, rate of oviposition and egg-laying sequence of different mating types in the *Mimusops* gall thrips are indicated in Table 8. The existence of polymorphic forms within a population of the Mimusops gall thrips is a recognizable feature, with such forms as major, normal and minor females as well as oedymerous, normal and gynaecoid males. As

TABLE 8. Fecundity, oviposition rate and egg laying sequence in the mating types of *Arrhenothrips ramakrishnae*.

| Mating types | Fecun-dity | Oviposi-tion rate/day | Egg-laying sequence |
|---|---|---|---|
| Major female vs. gynaecoid male | | | |
| Field | 68 | 5.6 | 2,7,8,8,7,6,6, 5,5,4,3,3 |
| Laboratory | 48 | 5.3 | 3,5,6,6,6,5,6, 4,5 |
| Major female vs. oedymerous male | | | |
| Field | 47 | 4.8 | 3,4,2,5,6,6,4, 7,8,2 |
| Laboratory | 30 | 5.0 | 3,4,7,8,6,2 |
| Major female vs. gynaecoid male | | | |
| Field | 29 | 3.0 | 2,1,4,6,4,5,4, 2,1 |
| Laboratory | 18 | 3.3 | 2,4,3,2,5,2 |
| Normal female vs. oedymerous male | | | |
| Field | 40 | 4.6 | 2,5,1,2,7,8, 5,7,3 |
| Laboratory | 22 | 3.6 | 3,5,2,5,5,2 |
| Minor female vs. gynaecoid male | | | |
| Field | 42 | 5.0 | 3,4,5,4,6,7,6, 5,2 |
| Laboratory | 20 | 3.0 | 2,3,4,5,4,2 |
| Major female vs. oedymerous male | | | |
| Field | 25 | 3.0 | 2,2,3,6,5,4, 2,1 |
| Laboratory | 18 | 3.0 | 2,3,5,4,2,2 |

such there occurs considerable reshuffling in mating patterns coupled with behavioural differences and differences in fecundity as well as in egg size. It is evident that the major female/gynaecoid male pairing resulted in the largest number of eggs both in the laboratory and the field (Varadarasan and Ananthakrishnan, 1981). The relationship between fecundity and size appears to be more in terms of the phenotype than the genotype, so that changes in the phenotype size of the adult will change the fitness of the genotype by altering the fecundity parameters (Roff, 1981). More such instances are evident in the mycophagous species which show profound oedymerism and gynaecoidism, details of which are discussed in the chapter on the ecology of mycophagous thrips.

Depending on the conditions of temperature, the general range of egg-duration is 3-16 days. The Terebrantia during metamorphosis pass through larval instars I and II, a prepupal, and one pupal stage; in Tubulifera there are two pupal stages- Pupa I and Pupa II after the pre-pupa (Plate 16). Pupation as mentioned earlier may be on plant surfaces, in leaf axils, leaf sheaths, floral parts, and fruits and other tender

58

Plate 18. *Leeuwenia ramakrishnae* - 1. Female, 2. Eggs and emerging larvae, 3. Pupae with heads converged towards the centre.

TABLE 9. Number of eggs laid, duration and total life cycle in some cereal thrips from Europe (after Koppa, 1970).

| Species | No. of eggs laid | Oviposition period | Duration of eggs laid | Total life-cycle |
|---|---|---|---|---|
| *Anaphothrips obscurus* | 51–216 | 2–7 weeks | 4–10 days | 14–35 days |
| *Frankliniella tenuicornis* | 53–252 | 13–50 " | 4–8 " | 12–29 " |
| *Limothrips denticornis* | 58–742 | 14–33 " | 3–9 " | 10–31 " |
| *Haplothrips aculeatus* | 38–115 | 21–73 " | 5–13 " | 21–49 " |

TABLE 10. Duration of life cycles (in days) of thrips inhabiting diverse habitats (from various sources).

| Thrips species | Incubation period | Larva I | Larva II | Prepupa | Pupa I | Pupa II | Total duration (egg to adult) in days |
|---|---|---|---|---|---|---|---|
| **Phytophagous species** | | | | hrs. | | | |
| *Frankliniella schultzei* | 2-4 | 1.5-3 | 3-5 | 20-28 hrs | 1.5-3 | - | 9-16 |
| *Microcephalothrips abdominalis* | 3-4 | 2 | 2-4 | 19-22 hrs | 2 | - | 10-13 |
| *Sciothrips cardamomi* | 6-14 | 3-5 | 8-10 | 2-4 | 4-6 | - | 23-39 |
| *Scirtothrips dorsalis* | 4-7 | 2-4 | 3-6 | 1-2 | 2-3 | - | 12-22 |
| *Thrips tabaci* | 3-7 | 3-6 | 3-6 | 1-2 | 1-5 | - | 11-26 |
| *Retithrips syriacus* | 4-5 | 2-4 | 2-4 | 1-3 | 2-3 | - | 11-19 |
| *Rhipiphorothrips cruentatus* | 2-8 | 3-5 | 3-6 | 1 | 2-3 | - | 11-23 |
| *Zaniothrips ricini* | 5-6 | 2-3 | 4-5 | 1 | 5-6 | - | 17-21 |
| *Euryaplothrips crassus* | 2.5-4 | 2-3 | 5-6 | 20-26 | 2 | 2.5 | 14-18.5 |
| *Haplothrips tardus* | 2-3 | 2-4 | 6-7 | 1 | 2-3 | 2 | 15-20 |
| **Gall Thrips** | | | | | | | |
| *Arrhenothrips ramakrishnae* | 5-6 | 3-4 | 4-5 | 1 | 2-3 | 1-2 | 16-21 |
| *Austrothrips cochinchinensis* | 6-8 | 3-4 | 4-6 | 1-2 | 1-2 | 3-4 | 18-26 |
| *Crotonothrips dantahasta* | 6-8 | 3-4 | 3-4 | 1 | 3-4 | 3-4 | 19-25 |
| *Gynaikothrips flaviantennatus* | 7-9 | 4-5 | 4-5 | 1-2 | 1-2 | 2-4 | 19-27 |
| *Liothrips furvus* | 5-6 | 4-5 | 1-2 | 1-2 | 2-3 | 2-3 | 15-21 |
| *Schedothrips orientalis* | 5-8 | 1-3 | 4-5 | 1-2 | 1-2 | 3-4 | 15-26 |
| *Teuchothrips longus* | 4-7 | 3-5 | 3-6 | 1-2 | 1-2 | 3-4 | 15-26 |
| *Thilakothrips babuli* | 5-6 | 3-4 | 2-3 | 1 | 2 | 2-3 | 15-19 |
| **Predatory species** | | | | | | | |
| *Androthrips flavipes* | 4-6 | 3-4 | 2-3 | 1 | 2-3 | 1-2 | 13-16 |
| *Scolothrips sexmaculatus* | 5-7 | 2-3 | 2-3 | 1-1.6 | 1.6-3 | - | 7-10 |
| *Trichinothrips breviceps* | 6-8 | 3-4 | 3-6 | 1 | 1 | 2-3 | 16-23 |
| **Mycophagous species** | | | | | | | |
| *Azaleothrips amabilis* | 6-8 | 2-3 | 3-4 | 1 | 1 | 1-2 | 14-19 |
| *Ecacanthothrips tibialis* | 3-5 | 2 | 6-8 | 1 | 2-3 | 2-3 | 16-22 |
| *Stigmothrips limpidus* | 2-7 | 3-5 | 4-8 | 1 | 1 | 1-2 | 12-24 |
| *Bactridothrips brevitubus* | 5-7 | 3-6.5 | 7.5-13.5 | 1-1.5 | 2-4.5 | 2.5-7 | 20.5-40 |
| *Elaphrothrips procer* | 1 | 2-3 | 8-12 | 1 | 1 | 2-5 | 15-23 |
| *Neosmerinthothrips indicus* | 5-7 | 2-3 | 5-6 | 1 | 1-2 | 2-3 | 16-22 |
| *Tiarothrips subramanii* | 6-7 | 2-3 | 4-5 | 1 | 4-5 | 3-4 | 20-25 |

plant parts, as well as under bark where they remain quiescent; sometimes they fall to the ground and pupation takes place in the soil (Plate 17). Aeolothripids have a peculiar habit of making a silken cocoon within which the wings and other organs develop (Bailey, 1940). Drebneva (1967) cites the instance of *Aeolothrips intermedius* second larvae entering the soil before pupation and spinning a silken cocoon made of material emanating from its anus. *Franklinothrips* also spins a loosely woven cocoon either in soil or on leaves in litter. Cocoon spinning has also been reported in heterothripids and one species of *Merothrips*, and in a rudimentary way in *Odontothrips confusus*, while in *Odontothrips loti* the larvae make a more elaborate cell to which soil particles are bound with silken threads (Obertel, 1963).

Prior to moulting each larval instar assumes the morphology of the succeeding instar, so that second stage larvae may be visible within the cuticle of the first stage larva just before the moult. Each of the immature stages usually becomes dark coloured as it reaches the end of its stadia. This feature is also very characteristic of the adults where the newly emerged insect is paler, and subsequently turns darker. The first larval stage generally lasts only for a very short period, but the second larva which differs from the first in its greater size, colouration, cuticular structure, chaetotaxy and antennal segments, feeds actively till it assumes its full size. The duration of this instar varies depending upon the species, environment and season, lasting two to three days in *Thrips tabaci* in summer, to several months in overwintering species. Prepupal and pupal instars do not feed, but move slowly and avoid light. Aggregation of the pupae of *Leeuwenia ramakrishnae* infesting leaves of *Syzygium jambolanum* interestingly enough remain oriented with their tube outwardly directed in a radial fashion (Plate 18). The longevity, fecundity and total duration of life-cycles in females of the three species, *Frankliniella fusca*, *Frankliniella tritici* and *T.tabaci* have shown that *F.fusca* has the shortest cycle (15.01 days), laid fewer eggs (41.25) and adults lived for 21.42 days (Watts, 1936). In *Frankliniella tritici*, there is a continuous overlapping of generations in the field, 12-15 generations developing in a year, adult females living for 64 days and males for 3-36 days, the average life of the female being 25-28 days and males 14.67 days. 50-100 eggs are laid, with an average of 15 eggs per day. A comparative account of the number of eggs laid, oviposition period and duration of eggs stage and total life-cycle in the cereal thrips in Europe is indicated in Table 9 (Koppa, 1970). Larval development is more rapid in males than females in *L.denticornis*, 4-8 days for males and 6-10 days for females at the same temperature.

A comparative picture of the duration of the different instars of some phytophagous, mycetophagous, sporophagous, predatory and gall thrips is provided in Table 10.

\* \* \* \* \*

## THRIPS AND AGROECOSYSTEMS

The degree of utilization of different crops for food, oviposition and shelter, as well as the suitability of the crop for survival and build-up of thrips populations may well indicate the extent of damage caused to crops. At the same time crops are not to be considered as isolated islands, but as forming an integral unit with the adjacent vegetation, the two together constituting the agroecosystem, encompassing the abundance, distribution and coexistence of insect populations in cultivated areas. The increasing tendency for a wide variety of weeds to multiply at a fast rate in well-fertilized soils in and around cultivated fields, competing with the crops plants for nutrients, causing considerable economic losses every year directly through competition for space, light and nutrients and indirectly through acting as reservoirs of several pest species, has come to be recognized as an important factor governing agroecosystems (Ananthakrishnan, 1980). The pest fauna of crops like paddy, sorghum and maize result from the segregation of a few local species associated with related wild plants and their adaptation to the crop which often present very similar, but vastly improved conditions for existence (Uvarov, 1964). In spite of their continued migration to the crops, these weeds or wild plants still continue to serve as reservoirs from which there is a replenishment of the species whenever pest populations go down due to artificial control measures. Several polyphagous thrips species like *Thrips tabaci, Scirtothrips dorsalis, Franliniella schultzei, Megalurothrips distalis, Haplothrips ganglbaueri* etc., provide well-known instances of such pest species. In an attempt to understand their pest status, it would appear necessary to study the population fluctuations of pest species both within the crop as well as in the weeds or wild vegetation around, brought about through periodical or consistent to and fro movements. This voluntary migration which is an adaptation for survival has come to be universally recognized, ensuring an advantageous displacement for the concerned species (Lewis, 1980; Taylor, 1977). Migration to the crop may occur due to lack of sufficient or suitable food on the uncultivated land, and this takes place mainly through changes in the plants in the course of their seasonal cycles of growth or through the use of weed killers forcing the insect species out of the weeds. Conversely for many anthophilous thrips species, feeding on flowers in the adjacent uncultivated land is apparently necessary during the egg maturation cycle and subsequent migration to the crop for oviposition and commencement of a new generation. Movement of pest species from the wild vegetation in uncultivated land to the crop, is often also due to the normal extension of the area covered by a species during the seasons. In many instances the time between the appearance of a crop and its harvest, is often shorter than the annual feeding period of many pests which may include several generations as in aphids (van Emden, 1965).

It should also not be forgotten that the crop is a dynamic component of the agroecosystem particularly in view of the microclimate changing and becoming more complex with time, as has been demonstrated in the soybean crop (Irwin & Price, 1976) and in cereal crops (Cederholm, 1963). Throughout the growing season the composition of the crop changes in terms of its ground cover, volume and maturity characters, so that considerable movement of species also occurs both within the plant niches and among the plants. In the cereal crops like maize and sorghum, the panicles get exposed showing rapid microclimatic changes of temperature and light. With the ripening of the ears there is considerable change in the number of thrips caught at different times of the day as the species occupy different positions on the plant as a result of vertical migration and by seeking shelter in such places as sheaths and ears of the crop plants. Reference is made here to the role of thrips in agroecosystems involving cereal, millet and pulse crops cotton, and oil seed crops as well as some plantation crops.

## THRIPS AND CEREALS AND MILLET CROPS

The investigations of Oettingen (1942), Weitmeier (1956), Wetzel (1964), and Koppa (1970) in Europe on thrips infesting such cereals as wheat, oats, barley, rye, etc., as well as of thrips infesting cereals and millet crops in India (Ananthakrishnan and Kandasamy, 1977; Ananthakrishnan and Thirumalai, 1977, 1978; Ananthakrishnan and Thangavelu, 1976; and Patel and Patel, 1953) to mention the major contributions, go a long way in our understanding of the biology as well as population dynamics of the concerned species, particularly with reference to their overwintering and migratory abilities from wild vegetation to the crops. As such in assessing their damage potential in terms of their abundance, the degree of infestation in the crop and weeds appears to be of significance. The importance of thrips as pests of cereals has been recognised for a long time. In parts of Europe, *Frankliniella tenuicornis* has long been regarded as one of the worst pests of barley, *Limothrips denticornis* of rye and wheat, *Anaphothrips obscurus* and *Stenothrips graminum* of oats and barley. In India some of the more important cereal thrips are *Stenchaetothrips biformis* on paddy seedlings, *Haplothrips ganglbaueri* in paddy inflorenscence, *Anaphothrips sudanensis* on wheat, *Florithrips traegardhi*, *Exothrips hemavarna* and *Chirothrips mexicanus* on Sorghum. Many other species are also known to inhabit cereals and grasses, like species of *Chirothrips*, *Aptinothrips*, etc.

An abundance of thrips species living on cereals and fluctuations in population size during the growing season are noticeable with longer seasons allowing additional generations, so that the appearance of a new generation usually causes a peak of abundance, although an overlapping of different generations may largely level out the peaks (Koppa, 1970). The interaction between grasses and cereal crops is reflected in the population fluctuations of species such as *Limothrips denticornis* favouring meadow foxtail and timothy grasses, in which the emergence of a new generation brings about a period of great abundance of this species. In view of the perennial nature of the meadows, there is a good build-up of population in these grasses. During the growing season, thrips may move to cereals from the meadows and then return in autumn, accentuating the fluctuation in the size of thrips populations, along with the formation of new generations (Koppa, 1970). A warm, dry summer usually speeds up the development of the species, and new generations will reach periods of abundance earlier than the cool, rainy summers. Migration of thrips to new food plants also causes periods of great abundance depending on the prevailing weather conditions and factors such as high temperature, lower RH, calm weather and high light intensity. During cold, windy weather, thrips take shelter in protecting parts of plants, moving towards the lower parts of the plant. In winter cereals and barley, *Limothrips denticornis* and *Haplothrips aculeatus* occur in abundance, most of the thrips sheltering between parts of the ears, the former forcing its way into the sheaths and the latter between and into the spikelets. *L.denticornis* will feed and reproduce on all species of cereals and several species of cultivated and wild grasses. Adult females overwinter mainly on grasses growing on the roadsides and forest edges and migrate in spring to their first host plants viz., meadow foxtail and rye. *Frankliniella tenuicornis* overwinters in winter cereal sprouts and cereal stubbles, smaller numbers occuring in winter cereals and a great majority migrating to spring cereals where most of the second generation develop. *Anaphothrips obscurus* occurs on oats and other spring cereals and several cultivated and wild grasses. Macropterous forms appear on sprouts of winter cereals, the brachypterous forms generally developing faster. *Haplothrips aculeatus* reproduces on all cereal crops and several grasses, adults overwintering in grass on the roadsides and forest edges. In general it has been observed that *Limothrips denticornis* is mainly univoltine, (partly bivoltine), *Anaphothrips obscurus* mostly trivoltine, *Frankliniella tenuicornis* mainly bivoltine (partly trivoltine), while *Haplothrips aculeatus* is only univoltine. The peaks of abundance of these species in Europe show considerable variation (Koppa, 1970).

Examining the picture of thrips infestation in rice crop in India, it is found that *Stenchaetothrips biformis* occurs as a serious pest of rice seedlings in all rice growing areas of the world, particularly in the nursery stage up to 2-3 weeks after transplantation. In view of the high rate of multiplication, and comparatively short duration of life cycle of *S.biformis* with an average of two weeks, severe infestation causes serious damage resulting in the longitudinal curling of leaves which subsequently dry up (Ananthakrishnan, 1971, 1973; Grist and Lever, 1969). Information on the population trends of this species prior to transplantation of rice seedlings, as well as that in the weed host of the species, appear to be important criteria in assessing the role of weeds in *Stenchaetothrips biformis* infestations. Regular examination of seedlings in the nursery stage up to the transplantation period, indicate the beginning of infestation from eighth to tenth day after germination, followed by the build-up of populations and then a gradual decline till the twenty-fifth to the twenty-eighth day, when transplantation commenced in the fields under investigation. Two weed species *Echinochloa colona* and *Cyperus iria* were abundant, with an estimated density of 221.4/sq.m. and 133.9/sq.m. respectively, along with a sparse distribution of *Cyperus rotundus* all along the bunds, the density of paddy seedlings being of the order of 671.8/sq.m. (Ananthakrishnan & Kandasamy, 1977).

Analysing the trends of infestation of seedlings, a gradual build-up of populations is evident, the total population inclusive of adult males, females and immature stages showing the maximum during 18-20 days and gradually declining thereafter till the time of transplantation. The comparative trends of infestation of the adult males, females and immature stages with the peak of immature and adult infestation on the sixteenth and seventeenth days and nineteenth and twentieth days respectively after germination, as was observed in the fields under observation, is indicated in Fig. 12.

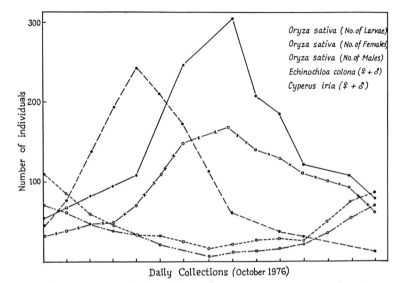

Fig.12. Trends of infestation of *Stenchaeotothrips biformis* on the paddy plant, *Oryza sativa*, and the weeds *Echinochloa colona* and *Cyperes iria*.

The polyphagous species *Haplothrips ganglbaueri* causing sufficient damage to the inflorescence of paddy is known to occur on more than fifty species of graminaceous and cyperaceous weeds in and around the culti-vated fields in Southern India.  A distinct correlation has also been known to exist between the population of *H.ganglbaueri* on the paddy inflorescence, with those of the major weeds *Echinchloa colona*, *Cyperus iria*, *C.rotundus* and *Cyperus difformis*.  Thrips infestation occurred nor-mally during the inflorescence stage from 40-45 days to 60-65 days, some-times extending till the paddy was 80-85 days old.  Infestation rates indicated the maximum infestation of *H.ganglbaueri* to be 27.5% in *Oryza sativa*, 35.3% in *E.colona* 33.9% in *C.iria* and 25% in *C.difformis*.  Obser-vations during the flowering period and after, on the densities of weeds inside the paddy fields and on the bunds, also indicated that in the fields the population density of weeds and paddy to be: *E.colona*  75-90 plants/sq.m., *C.difformis* 60-75 plants/sq.m., *C.iria*  50-70 plants/sq.m., all along the bunds, and the density of paddy plants being 67-74 plants/ sq.m.  The increasing incidence of *H.ganglbaueri* as a pest of paddy in this country and consequent high percentage of damage due to chaffiness of grain appears to be directly correlated both with the type and density of the weeds.  In several areas *Echinochloa crusgalli*  occurred amidst the paddy plants and harboured heavy populations of thrips.

In mixed type of crops as barley and oats involving *Limothrips cerealium*, *Limothrips denticornis*, *Stenothrips graminum*, *Frankliniella tenuicornis*, the species are localized to panicles and sheaths, and rarely may also be found in exposed situations.  The distribution of the species naturally varies in relation to microclimate, exposed species showing varied movements on or between different food plants in terms of copulatory and oviposition activities.  Only during the onset of unfavourable conditions like the drying up of plants, do the species become sensitive to the changing conditions so that females migrate to a more favourable weed environment (Cederholm, 1963).

## MILLET CROPS

*Florithrips traegardhi, Frankliniella schultzei, Exothrips hema-varna* and *Chirothrips mexicanus* occur in the inflorescence of sorghum, in parts of South India, along with *Haplothrips ganglbaueri*. The rise and fall in number of different species of thrips populations appeared independent of each other following the conditions of the environment, the maximum temperature ranging from 31.6°C to 36.0°C during the period of study. *F.schultzei, E.haemavarna* and *C.mexicanus* show their peak abundance during the last week of September with RH 62%, and during the first week of October with RH 93%. *Haplothrips ganglbaueri* which occurred in fewer numbers during the first two weeks of the study period showed a sudden increase, with the decline of populations of the other species. A high incidence of *Florithrips traegardhi* occurred from the 105th day of duration of the crop and the population was maintained till the 160th day, the maximum infestation occurring when the crop was 120-130 days old.

Analysis of the populations of different species of Thysanoptera on sorghum and on the weed hosts indicates the importance of weeds in the infestation of crops by thrips (Ananthakrishnan and Thirumalai, 1977). It is significant that during September-October 1977, when the fields were crowded with the weed-host *Echinochloa colona*, the main infestation of thrips on sorghum crop was by *Florithrips traegardhi*. On the contrary, during the same period in the next year when the grass weeds *Eleusine aegyptica* and *Eragrostis uniloides* were abundant, *Florithrips* population was completely absent and the crop was infested with *Frankliniella schultzei, Chirothrips mexicanus, Exothrips hemavarna* and *Haplothrips ganglbaueri*. This appears to agree with the view that the cultivation of natural vegetation quickly alters the structure of the thysanopteran community living in it (Lewis, 1973). Observations presented above also strongly support the view of Post and Colberg (1958) that suitable niches when available can be exploited quickly.

The higher incidence of *Frankliniella schultzei* (62.9%) on sorghum indicates its preference to optimum temperatures and low humidities as suggested by Viswanathan and Ananthakrishnan (1976) for thrips on *Ruellia tuberosa*. On the other hand the relatively low incidence of *Exothrips hemavarna* (9.8%) and *Chirothrips mexicanus* (17.7%) was due to their preference to lower humidity and higher temperatures (Ananthakrishnan and Thirumalai, 1978). Similarly, Oettingen (1942) observed that *Chirothrips manicatus* was more abundant in dry months. The comparatively low incidence of *Chirothrips mexicanus* could also be attributed to their being parthenogenetic (Ananthakrishnan and Thirumalai, 1977, 1978), increasing in numbers in warmer seasons, because less time was needed to complete development, so that more generations were produced in the time available (Lewis, 1973). An increase in the incidence (7.1 to 16.7%) of *Haplothrips ganglbaueri* population later in the study season was due to the decline of other species and the reduction in humidity (from 93% to 70%) and temperature (36.0°C to 31.6°C).

66

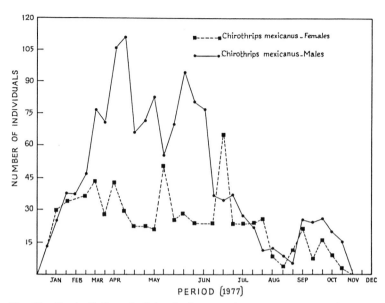

Fig.13. Periodicity of *Chirothrips mexicanus* males and females on *Pennisetum typhoides*.

*Florithrips traegardhi*, normally infesting the young leaves of sorghum, has been reported on the inflorescence of *Zea mays* which is raised as a summer crop, and on the inflorescence of the alternate weed hosts *Vernonia* sp. and *Amaranthus* sp. along with *Haplothrips gowdeyi*. Regular examination of *Zea mays* indicated that with the beginning of infestation from 114th day of the crop, the population of *Haplothrips gowdeyi* gradually increased to 68-72 individuals/flower within a period of 7-10 daus. Populations of *Haplothrips gowdeyi* started decreasing from 121st day onwards due to the infestation of *Florithrips traegradhi*. From the 121st day of the development of maize crop, *Florithrips* population occurred till the 139th day with the maximum infestation during the 132-135th day. Inspite of its infesting maize, the population *H.gowdeyi* was steadily maintained on the weed *Vernonia* indicating the latter as a potential reservoir for this pest species.

A very good correlation appears to exist between the degree of infestation of *Chirothrips mexicanus*, principally a seed feeder in very young earheads of *Pennisetum typhoides*, and the graminaceous weed *Chloris barbata* abundant in *Pennisetum* fields. The incidence of this species in *Chloris barbata* indicated a range of 25-30 individuals/branch of the four-branched spike, each with 45-50 spikelets, presenting an unusual preponderance of males resulting in a sex ratio of 2:1 to 5:1 (Males: Females), suggesting an arrhenotokous parthenogenetic mode of reproduction occurring side by side with the normal sexual reproduction. The periodicty of males and females of *Chirothrips mexicanus* on *Pennisetum* as

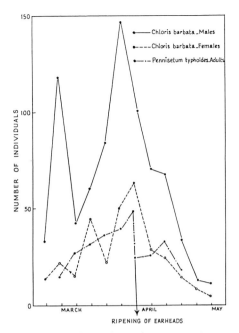

Fig.14. Trends of infestation of *Chirothrips mexicanus* on
*Pennisetum typhoides* and the weed *Chloris barbata*.

well as the trends of their infestation on *Chloris barbata* are indicated
in Figs. 13 and 14. Only one egg is laid per floret, the larva feeding on
the growing ovarian tissues, preventing seed formation. Of 176-200
growing florets of *C.barbata* examined in a complete branched spike, 57-75
individuals of *C.mexicanus* occurred in various stages of development,
there being only one individual per floret. The population of adult
males of *C.mexicanus* reaches its peak in the first few days of adult
emergence and declines rapidly thereafter. But the female population
builds up gradually within 2-4 days of adult emergence. In addition, the
females survive longer (30-35 days under laboratory conditions) than the
males (6-7 days) (Fig. 15). The overall seed damage in *Pennisetum* was of
the order of 5-10%, while in *C.barbata* the very heavy incidence indicating a total damage of 60% of the seeds. While the young *Pennisetum*
inflorescence and the grass *Chloris barbata* mostly harboured *Chirothrips*
very few *H.ganglbaueri*, *H.gowdeyi* and *Frankliniella schultzei* occurred.
*Exothrips hemavarna*, a graminivorous species infesting the weeds *Panicum
maximum*, *Andropogon pertusus*, etc. has also been reported as a pest of
*Pennisetum* earheads, with the grass *Chloris barbata* also as its alternate
host.

## THRIPS AND PULSE CROPS

Interesting information is available on thrips infestation in cowpea
in Nigeria, where the flowers are very heavily infested with *Megalurothrips sjostedti*, immigrant populations of adults coming mainly from

68

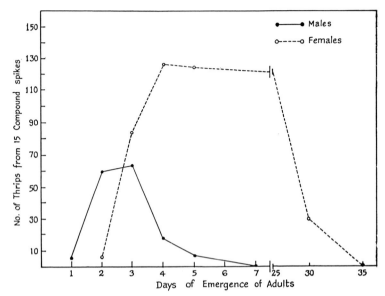

Fig.15. Emergence sequence and survival of males and females of *Chirothrips mexicanus*.

alternate host plants as indicated in Table 1. Within 12–34 days, the population build-up on cowpea occured, the build-up being correlated with cumulative flowers on the plant and to the flowering duration pattern. *Centrosema pubescens*, a perennial cover legume pasture and hedge crop is the only species in which flowering occurs intermittently for many months in the year. The main flowering cycle from November to December resulted in high populations in *Centrosema* and studies on the population dynamics of *M.sjostedti* indicated that two or three peaks existed on *Centrosema* from where they infest cowpea crops. *Centrosema* therefore appears to be the major reservoir of *M.sjostedti* from which migrant populations invade cowpea in the immediate pre-flowering stage leading to a population explosion on both the early and late crops (Taylor, 1974). The reverse situation occurs when the thrips migrate from senescent crops of cowpea contributing to the increase in thrips population on *Centrosema* and other weed-hosts (Figs. 16, 17).

Thrips compostion in pulse crops in India appears to present a more varied picture, with *Megalurothrips distalis* and *Frankliniella schultzei* infesting flowers of *Cajanus cajan*, *Phaseolus indicus*, *Phaseolus mungo* and *Vigna catjang*; leaf infesting species involve *Ramaswamiahiella subnudula*, *Hydatothrips ramaswamiahi*, *Ayyaria chaetophora*, *Scirtothrips dorsalis* and *Caliothrips indicus*. The Papilionaceous weeds *Indigofera tinctoria* and *Tephrosia purpurea* which blossom in the month of May every year after the removal of the pulse crops, act as effective alternate hosts for *M.distalis*, *H.ramaswamiahi* and *R.subnudula*.

Populations of *M.distalis* in parts of Southern India start building up on these weeds by May and reach the peak by August following summer showers and disappear after October. Following this, *M.distalis* migrates

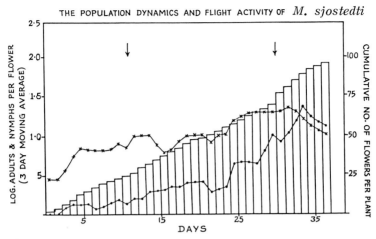

Fig.16. Population trends of adults and nymphs of *Megalurothrips sjostedti* in relation to flower production in cowpea (after Taylor, 1969).

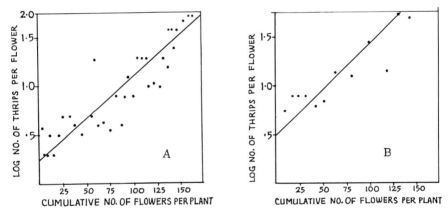

Fig.17. Relationship between log number of *Megalurothrips sjostedti/*flower/cumulative numbers/plants of (a) early cowpea (b) late cowpea (after Taylor, 1969).

from these weeds to *Phaseolus trilobus*, another weed which flowers till December. With the flowering of the crop commencing after December, thrips from *P.trilobus* migrate towards the flowers of the crop. *Frankliniella schultzei* being a highly polyphagous species spreads to the flowers of weeds such as *Leucas aspera*, *Portulaca plerocea*, *Cleome viscosa*, *Crotalaria recurvosa* and *Croton sparsiflorus* after the removal of the crop.

TABLE 1. The Incidence of *Megalurothrips sjostedti* on alternative host plants during the years 1970-1972.

| HOST PLANT | MONTHS | REMARKS |
|---|---|---|
| *Phaseolus vulgaris* | May–July, November and December | Adults and Nymphs |
| *Glyricidia* sp. | January–March and December | Adults only |
| *Thoningia* sp. | February and March | Adults only |
| *Newboldia laevis* | February and March | Adults only |
| *Crotolaria juncea* | May–July, October and December | Adults and Nymphs |
| *Vigna triloba* | September–November | Adults and Nymphs |
| *Lycopersicon esculentum* | May–July, October–December | Adults only |
| *Caesalpinia pulcherrima* | January–April and December | Adults only |
| *Cola* sp. | February–April, September–November | Adults only |
| *Cajanus cajan* | January–March, June–December | Adults and Nymphs |
| *Glycine max* | May–June, October and November | Adults only |
| *Psophocarpus tetragonolobus* | April–June, October–December | Adults and Nymphs |
| *Centrosema pubescens* | throughout the year | Adults and Nymphs |

(after Taylor, 1974)

## THRIPS AND FIBRE CROPS

Watts (1937) reported thirteen species of thrips infesting cotton in America causing considerable injury, but the activities of four principal species *Frankliniella fusca*, *F.tritici*, *F.occidentalis* and *Thrips tabaci* appear to cause retarded plant growth, and delayed fruiting, maturity and harvest (Watson, 1965). Thrips injuries are known to reduce the total leaf area in young plants by 50-70%. In the seedling stages the leaves are often tightly curled, later becoming irregular and rugged. The Primordia of seedling leaves often become destroyed stopping further growth.

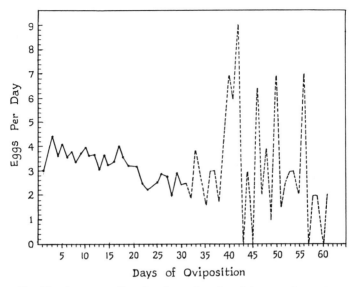

Fig.18. Average distribution of oviposition during life of the female *Frankliniella tritici* (after Watts, 1937).

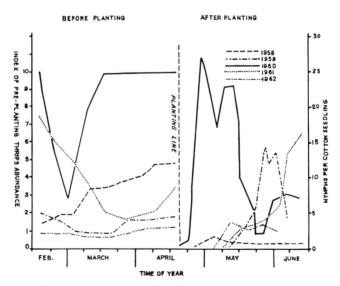

Fig.19. Abundance of *Frankliniella occidentalis* before and after cotton planting in New Mexico (After Race, 1965).

*Thrips tabaci* is more predominant in cotton seedling and species of *Frankliniella* take over at the flowering stage, forming 80% of the total. Infestation levels vary from year to year considerably and from field to field within the same year and severe infestation results in destruction of leaf buds and cause plants to become excessively branced and distorted (Watson, 1968). Among the more important alternate hosts, in the United States, from the viewpoint of suitability of thrips development are the white clover *Trifolium repens*, the crimson clover *Trifolium incarnatum* and alfalfa, *Medicago sativa*. With the exception of alfalfa, the other hosts begin to mature or have matured during the period when cotton is in the seedling stage, and is susceptible to thrips injury, so that *Frankliniella fusca* moves to seedling cotton from other hosts. Important summer hosts are alfalfa and *Lespedeza striata* which are extensively grown as increased feeds, and contribute towards maintaining high populations of thrips at a time when it is adverse for thrips development in cotton. Alfalfa is the only crop observed to furnish a satisfactory alternate host for the development of the cotton thrips throughout the year. The grass *Brachiaria extensa* is also an important summer host, the other hosts near the cotton fields being *Sorghum halipensa*, the Johnson grass and red sprangletop *Leptochloa filiformis*. As such *Frankliniella fusca* breeds throughout the year and in particular brachypterous forms were found to be very active throughout winter months and developed heavy populations in various hosts. Beginning from March, there was a gradual change to the macropterous conditions and by May all the adults are macropterous, the proportions between brachypterous and macropterous forms being: 363:3 (January), 259:5 (February), 243:22 (March), 239:97 (April) and by May it is about 100% macropterous (Newsom *et al.*, 1953).

In India and Egypt where the cotton crop is infested by *Thrips tabaci*, cotton seedlings suffer badly from the attack. The smooth brand Egyptian cotton is more susceptible to thrips attack than the Indian and American varieties. Because of the variable degree of infestation, periodicity of occurrence and injuries inflicted, cotton seedlings suffer from thrips attack. Particular mention may be made of the interaction of thrips species in a crop community, wherein mixed cropping occurs and where cotton, chillies and onion and to a limited extent tomatoes are cultivated. The major species *Thrips tabaci*, *Scirtothrips dorsalis*, and *Frankliniella schultzei* infesting these crops are very highly polyphagous and are maintained in considerable numbers on various weeds and other vegetation including *Prosopis* trees growing around fields. While chillies and onions are not attacked by other species of thrips, there is a concentrated infestation on the cotton seedlings by all the three species resulting in large-scale mortality of cotton seedlings. Several weeds such as *Acanthospermum* sp., *Ageratum conizoides*, *Synedrella nodiflora*, *Bidens pilea*, *Tridax procumbens*, species of *Amarantus* etc., act as alternate hosts for thrips species serving to maintain a steady population (Ananthakrishnan, 1980a).

Studies on the incidence and intensity of infestation of *Scirtothrips dorsalis* in different ecological conditions in cotton fields in southern India have also clearly revealed, that the overall monthly fluctuations of incidence of this species involving (a) populations in cotton fields adjacent to *Prosopis spicigera* on the windward side (b) populations in fields adjacent to *Prosopis* but on the leeward side, and (c) populations in fields totally isolated from *Prosopis* trees, was the highest in the month of October during the years 1977-78. Prediction of thrips population on seedling cotton has been made, as indicated in Figure 19, by comparing the relative abundance of *Frankliniella occidentalis* populations during the pre-planting period on adjoining host plants such as onions, alfalfa and lettuce with the populations during the post planting period (Race, 1965).

Flax is an important fibre crop in the Netherlands and the two major species occurring frequently and regularly are *Thrips angusticeps* and *Thrips linarius* which breed on this plant. *Thrips angusticeps* have both a brachypterous and a macropterous generation, the former hibernating in the soil and emerging from it in spring, long before the emergence of the flax seedlings. Although *Thrips angusticeps* has many host plants, the macropterous forms migrate mostly to flax and to a lesser extent to pea, barley and wheat on which also they tend to lay eggs. The heaviest soil infestation occurs under flax. The damage to a young flax crop caused by the brachypterous thrips results in silver spots on the stalks and the fibres later break at the points. The larvae of the macropterous generation and adults of *Thrips linarius* appear in the half-grown crop and the infested plants have a yellowish grey colour, and the leaves become dark spotted (Frannsen and Mantel, 1960, 1961) (Fig. 20).

## THRIPS AND OIL SEED CROPS

Oil seed crops like *Ricinus communis*, *Arachis hypogaea* and *Sesamum indicum* are known to be infested by several species of thrips, the periodicity of which varies according to the season as well as the type of weeds associated with the crop during different times of the year. *Caliothrips indicus*, the polyphagous panchaetothripine species is known for its severe infestation on groundnut, causing the leaves to be spotted, pale and sickly. Since its life-cycle is very short, being of the order of 11-14 days, it can pass through several generations in a year, and can reproduce mostly by parthenogenesis. In the cultivated areas of the groundnut crop in southern India, *Caliothrips indicus* builds up its population on the annual weed *Achyranthes aspera* before the appearance of the crop. The density of the weed starts declining in June and completely disappears in the fields by July, following the appearance of *Arachis hypogaea* seedlings in the fields. During this period migration of *Caliothrips* towards the 15-45 days old seedlings of groundnut occurs, the infestation remaining for three months from July-September, with the population peak in September. With the decline in the population of thrips in the groundnut crop they switch from September, over to fresh *Achyranthes aspera* plants, which appear after the rains. *Hydatothrips ramaswamiahi* also infests this oil seed crop in large numbers during February, followed by their heavy build-up in the weed *Tephrosia purpurea* in the same field. During the flowering of the crop in the months of December-February, *Megalurothrips distalis* also appears, its maximum infestation being in February. Blooming of the papilionacous weeds *Tephrosia purpurea* and *Indigofera tinctoria* follows the flowering of the crop, which enables migration of this species to both these weeds, which act as alternate host for this species till June. *M.distalis* moves to another papilionaceous weed *Phaseolus trilobus* which blooms by June. In the same fields *Ruellia tuberosa* also showed infestation of *M.distalis* during the period, along with the other highly polyphagous species *Frankliniella schultzei* and *Scirtothrips dorsalis*.

It was mentioned earlier in the chapter on thrips communities that the castor crop *Ricinus communis* harbours seven species of thrips during different periods of their growth (Fig. 3). Three to four months after the planting of the crop, *Toxothrips ricinus* and *Scirtothrips dorsalis* appear showing a peak in summer. With the removal of the crop *S.dorsalis* migrates towards *Prosopis spicigera* where heavy population occurs in May and June. By September two more species *Ayyaria chaetophora* and *Zaniothrips ricini* infest the castor crop. A build-up of *A.chaetophora* population in the weed *Melochia* sp. occurs by August, subsequently migrating to the crop. No such migration was seen to occur in *Z.ricini*, but following the decline in its population during March-April, it appeared on its alternate hosts *Datura* sp., and *Calotropis gigantea*. From January onwards the species *Astrothrips tumiceps*, *Retithrips syriacus* and *Rhipiphorothrips cruentatus* occur on the crop. *R.syriacus* attains its maximum population in May declining thereafter and migrating to several alternate hosts such as *Croton sparsiflorus*, *Cassia auriculata*, *Acalypha indica*, etc.

*Sesamum indicum* is also known to be infested by two major species, *Thrips palmi* inhabiting flowers and *Hydatothrips ramaswamiahi* infesting leaves. The common weeds in the *Sesamum* fields which show populations of the species are *Croton sparsiflorus* and *Tephrosia purpurea*. Infestation of *T.palmi* commences on the crop by early January and a sudden decline is noticed in February, after which they switch on to the alternate hosts.

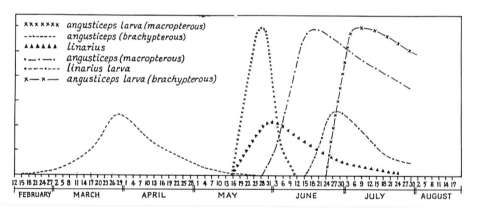

Fig.20. Seasonal incidence of flax thrips (after Franssen and Mantel, 1962).

## PLANTATION CROPS

Consideration is made here of the cardamom crop generally grown in the high ranges of Kerala, Tamil Nadu and Karnataka of India in view of it's being very severely infested with *Sciothrips cardamomi* which feed and breed mostly in the pseudostems concealed by the leaf axis. In plants of about 10 years growth, thrips populations usually concentrate upto the eighth leaf axis when counted from the base. They migrate from

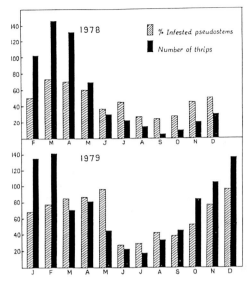

Fig.21. Percentage of infested pseudostems and number of thrips on cardamom.

one leaf axis to another for fresh food and better protection. During March and April the migration from pseudostems to panicles is at its maximum and during these months the bracts on the panicles open providing shelter and fresh food. The colonies under the leaf sheaths on pseudostems contain 10–30 individuals, whereas in each bract on the panicles only 5–15 individuals generally occur.

Biological studies of this species have shown that these thrips are able to reproduce both sexually and parthenogenetically, there being as many as eight generations, the females predominating the males. The build-up of thrips populations generally attains a maximum in March/April on pseudostems and they show a gradual decline, reaching the minimum during August-September. Regarding the relationship between the age of the plantation and the degree of incidence of cardamom thrips, observations made in southern India in a 30-year old plantation and a four-year old plantation showed that both the young as well as the old plants were equally attacked showing no preference to the age of the plantation. However, the relative population of thrips was more in the thickly shaded areas than in the thinly shaded ones. In 150 fascicles examined, the fluctuations of thrips populations in overhead thickly and thinly vegetated areas showed considerable variation with around 800 thrips/100 panicles in thickly shaded ones and around 550 in the thinly shaded areas (Figs. 21,22). The periodicity of populations generally vary and there appears to be a correlation between *Sciothrips cardamomi* populations on cardamom and that on some of the alternate hosts like *Panicum longipes*, *Hedychium flavescens*, *H.coronariam*, *Amomum cannecarpum*, *Colocasia* sp. to mention a few. However more authentic data on this correlation is lacking at present, but consistent observations all through the year should produce interesting results.

76

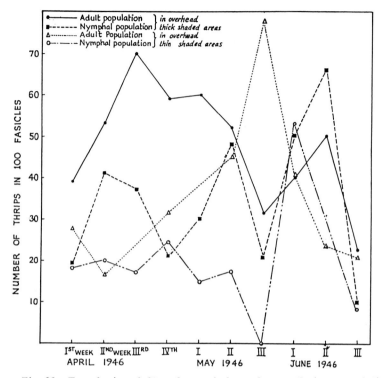

Fig.22. Trends in adult and nymphal cardamom thrips populations in overhead, thickly shaded and thinnly shaded areas.

Another plantation crop suffering from thrips infestation is coffee and in recent years *Scirtothrips bispinosus* has proved to be a major pest. Heavy infestation results in lacerations in the form of irregular brownish areas on the under surface, causing the leaves to turn leathery, brittle, and subsequently to crinkle. In the coffee growing areas in S.India, it has been found that the population density varies throughout the year with a gradual increase from July-December followed by a sharp decrease and again increasing in May and reaching its peak in June. Frequently the buds are badly damaged resulting in the development of adventitious buds, which when attacked by this thrips leads to rosetted growth. The average life-cycle takes 19 days with a range of 15-28 days and 12 generations per year, reproduction being by both sexual and parthenogenetic means. The maximum activity of this thrips has been known to be between 14.30 and 15.30 hrs. and plants with a high population density even when they were interspersed with those having negligible infestations showed that the total infestation remained almost like the exposed and shaded areas (Sekhar *et al*, 1965).

At temperatures of 25-31°C, thrips incidence was high and above 31°C, it was low. Leaves of the first node carried the highest number of thrips, more than twice as much as in the leaves of the second node. Counts showed that the total population on 15 leaves of each of the 24

TABLE 2. Population of *Scirtothrips hispinosus* in three shade patterns at stipulated periods (Sekhar *et al.*, 1965).

| Shade pattern | Total average population per plant of 20 leaves | | | Grand total |
|---|---|---|---|---|
| | 8.30–9.30 | 2.30–3.30 | 4–5 | |
| Exposed | 31.5 | 42.5 | 32.3 | 106.3 |
| Medium | 32.6 | 33.8 | 37.9 | 104.3 |
| Thick | 26.5 | 33.2 | 31.0 | 90.7 |

plants examined was 1653 in December, 1028 in January, 2859 in June and 305–591 in other months (Sekhar *et al.*, 1964, 1965) (Table 2). Numerous weeds are also known to harbour this thrips in the coffee plantations, but information on their interactions is lacking. The coffee thrips of Kenya, *Diarthrothrips coffeae* has similarly been known to depend on outbreaks of dry weather. Heavy infestation of this species has been shown to be due to the density of migrants over the crop, particularly occurring on the leeward slopes and behind wind breaks in coffee fields (Lewis, 1973).

A close parallel to thrips in coffee fields is seen in those species infesting tea in the hilly areas of North Eastern India as well as various parts of southern India, where *Scirtothrips dorsalis* as a result of heavy infestations has been known to damage buds, young leaves, and occasionally older leaves. The injured tissues harden and turn brownish and due to repeated feeding in more or less continuous lines in the buds, the wound marks appear later as 'sand papery lines' on the epidermis of the leaves. In some cases of infestation leaf growth is arrested, the leaves becoming crinkled and corky and often resulting in a premature fall. Its occurrence on the leaves of young *Albizzia odoratissima* and *A.falcata* used as shade trees in tea plantations, indicates its ability to build up populations in these hosts during the off-seasons. *Scirtothrips dorsalis* appears on pruned tea with the development of new growth and the population, reaches its peak during May. A sudden decline in the population occurs from August to October with the onset of monsoon. Both adults and nymphs prefer sheltered places mostly in the partly opened buds and young nymphs usually occur in large numbers on the underside of the second and third leaves. Pupation takes place on the lichens and mosses growing the stems of the tea plant (Dev, 1964).

Banana plantations in various parts of the world are also subject to attack by different species of thrips, *Chaetanaphothrips orchidii* infesting the pseudostems, *Frankliniella parvula* and *F.musaeperda* causing damage to the banana fruit by ovipositing on young fingers, *Helionothrips kadaliphilus* feeding on the young leaves causing yellow spots and *Thrips hawaiiensis* within flowers. Studies in several banana growing areas in the French Antilles have yielded some information on the population and distribution of *C.orchidii* in the pseudostems as well as in banana plots in general regarding the migration of adults and the methods of settling

78

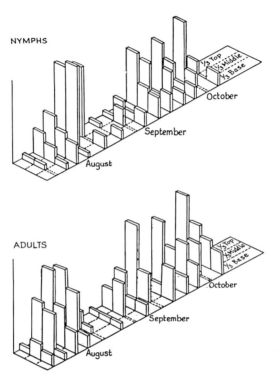

NYMPHS

ADULTS

Fig.23. Distribution of populations of *Chaetanophothrips orchidii* in banana (after Delattre and Toregrossa, 1978).

on the banana stems as well as the population dynamics of larvae and adults (Delattre and Torregrossa, 1975, 1978). Studies on the build-up of this species on various host plants and its subsequent migration to banana has been discussed and the principal host plants of this species in and around banana fields are *Paspalum paniculatum*, *Brachiaria purpurescens*, (Graminea), *Torilinium ferax* (Cyperaceae) *Ageratum connizoides*, *Bidens pilosa*, *Sonchus oleraceus* (Compositae), *Croton lobatus* (Euphorbiaceae), *Ipomea tiliacea* (Convolvulaceae), *Commelina erecta* (Commelinaceae), *Portulaca oleracea* (Portulacaeae). Of these *Commelina* and *Brachiaria* harbour enough populations so that dispersion to the banana plant is assured (Fig. 23).

*Frankliniella parvula* is an equally important pest in the Dominican Republic and has become a dominant thrips in the banana plantations there. Oviposition takes place in the young banana fingers, petals, pistils, bracts and in the stems of the fruits while these structures are still enclosed in the bracts. The flower parts and bracts fall to the ground carrying the larvae with them. Before pupation they crawl from these old bracts and flower parts into the ground to pupate, 1.5 to 7.5 cms. beneath the soil surface (Harrison, 1963). In India *Helionothrips kadaliphilus* is known to be very specific to certain varieties of bananas, generally found distributed singly over the ventral sides of the young leaves causing yellowish blotched areas. Heavy populations of this species has been recorded from *Colocasia* leaves generally common in and around the banana fields which appears to be a source for infestation to the banana crop (Ananthakrishnan, 1969, 1973).

The abundance, the pattern of distribution of various host plants involving crops as well as alternate weed hosts in space and time is an important factor in the population dynamics of thrips. As mentioned earlier, the changes occurring when a crop matures and the influence of host plant on intraspecific competition in the insect population is affected by several factors. Plant growth is continuously altering the space available and the amount of food changing with it along with the physical factors which impose severe restrictions on thrips populations. At the same time the growing insect populations are making increasing demands on the plant affecting its growth and quality (van Emden & Way, 1972).

Agroecosystems when viewed as a whole, presents a picture of dynamism of both the crop plant and the weeds as well as of thrips infesting them. Ploughing the field at different times of the year affects the species composition and abundance not only of the weed complex, but also of the thrips fauna. Such a seasonal disturbance of weeds also results in changes in the predatory complex which fluctuates according to the availability of alternate prey as determined by the presence of weed hosts (Altieri & Whitcomb, 1978/79). The presence of specific weeds in habitats adjacent to crop fields determines to a considerable extent the type of predatory species inhabiting particular crop fields. It is therefore evident that the interaction of predators, prey and host plants may differ not only from one crop field to another, but also from one region to another, as well as from year to year. Manipulation of plant diversity in agroecosystems through seasonal disturbances of the soil by ploughing has now been attempted in many parts of the world.

* * * * *

# THRIPS AND NATURAL CONTROL AGENTS

Natural ecosystems abound in predators and parasites as well as microorganisms whose action tend to regulate natural imbalances in communities enabling injurious species in particular, to be maintained at levels below the economic threshold. Predation and parasitism are two aspects of biological control of organisms, although in recent years a tendency exists to regard the total consumption of any organism, plant or animal as predation. Price (1975) clearly indicates that 'predation must be considered as the heart of ecological thinking', in view of its forming 'the central issue of our understanding of how energy moves through the food chains, as also of both the adaptive strategies in getting food and for avoidance of becoming food'. This is clearly evident in the action of several anthocorid predators of thrips discussed in this chapter. It is interesting that while many Hemiptera, Coleoptera, Neuroptera etc., are efficient predators of thrips, several species of thrips themselves are also known to be active predators. Parasitism by Hymenoptera and Diptera are equally well-known in Thysanoptera, as also the utilization of parasites like *Ceranisus brui* for the control of the onion thrips *Thrips tabaci*, and other species in the control of thrips pests. In recent years it has also come to be recognized that habitat manipulation with a view to increase alternate food sources for predators helps in maintaining a natural balance of predator populations within particular cropping communities - an aspect which is being practiced in soyabean fields in the United States of America. The utilization of these parasites and predators from their natural weed reservoirs to their specific hosts in adjacent crops, reveal the ecological basis of natural control, so that the inherent stability in an ecosystem forms the basis for successful operation of biological control agents. At the same time it may be mentioned that predator/prey systems involving species feeding on more than one trophic level are likely to be unstable. In general, as the number of possible interactions within a random-web increases, so does the probability that the system would be unstable. With the increase in the number of trophic levels, the relative time for the system to return to equilibrium after disturbance also increases (Pimm, 1979).

Studies on natural control agents of thrips involve consideration of predators, parasites and microorganisms such as protozoa, bacteria and fungi. Aspects of host/predator interactions essentially comprise consideration of predatory thrips involving acariphagous, coccidophagous and thripiphagous species, as well as of thrips predators involving thripiphagous acari, and other arachnids such as Chelonethi, and Hemipteran predators such as species of anthocorids, lygaeids, mirids and the like, species of Neuroptera, Coleoptera, Hymenoptera and Diptera. Parasitism in thrips is equally well-established with many species of chalcids, eulophids, mymarids, trichogrammatids etc. acting as efficient parasites. Besides parasitic nematodes are known to infect thrips. Many protozoan, bacterial, and fungal pathogens are also known to play an important role in the natural control of thrips populations.

PREDATORY THRIPS

(1) *Acariphagous thrips* :

Thrips feeding on mites mostly belong to species of *Aeolothrips*, *Scolothrips*, and *Haplothrips*, though species such as *Cryptothrips nigripes* and *Leptothrips mali* are also known to be efficient predators of mites. *Scolothrips acariphagus* has been reported to feed on cotton mites in Russia (Yakhantov, 1935), *Scolothrips sexmaculatus* on the six-spotted mites (Muma, 1955, 1958) and Mori (1967) reports its predatory activity on *Tetranychus kurazawai* in Japan. *Scolothrips longicornis* is found to prey on *Tetranychus urticae* in East Germany on beans (Fritzsche, 1958), an adult thrips consuming 5 mites or 8 eggs/day. *Scolothrips indicus* in India is a well-known predator of the cotton mite, while *Parascolothrips priesneri* is reported to feed on *Tetranychus atlanticus* on apple trees in Baghdad (Mound, 1967).

Though Bailey (1939) briefly indicated the life-history of *Scolothrips sexmaculatus*, an outstanding contribution regarding the bionomics of this species feeding on spider mites is that of Gilstrap and Oatman (1976). *S.sexmaculatus* has been found to be the earliest and most abundant predator and has been recognized as a specialized predator of spider mites causing considerable reduction in mite populations on peach, cotton, strawberry, etc., in California (Gilstrap & Oatman, 1976). After an incubation period of 6.3-8.6 days, the unhatched larvae force their respective eggs to protrude nearly 2/3 of their length from the leaf surface and within 5 minutes the larvae become free of the chorion, eclosion taking about 6.7-8.7 minutes. Post-eclosion period is usually spent close to the spider mite webbing, and 18.1-79.4 minutes after eclosion, the larvae killed their first mite egg, the first feeding activity lasting 16.8-66.6 minutes when most of the egg contents were consumed. The first stage larvae feed on all stages and both sexes of spider mites, the first larval duration being 2.3-3.0 days. The second larva lasts for 2.0-3.3 days. The various developmental stages of the prey were usually held by the prothoracic tarsi of larvae and active mite stages were usually fed on at a median point between eye spots. First and second stage larvae are well-adapted behaviourally to accommodate the copious webbing produced by some members of the Tetranychidae. Feeding ceased 16-24 hours prior to moulting with the non-feeding, but mobile prepupa lasting 1.0-1.6 days, after which they moulted into the pupae, also non-feeding and mobile, lasting 1.6-2.6 days. The total developmental period for the active immature stages was 7.6-10.3 days. The first prey was killed within 1.5 hours after imaginal moult. Cannibalism occurs under scarcity of prey conditions, the first stage larvae cannibalizing larvae in the process of hatching, the 2nd stage consuming weak individuals of first and second stages. The peak mean numbers of eggs killed per day were 143.60 (at 40.6°C), 111.95 at 35°C, 64.83 at 29.4°C, 62.30 at 23.9°C and 22.40 at 18.3°C (Fig. 24). Males killed only about one quarter as many mite eggs daily as did females at the same temperature (Gilstrap & Oatman, 1976). The predatory efficiency of *Scolothrips sexmaculatus* naturally depends on such factors as voracity of predators, rate of reproduction of prey, and synchronization of predator/prey populations.

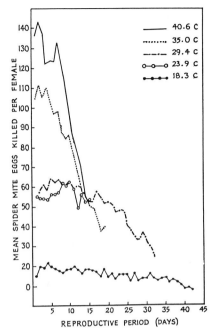

Fig.24. Mean daily number of eggs of *Tetranychus pacificus* killed by *Scolothrips sexmaculatus* at several constant temperatures (after Gilstrap and Oatman, 1976).

Putman (1942) records *Haplothrips niger* consuming eggs of various insects and mites, and both adults and larvae feeding on the eggs of the oriental fruit moth, European red mite and the common red spider mite, *Tetranychus telarius* in orchards. Putman and Herne (1966) observed larvae of *Aeolothrips melaleucus* feeding on *Tetranychus urticae* and more rarely on *Panonychus ulmi* in peach orchards. *Leptothrips mali* is also known to largely feed on eriophyid mites (Bailey, 1937), consuming mainly the silver or rust mites and red spider eggs. It has also been found to be associated with the citrus rust mites *Phyllocoptrita oleirosa* and the purple mite *Metatetranychus citri* (Muma, 1955). *Leptothrips mali* is the most abundant predator on *Panonychus ulmi*, a perennial pest of apples in Virginia, 73-86% of mites being reported to be killed and in combination with the coccinellid *Stethorus punctum* 93% mites were killed (Parella *et al.*, 1980). *Haplothrips faurei* is an equally important predator of *Panonychus ulmi* on apple in Novascotia, (Lord, 1949; Lord *et al.*, 1952), and is a density dependent factor in the regulation of mite populations. Putman (1965) records *H.faurei* feeding on winter egg pupulations of *P.ulmi* on peach and *Bryobia arborea*. Larvae consumed on an average 143 eggs of *P.ulmi* during a developmental period of 8-10 days at 24°C. Adult females at the same temperature consumed 43.6 eggs (Putman, 1965; Huffaker *et al.*, 1970). *Cryptothrips nigripes* is reported to occur only in the hibernation sites of *Tetranychus urticae* in East Germany (Fritzche, 1958), larvae being active even at 0°C causing high mortality of hibernating mites.

(2) *Coccidophagous thrips*:

Several species of thrips are well-known predators of coccids and
aleyrodids and as early as 1912, Back reported *Aleurodothrips fasciatus*
feeding on eggs, nymphs, and pupae of citrus white flies (*Dialeurodes
citri*) and cloudy winged white flies (*Dialeurodes citrifolii*) and producing 95.5% egg mortality in rearing cages.   Taylor (1935) reports it as
feeding on the coconut scale (*Aspidiotus destructor*) and other armoured
scales (Diaspidae).   Muma (1955) recorded associations of the thrips with
the purple scale (*Lepidosaphes beckii*) and the Florida red scale
(*Chrysomphalus aonidum*) in citrus trees.   Eggs are deposited in groups
varying from 1 to 7 under scale armours, in the cast skin of white fly
nymphs, under trash and under sooty mould on scale infested leaves.   Larvae of *Aleurodothrips* vary in colour from light lemon yellow when fed on
the purple scales, Florida red scale or cloudy winged scale; and white
with orange red to purplish red pigment spots when fed on chaff scale
(*Parlatoria pergandei*).   Development of *Aleurodothrips* takes place in 23
days at 80°F, some taking 14, others 36 days.   Laboratory experiments on
the development of *A.fasciatus* isolated with and allowed to feed on different suspected hosts showed that eggs of Florida red scale, purple and
chaff scale were preferred, 56.4, 56.6 and 46.9% respectively completing
development on these scales (Selhime *et al.*, 1963).   *Aleurodothrips
fasciapennis* has been introduced into parts of the Orient for the control
of the scale *Aspidotus destructor*.   It has also been found in association
with the pyriform scale *Prosopulvinaria pyriformes*  and the cotton
cushion scale *Icerya purchasi*.   Other coccid feeding thrips are *Veerabahuthrips bambusae* found in the company of *Asterolecanium* sp., *Karyothrips*

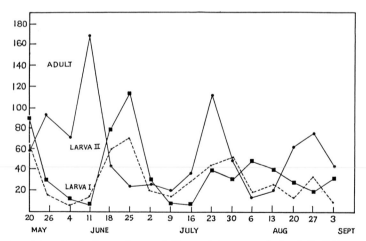

Fig. 25.  Evolution of population of larvae of *Aeolothrips
intermedius* - No. of individuals/200 inflorescences (after Bournier et
al., 1978).

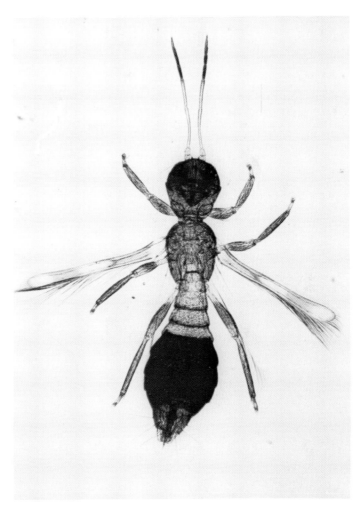

Plate 19A. Predatory aeolothripid  - *Franklinothrips megalops.*

*flavipes on Asterolecanium* sp. and *Saissettia* sp. hiding under their scales. *Podothrips graminum* and *P.aegyptiacus* are also known to occur under
the leaf sheaths of gramineae feeding on *Ripersia Oryzae* (Ananthakrishnan,
1973.)


(3) *Thripiphagous thrips*:

Aelothripids are known to be active predators of thrips, *Aeolothrips
fasciatus* being recorded as early as 1913 devouring the wheat thrips
(Kurdjumov, 1913). Subsequently species like *Aeolothrips intermedius*

have been reported as efficient predators of thrips. Various species of thrips were offered to the larvae of *A.intermedius* and duration of larval development was used as an indicator of their nutritive value. Larvae of *Thrips tabaci, Heliothrips haemorrhoidalis* and *Odontothrips confusus* allowed the fastest development (12 days average), while mites like *Tetranychus cinnabarinus, T.urticae, T.atlanticus, Panonychus ulmi* gave comparatively poor results (19 days average). *A.intermedius* when fed on *Thrips tabaci* larvae and reared at 26°C, the average fecundity of females was 29 eggs with a maximum of 73 (Bournier *et. al.*, 1978) (Fig. 25). Species of *Franklinothrips* such as *F.vespiformes* and *F.tenuicornis* are known to be common predators of cocoa thrips in Trinidad, both larvae and adults being very active and predacious, sucking the juices of thrips and other small insects (McCallan, 1943) (Fig. 26). In India, *F.megalops* is a common predator on *Retithrips syriacus* and *Scirtothrips dorsalis* on castor plants (*Ricinus communis*) each larva consuming 4-5 thrips per day. *Erythrothrips asiaticus*, a highly seasonal species is also predaceous on *Scirtothrips dorsalis* (Ananthakrishnan, unpublished observations) as also *Mymarothrips garuda* (Plate 19A&B).

Plate 19B. Predatory aeolothripid - *Mymarothrips garuda*.

*Androthrips flavipes* is a recognized thrips predator feeding actively on the eggs and immature stages at several gall thrips, the only
other species known to be predatory within galls being *Mesandrothrips
inquilinus* predatory on *Liothrips kuwanai* in galls on the leaves of *Piper*,
sp., *Gynaikothrips uzeli* in Ficus galls, *Mesothrips claripennis* in
*Bladhia* galls and of *Liothrips brevitubus* (Ananthakrishnan, 1978).
*A.flavipes* is invariably present within the galls of *Mimusops elengi*,
*Casearia tomentosa*, *Ficus retusa* etc. and Table 1 provides an idea of the
nature of predation of this species on the eggs of some gall thrips.

## THRIPS PREDATORS/PREDATORY THRIPS

Anthocorids have been long known to be efficient predators of
thrips, Bailey (1937) recording *Orius tristicolor* feeding on *Microcephalothrips abdominalis*. Detailed information on the biology and predation
efficiency on *Orius minutus* and *Carayonocoris indicus* on the anthophilous
thrips *Montandoniola moraguesi* on several species of gall thrips, *Xylocoris clarus* on litter inhabiting thrips, *Scoloposcelis parallelus* on
bark infesting species in India was provided by Muraleedharan and
Ananthakrishnan (1977). *Orius insidiosus* a well-known predator of *Sericothrips variabilis* on soyabean in Illinois (Irwin & Kuhlman, 1979), and
*Orius tristicolor* mostly on cotton-thrips *Frankliniella occidentalis*
(Stoltz & Stern, 1977) in the United States of America, appear to be some
of the more important species, through several other species are also on
record, feeding on different species of thrips. Among these are *Orius
albidipennis*, *O.persequens*, *O.niger* (on *Thrips tabaci*), *Orius indicus*,
*O.maxidentex* (on *Megalurothrips distalis*), *O.insidiosus* (on 9 species of
thrips), *O.tristicolor* (on *Frankliniella occidentalis*) *Montandoniola moraguesi* (on most gall-thrips); *Carayonocoris indicus* (on *Haplothrips
ganglbaueri* and *Frankliniella schultzei*), *Scoloposcelis parallelus*
(on *Ecacanthothrips tibialis* and *Androthrips flavipes*), *Xylocoris clarus*
(on *Apelaunothrips indicus*, *Allothrips bicolor*), on *Macrotrachelliella
laevis* (on *Gynaikothrips ficorum*) and *Cardiastethus rugicollis* (Carayon
& Steffen, 1959; Ghabn, 1948; and Ananthakrishnan, personal
observations).

Observations on the feeding rates of *Carayonocoris indicus*, *Montandoniola moraguesi*, *Xylocoris clarus* and *Scoloposcelis parallelus* have
shown that the first and second instar nymphs prefer thrips larvae,
whereas the later stages including adults did not show any preference.
*C.indicus* and *Montandoniola moraguesi* were found to consume and 71-93
thrips during postembryonic development. The prey species, duration of
the life cycle, fecundity and longevity of females are indicated in
Table 2.

Observations on *Orius minutus* within the inflorescence of *Glyricidia
maculata* (Fabaceae) indicate that this anthocorid effectively pre-      -
dates on *Megalurothrips distalis*, *Frankliniella schultzei* and *Haplothrips
ganglbaueri*, consuming a good number of immature and adult thrips.
Increase in thrips population was followed by a rise of anthocorid population which in turn resulted in a decline of thrips populations
(Viswanathan & Ananthakrishnan, 1974). *Orius tristicolor* predates on
cotton thrips and Stolz and Stern (1977) report that the longevity
*O.tristicolor* adults and nymphs increased and more nymphs were produced
per female as food supply of *Frankliniella occidentalis* increased.

TABLE 1. Nature of predation of *Androthrips flavipes* on the eggs of gall thrips

| | Host plant gall species | | | |
|---|---|---|---|---|
| | *Memecylon edule* (*Crotonothrips dantahasta*) | *Mimusops elengi* (*Arrhenothrips ramakrishnae*) | *Ventilago maderasapatana* (*Schedothrips orientalis*) | *Casearia tomentosa* (*Gynaikothrips flaviantennatus*) |
| Total no. of eggs | 169 | 144 | 110 | 250 |
| % of eggs predated | 74 | 38 | 38 | 49[1] |
| % of eggs intact | 26 | 62 | 62 | 51 |
| No. of adult *A.flavipes* | 29 | 4 | 22 | 1[2] |

[1] Predation due to feeding of anthocorid bug *Montandoniola moraguesi*.
[2] Heavy predation of eggs even with meagre number of *A.flavipes* due to large number of anthocorid bug which feed both on the predatory inquiline and its prey.

TABLE 2. Life cycle duration, fecundity and longevity of females of some anthocorids.

| Species | Prey | Duration of life-cycle from egg-adult | Max. no. of eggs laid by a female | Longe-vity of male |
|---|---|---|---|---|
| *Montandoniola moraguesi* | *Gynaikothrips flaviantennatus* *Arrhenothrips ramakrishnae* | 25–31 | 30–74 | 52 |
| *Carayonocoris indicus* | *Haplothrips ganglbaueri* *Frankliniella schultzei* | 26–32 | 53 | 52 |
| *Xylocoris clarus* | *Apelaunothrips madrasensis* | 32–42 | 63 | 59 |
| *Scoloposcelis parallelus* | *Ecacanthothrips sanguineus* | 28–32 | 40–86 | 61 |

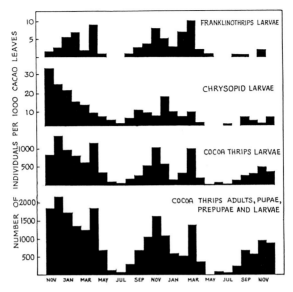

Fig. 26. Histogram depicting population of the Cacao thrips and its more important predators (after McCallan, 1941).

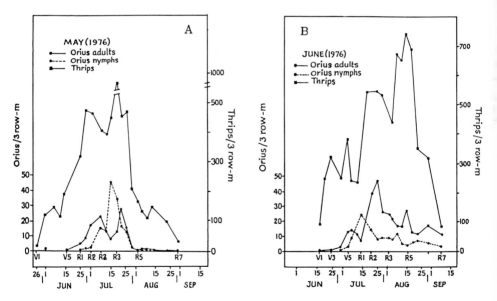

Fig. 27. Number of *Orius insidiosus* and total thrips in Soyabeans (after Isenhour & Marston, 1981).

Increase in number of thrips led to subsequent increases in the bug populations. *O.tristicolor* population maintained its high correlation with
prey food source and increase in thrips seemed to follow the insecticide
kill of predators. It was suggested that when thrips are abundant in
cotton fields, *O.tristicolor* would increase its numbers and provide a
resident population of biotic agents helping to suppress mid, and late-
season cotton pests. A more plausible explanation of the food chain in
the cotton fields is that they act as food for predatory insects which in
turn feed on other pests. Similarly the insidious flower bug, *Orius
insidiosus* is also an important predator of *Sericothrips variabilis* in
various agro-ecosystems in the United States of America and in soyabean
crop forming 55% of the total predators in Missouri soyabean fields.
(Fig. 27). A strong correlation has been reported between the number of
larval *S.variabilis* and *O.insidiosus* indicating the mean densities of
former and all stadia of the latter per central leaflet of soyabean trifoliates (Irwin & Kuhlman, 1979). (Fig. 28). The late season decline in
the densities of *O.insidiosus* and thrips detected in soyabean plantings
appear to have been the result of a combination of predation by
*O.insidiosus* and outward migration by both thrips and predators. The
number of adult *Orius* present prior to any of the observed declines in
thrips density could have caused the reduction (Isenhour & Marston, 1981).

Prey searching strategy of *O.insidiosus* has been studied by Isenhour
and Yeargan (1981), and they indicate that the searching speed of
*O.insidiosus* decreased with the increase in soyabean thrips density from
1 to 45. Predators are known to search certain areas more thoroughly
when prey are abundant, which may result in a decrease in their searching
speed (Hassel, 1978). More predator-prey encounters occurred along the
midrib of the upper trifoliate than at any other location for both sexes
of *Orius*. The greater length and density of trichomes on the lower

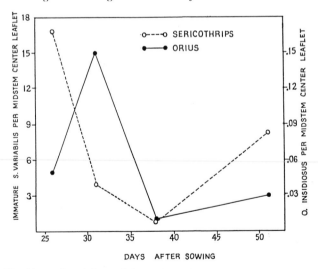

Fig.28. Mean densities of larval *Sericothrips variabilis* and all
stadia of *Orius insidiosus*/centre leaflet of Soyabean trifoliate (Irwin
and Kuhlman, 1979).

aspects of the soyabean trifoliate appeared to be the primary
reason. Adult *Orius* had a capture success of 50% in their encounters
with adult *S.variabilis* and the avoidance reaction employed by
*S.variabilis* in response to attack was running and not through flying
(Isenhour & Yeargan, 1981).

Regarding the other hemipteran predators of thrips, the mirid bug
*Termatophylidea pilosa* is a known predator of the cocoa thrips in Trinidad, while another species *Termatophylidea opaca* lives with its nymph on
the underside of cocoa leaves mostly in colonies of *Selenothrips rubrocinctus*. This mirid punctures thrips with its rostrum suspending the
thrips on it, sucking it for 10-15 minutes. The number of thrips they
consume is considerable and a small colony can be wiped out by a single
mirid (Doesberg, 1964). The capsid bug *Paracaranus* sp., has also been
known to feed on the cocoa thrips. Though not many mirids are known to
predate on thrips, the mirid *Psallus* sp., has been reported to consume
*Megalurothrips distalis* (Rajasekara *et al.*, 1970). Lygaeids have also
been known to be efficient predators, and two species of *Geocoris* –
*G.ochropterus* and *G.tricolor* appear to feed avidly on nymphs and adults
of *Caliothrips indicus*. *G.tricolor* completes its life-cycle in 32-39
days, a single female laying 5-8 eggs/day. All the immature stages and
adults feed on *Caliothrips indicus* both on the weed *Achyranthes aspera*
and on *Arachis hypogaea*. Newly emerged nymphs consumed larvae only, but
2-3 days after emergence they fed on adults as well, adults and 5th
instars nymphs consuming the maximum number of thrips. Newly emerged
instar nymphs consumed 3-4 larvae later, instars and, fed adults on 25-30
thrips (Ananthakrishnan, unpublished observations).

Many species of coccinellids are known to feed on the immature stages of thrips, *Hippodamia corvergens* and *Coccinella novumnotata* being
known to be predaceous on *Thrips tabaci* in Iowa. In the USSR, *Adonia
variegata* is predaceous on the larvae of thrips infesting on *Avena* spp.,
while *Propylaea 14-punctata* is predatory on the larvae of *Haplothrips
knetcheli*, *H.subtilissimus* and *H.reuteri*. Larvae and adults of *Scymnus
frontalis* suck the contents of *Kakothrips robustus*, *Odontothrips loti*
and *Odontothrips phaleratus* (Dyadechko, 1977). *Scymnus thoracicus* is
known to regulate populations of *Chaetanaphothrips orchidii* in banana
plantations (Delattere & Torregrosse, 1978).

Among other beetles, *Malachius viridis* (Melyridae) has been reported
feeding on the immature stages of the wheat thrips consuming 10-12 thrips
and adults (Tansky, 1958). Several staphylinids are also reported prey-
ing on larvae and pupae of thrips living beneath barks of trees, such as
*Hoplothrips pedicularius*, *H.propinquus*, *H.corticus*, *Acanthothrips nodicornis* and *Hoplandrothrips pillichianus* (Dyadechko, 1977).

Neuropterans appear good predators, *Chrysopa vulgaris* and *C.perlia*
being known to feed on the larvae of *Odontothrips intermedius* and
*O.phaleratus* in the USSR. Reyne (1921) indicated that predaceous larvae
of such chrysopids as *Leucophrysa marguezi*, *L.submacula*, *Chrysopa cla-
veri*, *C.iona*, *C.varia* and *C.alobana* feed on the cocoa thrips *Selenothrips
rubrocinctus*. On hatching, the larvae of these chrysopids immediately
begin to search their first prey comprising all stages of the cocoa
thrips.

Among the Diptera, the immature stages of *Sphaerophoria quadrituber-culata* are recorded as predatory on *Cercothrips afer* (Stuckenberg, 1954), consuming only nymphs and pupae of thrips. Other dipteran predators on record are the cecidomyiid, *Thripsobremia liothrips* feeding on *Liothrips urichi* (Barnes, 1930) in Trinidad and *Adelgimyza tripidiperda* on *Phlaeothrips oleae* in Italy. The Asilid or the robber fly *Machinus annulipes* feeding on the first instar larvae of *Haplothrips* sp., is also on record (Kurkena, 1979).

Among the Hymenoptera, sphecids are predaceous, *Spilomena barberi* being known to carry the prey comprising the first or second instar nymphs of *Frankliniella*, *Thrips* or *Sericothrips* to their nests (Krombein, 1962). Another sphecid, *Mysma ceanothae* is known to transport thrips larvae, its mandibles clutched around the neck of thrips (Krombein, 1958), and *Spilomena pusilla* has been observed to hold in her mandibles,a paralyzed second instar larva possibly of *Sericothrips variabilis*. *Microstigmus thripictenus* is a thrips hunter sphecid, from the Costa Rican rain forests occurring within nests at heights of 1-2 m. from the ground and hanging firmly from the midrib of leaf of a palm and within each nest are six pocket-like cells which are mass-provisioned. Three cells contained 171 thrips and an incompletely provisioned cell, 58 thrips. Another nest with 70 thrips in a cell and yet another with a dozen thrips as prey has also been reported. More than 300 thrips in the nest were immature, apparently belonging to four species, presumably of *Leucothrips*, *Bradinothrips*, etc. (Matthews, 1970). The thrips were piled loosely in the cells and not packed. The ant *Wasmania auropunctata* is reported to carry away young cocoa thrips on Trinidad, and in Brazil the ant *Azteca chartifox* is used to control thrips.

Several species of mites are ectoparasitic and their larvae are pre-datory, clinging to thrips at the bases of their legs for 5-6 days. Adults of the pyemotid mite *Adactylidium nicolae* are also known to be efficient egg predators of thrips, predating on the eggs of *Gynaikothrips ficorum*, a single mite in its mature feeding stage being associated with a single egg of thrips. Each adult female mite feeds and reproduces on a single host egg and accordingly the life-cycle and reproductive behaviour of the mite are modified, with a reduction in the number of active deve-lopmental stages, permitting a new generation to develop every 4 days in the summer season, effecting efficient biological control (El Badry & Tawfik, 1966). Each viviparous female produced 6-9 individuals of which only one was a male. Another pyemotid mite known to attack *Gynaikothrips ficorum* is *Pediculoides* sp., (Bennet, 1965). While *Pyemotes ventricosus* is known to feed on eggs and nymphs of *Gynaikothrips* sp., the gamasid mite *Typhlodromus thripsi* and *Anystis astripus* (Anystidae) are known to feed on *Thrips tabaci* (MacGill, 1939). Several species of phytoseid mites are also reported to feed on *Thrips tabaci* in particular; *Ambly-seius mackenziei* in cucumber and *A.cucumeris* in sweet pepper appear to be associated with *Thrips tabaci* in Netherland (Ramaker, 1980). Dyadechko (1977) records larvae of *Hauptmania brevicollis* as an ectoparasite on several species of thrips in the USSR, like *Anaphothrips obscurus*, *Frankliniella intonsa*, *Haplothrips aculeatus*, *Odontothrips loti*, *Taeniothrips atratus*, *Thrips lini*, *Thrips tabaci*, *Thrips validus*, etc.

In general, most of the predatory thrips belong to the Phlaeothri-pinae and the Idolothripinae appear to be exclusively non-predatory, though a solitary instance indicated earlier has been noted in *Cryptothrips nigripes* feeding on dormant female mites. There is also a tendency among predatory thrips to become cannibalistic when they are crowded, and in several instances such as in *Haplothrips faurei* and *Androthrips flavipes*, they are known to feed on their own eggs when food is scarce. Alternately most predatory thrips being usually polyphagous, tend to survive for some time at least on plant food, except some of the aeolothripids which appear to be totally carnivorous.

## PARASITES

Internal parasites of Thysanoptera were first noticed in 1911 in Italy, a chalcid *Tetrastichus* sp. parasitising the olive thrips, *Phlaeothrips oleae*. Subsequently many other parasites have been recorded and described. Most of the parasites belong to the Eulophidae and apart from odd species of *Tetrastichus* and *Pediobius*, eulophids belong to the natural group within Etedontinae comprising four genera *Goetheana*, *Thripobius*, *Thripoctenoides*, and *Ceranisus* (Boucek, 1976). Bluck (1950), Thompson (1950), Ferriere (1958) and Boucek and Askew (1976) have listed parasites of thrips from Central Europe and Africa. An overall list of known parasites with their host species and distribution is provided in Table 3.

TABLE 3. Hymenopteran parasites of thrips species and their distribution

| Parasite | Host species | Distribution |
|---|---|---|
| Eulophidae | *Thrips Tabaci* | |
| *Goetheana parvipennis* Gahan 1927 | *Heliothrips haemorrhoidalis* | Java, Africa, Trinidad |
| | *Selenothrips rubrocinctus* | |
| | *Frankliniella parvula* | |
| *Ceranisus brui* (Vuillet) 1914 | *Kakothrips pisivorus* | |
| | *Thrips tabaci* | Europe, Japan, Java |
| | *Taeniothrips* sp. | |
| | *Microcephalothrips abdominalis* | |
| | *Frankliniella formosa* | |

| | | |
|---|---|---|
| *Ceranisus americensis* (Ishii) 1933 | *Frankliniella occidentalis* | USA |
| *Ceranisus bicoloratus* (Ishii) 1933 | *Thrips* sp. | Japan |
| *Ceranisus fernotatus* (Gahan) 1932 | *Taeniothrips longistylus* | Philippines |
| *Ceranisus maculatus* (Waterston) 1930 | *Rhipiphorthrips cruentatus* | India |
| *Ceranisus* sp. Saxena 1971 | *Thrips tabaci* | India |
| *Ceranisus nubilipennis* (Williams) 1916 | *Cryptothrips rectangularis* | USA |
| | *Megalothrips spinosus* | |
| *Ceranisus russeli* (Crawford) 1911 | *Frankliniella tritici* | Britain, USA, Hawaii |
| | *Caliothrips fasciatus* | Hawaii, Britain, USA |
| | *Taeniothrips simplex* | |
| | *T.inconsequens* | |
| *Ceranisus vinctus* (Gahan) 1932 | *Taeniothrips longistylus* | Philippines |
| *Ceranisus menes* (Walker) 1839 | *Kakothrips robustus* | Europe Korea Japan |
| | *Microcephalothrips abdominalis* | Philippines Taiwan |
| | *Taeniothrips alliorum* | |
| | *Thrips flavus* | |
| *Ceranisus pacuvius* (Walker) 1838 | *Kakothrips robustus* | Europe |
| *Ceranisus kutteri* Ferniere 1936 | *Kakothrips pisivorus* | Europe |
| *Ceranisus javae* (Girault) 1917 | *Thrips* sp. | Java |
| *Thripobius hirticornis* Ferriere 1938 | *Retithrips syriacus* | Africa |

| | | |
|---|---|---|
| *Thripobius semiluteus* Roucek 1976 | *Panchaetothrips indicus* | India |
| | *Brachyurothrips anomalus* | |
| *Thripoctenoides gaussi* Ferriere 1958 | *Liothrips setinodis* | |
| | *Cryptothrips nigripes* | Europe USSR |
| | *Phlaeothrips coriaceus* | |
| | *Hoplandrothrips pillichianus* | |
| *Tetrastichus gentilei* Del Guercio 1911 | *Liothrips oleae* | Europe |
| *Tetrastichus thripophonus* Waterson 1923 | *Liothrips urichi* | USA |
| | *Liothrips laureli* | |
| | *Gynaikothrips uzeli* | India |
| | *Schedothrips orientalis* | |
| *Tetrastichus rhipiphorothripsidis* Narayanan *et al.* | *Mallothrips indicus* | |
| | *Rhipiphorothrips cruentatus* | India |
| **Trichogrammatidae** | | |
| *Megaphragma mymaripennis* Timberlake 1924 | *Heliothrips haemorrhoidalis* | USA Hawaii |
| *Megaphragma priesneri* Kryfer 1932 | *Retithrips aegyptiacus* | Egypt |
| *Megaphragma ghesquieri* Novicky 1939 | *Panchaetothrips noxius* | Africa |
| *Megaphragma longiciliatus* SubbaRao 1969 | *Frankliniella lilivora* | India |
| **Mymaridae** *Camptoptera pulla* Girault 1910 | *Caliothrips fasciatus* | USA |

The parasite *Ceranisus brui* is known to be an efficient parasite of
*Thrips tabaci, Taeniothrips alliorum,* and *Microcephalothrips abdominalis*
(Sakimura, 1937). Its major host, however, is *Thrips tabaci* particularly
in onion fields. *C.brui* is an endoparasitic larval parasite, oviposition
taking place on the immature larvae and pupation in in the prepupal
stage of the host. This parasite is vital in reducing *T.tabaci* populations during late summer and autumn in Hawaii. Four broods of the parasite per season have been recorded and population peaks known to occur in
the middle of June, July and August, and from mid-, to late September.
Both natural climatic conditions as well as biotic factors act on the
population bringing the pest effectively under control. The percentage
of parasitism was found to be as high as 79% with an absolute maximum of
78.9%. Higher parasitic activity reduced the number of host emergence
causing a lower reproductive capacity of the total host population
(Fig. 29). An allied species *Ceranisus maculatus* has been reported from
India and laying their eggs inside larvae of *Rhipiphorothrips cruentatus*.
The females of this eulophid 3-5 days after mating are said to search for
the first and second instar larvae and pierce their abdomen with the ovipositor, to lay eggs. As the parasite grows inside the nymphs, patholo-
gical symptoms set in, resulting in the death of the host (Rahman &
Bharadwaj, 1937). *Tetrastichus thripiphonus* is on record (Ananthak-
rishnan & Swaminathan, 1977) as parasitising the second instar larvae of
*Schedothrips orientalis,* a gall thrips making roll galls on the leaves of
*Ventilago maderaspatana.* As much as 20% parasitization was recorded when

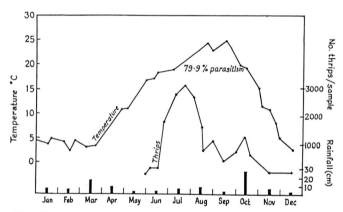

Fig.29. Changes and abundance of *Thrips tabaci* populations by parasitism by *Ceranisus brui* (after Sakimura, 1937).

thrips populations were high. The life-history of *Goetheana parvipennis*
another euloploid, is of interest in that it parasitizes *Selenothrips
rubrocinctus, Heliothrips haemorrhoidalis, Frankliniella formosa* etc., in
Java, Africa and Trinidad. In the host the female lays a single egg
which hatches in about 24 hours. The entire life-cycle takes 18-21 days
and reproduces by arrhenotokus parthenogenesis. This species has been
used in the control of the cacao thrips and has been successfully introduced into Trinidad and Puerto Rico. The female *Goetheana* attacks
nearby mature host larvae, but can reproduce more efficiently in younger
hosts. Laboratory observations indicate that the percentage parasitism

Plate 20. Ectoparasitic species of *Orasema* attached to the larva of *Microcephalothrips abdominalis* (Courtesy, Ramona Beshear).

in newly hatched larvae is double that of fully developed larvae. The parasite is known to take six days to devour the body contents of a thrips. The parasite after emergence pupates, hanging head down, and at an angle to the leaf from the skin of the host. Parasitism reaches the maximum during the highest infestation of thrips. At peak periods whole colonies of 50-60 individuals in one leaf are destroyed and in exceptional cases with severe infestation, parasitism reached as much as 70-80% (Entwistle, 1972).

Species of the genus *Megaphragma* (Trichogrammatidae) appear to be parasitic on the eggs of thrips, as also the mymarid *Camptoptera pulla*. Four known species of *Megaphragma* are *mymaripennis* (on *Heliothrips haemorrhoidalis*), *ghesquieri* (on *Panchaetothrips noxius*) *priesneri* (on *Retithrips aegyptiacus*), and *longiciliatus* (on *Frankliniella lilivora*).

98

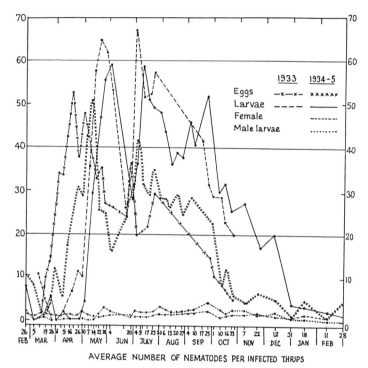

Fig.30. Average number of nematodes per infected thrips including eggs, larval females and males (after Lysaght, 1938).

Chalcidoid ectoparasites are also known to attack thrips. Wilson and Cooley (1972) record an eucharitid planidium ectoparasitic on larvae of *Frankliniella occidentalis*. The eucharitid *Psilogaster* sp., has been recorded from Malaya attached to *Selenothrips rubrocinctus* (Clausen, 1949). Beshear (1974) records *Orasema* sp., attached to 41 larvae with a mean of 3.4(1-18) larvae per larva of first and second stage *Microcephalothrips abdominalis* (Plate 20).

## NEMATODE PARASITES

Parasitisation by nematodes is not infrequent, the earliest record being on *Aptinothrips rufus* abundant in grasslands, and parasitized by *Anguillulina aptini* (Sharga, 1932). The adult female nematode is extremely efficient in its reproductive capacity and one parasitized thrips was found to contain a single female nematode, 111 eggs and 18 newly hatched larvae (Lysaght, 1938). (Fig. 30) Males were found leaving the anus of the host and after fertilization, the female finds a larval or pupal thrips and enters it through the delicate skin of the host, penetrating it by the stylet. Development of female nematodes in overwintering thrips is delayed and examination of 1650 infected thrips showed that in the great majority of cases one or two females occurred in each

TABLE 4. Fungi infesting thrips.

| Fungus | Thrips species |
|---|---|
| *Empoasca grili* | *Hoplothrips ulmi, Rhynchothrips hungaricus, Acanthothrips nodicornis, Phlaeothrips coriaceus, Zygothrips minuta, Taeniothrips atratus.* |
| *Aspergillus* sp. | *Thrips fuscipennis, Thrips validus, Thrips tabaci, Thrips physapus, Taeniothrips discolor, Frankliniella intonsa, Odontothrips loti, Odontothrips phaleratus, Anaphothrips obscurus, Limothrips denticornis.* |
| *Beauveria bassiana* | adult and larvae of *Haplothrips tritici, Aptinothrips rufus, Limothrips schmutzi, Chirothrips manicatus, Heliothrips haemorrhoidalis.* |
| *Cephalosporium* sp. | all stages of *Thrips tabaci* |
| *Cunninghamella* sp. | larvae and adults of *Elaphrothrips denticollis* |
| *Metarrhizium* sp. | adults of *Elaphrothrips denticollis* |
| *Penicillium* sp. | adults of *Elaphrothrips denticollis* |
| *Entomophthora sphaerosporum* | larvae of *Haplothrips tritici, Haplothrips aculeatus, Haplothrips subtilissmus, Phlaeothrips coriaceus.* |
| *Entomophthora thripidum* | *Thrips tabaci.* |

host and occasionally even up to eight. Infestation of nematodes is equally evident in *Microcephalothrips abdominalis* in India, with an infection rate of 40%, with each thrips harbouring on an average 25 eggs, 80 larvae and 35 adult nematodes (Ananthakrishnan, unpublished data).

## PROTOZOAN INFECTIONS

The first record of an endoparasitic protozoan is the occurrence of the microsporidian parasite *Mrazekia* sp., in larvae and adults of *Scirtothrips oligochaetus*. Infection was so intense as to occupy the entire haemocoelic space. The average number of thrips, adults and larvae on an infected plant was about 110 larvae and 25 adults/10 cotton leaves. At the peak of infestation by the microsporidian, the infestation rate was nearly 100% i.e., almost all the adults and larvae suffered from the infection. *Mrazekia* sp., can parasitize both the larvae and adults of thrips and cause heavy mortality. Under natural conditions, this microsporidian may be responsible for bringing about fluctuations in populations of this thrips (Raizada, 1976).

## FUNGAL INFESTATIONS

Information on fungal infestation of thrips is equally scarce, the earliest being that of Williams (1915) in the pea thrips *Kakothrips robustus*. Raizada (1976) has recorded fungal infestations from *Thrips flavus, Scirtothrips dorsalis* and *Microcephalothrips abdominalis*. Heavy infection of *Alternaria alternata* in *Thrips flavus* is known and 25-30 conidia per larva were seen in smears of the fungus. Mostly haemocytes were damaged by the fungus, with a certain degree of damage to the fat bodies and gonads. Raizada (1976) recorded *Cladosporium cladosporiodes* and *Trichothecium roseum* infesting *Thrips flavus* on cotton. A list of the more common fungi infesting different species of thrips are given in Table 4.

* * * * *

## ECOLOGY OF GALL THRIPS

Plant galls are characterized by a more intimate biological association between insects and their host plants, a feature well documented
among thrips. Thrips are well known cecidozoa, causing a variety of
structural abnormalities on a great variety of plants belonging to the
gymnosperms, dicotyledons, and some monocotyledonous plants as well.
Their ability to form galls on more than 150 host species involving about
90 Natural Orders, and more than 300 species of gall thrips have been
recogized (Sakimura, 1945; Ananthakrishnan, 1979, 1980). Among the dominant families of plants harbouring thrips galls are Araliaceae, Combreta-
ceae, Euphorbiaceae, Mimosae, Moraceae, Myrtaceae, Piperaceae, Rubiaceae,
Rutaceae, Urticaceae and Vitaceae. The families Liliaceae, Araceae, and
rarely Poaeceae (=Gramineae) too have been recognized as being susceptible
to gall-formation. This is also true with the family Gnetaceae, the species *Gnetum latifolium* being known to harbour 5-6 species of thrips.
Among the pteridophytes, rolling of leaflet margins by species of *Physothrips* on *Asplenium nidus*, *Pleopeltis superficialis*, and *Pteropeltis
pteropus* is also known. The factors which govern the occurrence and
abundance of thrips galls in plants of various families are not fully
understood, but are undoubtedly bound up with host selection phenomenon
and phylogeny of the gall thrips, among the other factors.

Almost 75% of the gall-thrips are confined to the genera *Liothrips,
Gynaikothrips, Liophlaeothrips, Eugynothrips, Eothrips,* and *Mesothrips.*
From the viewpoint of geographical distribution of gall thrips, it is
seen that though they are generally abundant in the tropics, they appear
to be particularly rich in the old world tropics, and relatively poorly
represented in the Neotropical areas. True gall-forming Tubulifera may
be said to be almost absent in Europe, though several species of
Terebrantia are on record, forming leaf rolls. North America is very
poorly represented by gall-thrips fauna. Southeast Asia, South Asia and
Australia are apparently the areas of incidence of gall-forming
Tubulifera and nearly all known species occur in these regions. Some
interesting forms are also known from the Ethiopian and Mediterranean
regions as well (Priesner, 1960).

A striking peculiarity of thrips galls is that a majority of them
arise on leaves and only very few bud and flowers galls are known.
Rarely thrips-galls occur on the shoot axis and only two such galls are
known at present. Most thrips galls conform strictly to a characteristic
pattern and are merely modifications of curling, folding, rolling and
other related horizontal growth movements of the leaf-blade, so as to
eventually enclose the thrips in the gall-cavity, often communicating
with the outside by a more or less well-developed ostiole or a lateral
slit. The great bulk of thrips galls are leaf rolls and leaf-folds, but
simple sac-like malformations as in *Terminalia chebula* to highly convolute pouch-galls as in *Calycopteris floribundus* and *Memecylon* sp. also
occur. The complexity of the gall depends not only on the species of

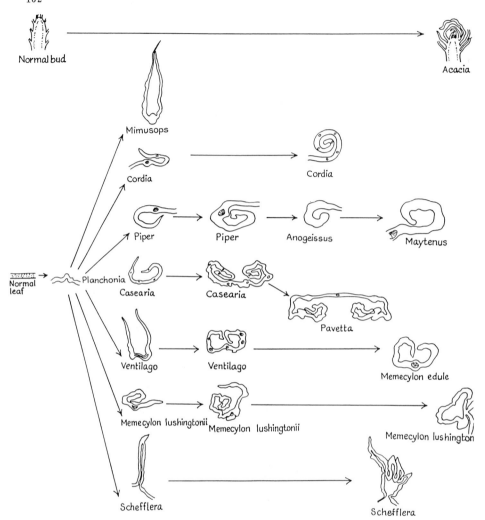

Fig.31. Pathways of complexity in Thyanopterocecidia.

thrips and their host plants, but also to a great extent on the number of individuals within the gall, since increasing complexities occur with the increase in thrips populations. Depending both on the time of infection as well as of the impact of thrips activity, varying organization patterns occur (Ananthakrishnan, 1981).

## BASIC GALL TYPES

Unlike the galls of dipteran and homopteran insects (Mani, 1964) thrips galls develop as a result of the cumulative feeding effects of a population, although during the initial stages of cecidogenesis very few individuals occur. Gall thrips prefer only very young plant tissue,

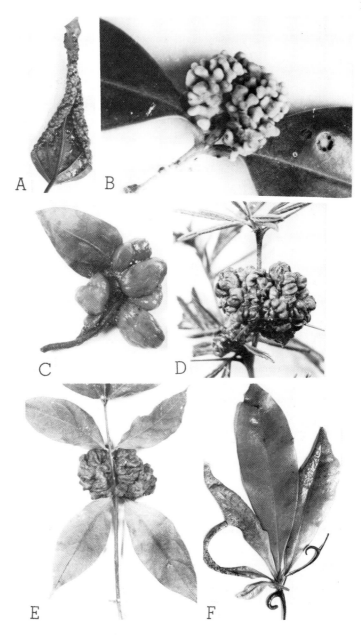

Plate 21. Some thrips galls - a. *Piper*, b.*Memecylon* sp., c. *Terminalia chebula*, d. *Acacia leucophloea*, e. *Calycopteris floribundus*, f. *Ancistrocladus heyneanus*.

Plate 22. Some gall thrips – *Thilakothrips babuli* (Top left), *Alocothrips hadrocerus* (Top right), *Tetradothrips foliiperda* (Bottom left), *Arrhenothrips ramakrishnae* (Bottom right).

mostly of leaves, since the well-organized galls with their characteristic morphology are not found in differentiated mature leaves.
Thrips galls are invariably 'open-gall systems' communicating with the
exterior, aiding in migration as well as enabling establishment of other
gall-associates which do have considerable influence on gall thrips populations. The tendency to form 'closed gall systems' is equally characteristic of thrips galls as evident in *Memecylon lushingtonii*, *Calycopteris floribundus*, *Terminalia chebula* and *Acacia leucophloea*. Open
galls such as the different leaf fold-gall types are developed when the
leaf is young and completed their marginal meristematic activity, but are
still to undergo laminar expansion. This appears to be the basic pattern. Gall induction during the late stage of ontogeny of the host organ
is perhaps primarily responsible for the simplicity in external gall-form
(Ananthakrishnan, 1980). Diversity in external and internal organization
exists in such partial and complete galls suggesting that gall initiation
occurring during the differentiation phase of the leaf results in a
complete gall; on the other hand, with the developing leaves having
crossed the stage of 'determination', coupled with a weak feeding impact
of low thrips population, partial or incomplete galls result. Besides,
it is also possible to recognize simple and complex galls types as in the
ceratonean galls of *Schefflera racemosa*, where the number of individuals
inhabiting a gall seem to control the form of the gall (Krishnamurthy et
al., 1975). Complex, highly branched fleshy galls result when thrips
inhabit the galls for a longer period and with more thrips per gall, as
against the simple tubular galls with very few individuals. The
influence of a single female in producing the different galls on a
leaflet of *Schefflera* and stoppage of gall development when the female is
removed is reported by van Leeuwen (1956).

An endless variety of thrips galls is evident from simple crinkles,
rolls and folds through more complicated pouch, rosette, tortuose and
ceratonean galls (Ananthakrishnan & Jagadish, 1969; Ananthakrishnan,
1973, 1978). The recognition of partial and complete gall types is peculiar to thrips galls, the two types being formed in response to varying
times of initiation as well as varying thrips populations. An overall
outline of the galling patterns by thrips involve (Plate 21, 22 & Fig.
31):
     (1) Marginal partial rolls - *Aneurothrips punctipennis (Cordia
dichotoma)* and *Alocothrips hadrocerus (Maytenus senegalensis)*
     (2) Marginal complete folds - *Liothrips karnyi (Piper nigrum)* and
*Lygothrips jambuvasi (Anogeissus latifolia)*
     (3) Typical leaf folds, the two halves meeting at middle.
*Gynaikothrips uzeli (Ficus retusa)* and *Arrhenothrips ramakrishnae
(Mimusops elengi)*
     (4) Complete leaf roll, end to end - *Gynaikothrips flaviantennatus
(Casearia tomentosa)*
     (5) Leaf rolling by each laminar half resulting in epiphyllous
rolls *Schedothrips orientalis (Ventilago maderasapatana)* and hypophyllous
rolls - *Teuchothrips longus (Pavetta hispidula)*
     (6) Twisted leaf rolls as in *Eothrips coimbatorensis (Jasminum
pubescens)*
     (7) Pouch galls
        (a)Bud galls developing into pouch or bladder galls by

106

*Austrothrips cochinchinensis (Calycopteris floribundus)*
  (b) Petiolar pouch galls as in *Dixothrips onerosus (Terminalia chebula)*
  (c) Phyllode pouch galls as in *Acacia* spp.
      (i) Spherical - *Oncothrips* sp. *(Acacia aneura)*
      (ii) Tubular - *Kladothrips* sp. *(Acacia homalaneura)*
      (iii) Flask shaped - *Koptothrips* sp. and *Oncothrips* sp. *(Acacia pendula)*
      (iv) Kidney shaped - *Kladothrips* sp. *(Acacia cambagei)* (Mound, 1971)
    (8)*Rosette galls* : Typical of *Acacia leucophloea* where the and terminal buds with their leaf rudiments becoming converted into a rosette-like structure.
    (9) Ceratonean galls or horn galls very characteristic of *Schefflera racemosa*, which are basically epiphyllous or hypophyllous tubular outgrowths.
    (10) *Midrib tubular gall*, the leaf blade on either side of the midrib becomes raised and fused all round to form a tube leaving the margins of the lamina free on either side as in *Linociera* sp.
    Well-defined, mature leaf folds of *Ficus retusa, F.benjamina* or *Mimusops elengi* may harbour as many as 25-200 young and adults, besides a very large number of eggs. Primitive leaf curls like those of *Planchonia valida* contain swarms of *Cercothrips nigrodentatus*, each leaf with more than 100 individuals of all stages, in addition to the associate species *Liothrips gracilis*. The leaf-rolls of *Ventilago maderaspatana, Walsura piscidia* and *Pavetta hispidula* also harbour countless numbers of adults and larvae. Complex galls, such as that of *Calcyopteris floribundus* (2-8cm. large), often contain anywhere between 200 and 50000 individuals. The pouch galls of *Terminalia chebula* formed by *Dixothrips onerosus* have an extremely dense population of thrips within them, as also those of some *Memecylon* sp. formed by different species of *Crotonothrips* and the rosette gall of *Acacia leucophloea* formed by *Thilakothrips babuli*. The largest thrips gall produced by *Tolmetothrips granti* in the Solomon Islands, is a convoluted leaf gall, 15cm. in diameter and harbouring about 10,000 individuals of a single species (Mound, 1970). On the other hand, in the horn galls of *Schefflera racemosa*, where numerous galls arise on a single leaflet, hardly 1-5 individuals occur within a gall.

## GALL ASSOCIATIONS

    Most thrips galls contain one or more secondary species, though they are fewer in number than the primary gall maker. Some of these secondary thrips species are true inquilines which are incapable of making galls by themselves, but are believed to be capable of inducing certain modifications in the galls of other thrips. The transition between an inquiline and a true-gall species does not seem to be sharply defined. The cecidophagous habit is perhaps primary and not strictly secondary as in some inquilines at least (Mani, 1964). It appears also that in some cases the inquiline thrips was primarily a cecidogenetic species that has come to be secondarily specialized for life in the gall of another species. Some inquilines like *Androthrips flavipes*, occurring in most galls seem to have even advanced towards definitive predatism on the primary cecidogenetic thrips species. Among non-predators, inquilines are monophagous, restricted to particular galls, like *Androthrips ramachandrai* in the galls of *Calycopteris floribundus*, *Aeglothrips denticulus* in *Maytenus senegalensis*, *Mesothrips melinocnemis* in *Pothos scandens* and *Corycidothrips inquilinus* in *Terminalia chebula*. The galls resulting from the activity of more than one species of thrips in which it is difficult to distinguish the gall-maker from the inquilines are generally referred to as company galls. In comparison with the one thrips-one inquiline association, the company gall associations are not numerous. Occasionally we find two species almost equally numerous, where both the species may be involved in gall formation, as in galls of *Santalum album* caused by *Mesothrips manii* and *Crotonothrips davidi*; of *Schefflera racemosa* by *Liothrips ramakrishnae* and *Liothrips associatus* and of *Memecylon* sp., by *Crotonothrips gallarum* and *Mesothrips cracens*. The best example of a gall containing several inquiline species, each although not very numerous, is the gall on *Ficus* sp. from Samoa, with four species of *Euoplothrips* (Table 1). Examples of monophagous gall species in Australian acacias are *Kladothrips acaciae* on *Acacia harpophylla*, *K.augonsaxxos* on *A.doratoxylon*, *K.ellobus* on *A.cambagei* and *K.rugosus* on *A.pendula*. But *Oncothrips tepperi* is known within the galls of several species of *Acacia* viz., *oswaldii*, *homalophylla*, *pendula*, *sclerophylla* (Mound, 1971). *Liothrips cognatus* is again polyphagous, known from galls of *Medinella horsefieldi*, *M.laevifolia*, *M. verrucosa* and *Aridisia javanica* (Priesner, 1968).

Thrips not only occur as inquilines in thrips galls, but also as inquilines in the galls made by other insects. Common examples of such inquiline thrips are *Mallothrips indicus* in the galls of the psyllid *Trioza jambolanae* on *Syzygium*, *Haplothrips atriplicis* in the gall of *Asphondylia conglomerata*, *Dolichothrips inquilinus* in the gall of a psyllid on *Ziziphus* sp., *Liothrips interlocatus* in psyllid galls of *Trichilogaster acacia-longifolia* on *Acacia floribunda*, and *Liothrips devriesi* in the cecidomyiid gall of *Elatostemma sesquifolia*. Kosztarab (1982) discusses the association of *Torvothrips kosztarabi* within galls produced by *Ollifiella cristicola* on *Quercus emoryi* (Plate 23).

Thrips galls, like most other insect galls contain a complex community, the size and composition of which varies with the plant bearing the gall, the gall thrips, and the other secondary species. Such communities are evident in the pouch, blister, rosette galls as well as fold galls, and seems to be comparatively limited to roll galls. The secondary organisms in thrips galls include other species of thrips, besides wasps, fungi and bacteria. There is a regular and characteristic sequence in which these organisms appear; commencing with the increase in individuals of the gall thrips connected with the growth of the gall, there follows an invasion of predatory bugs and beetles, parasites and hyperparasites in the mature galls, culminating in the entry of ants, spiders and lepidopteran larvae in the old gall that has already started to senesce after the escape of the gall thrips. One of the commonest species associated with thrips galls is the predatory anthocorid bug *Montandoniola moraguesi* which consumes eggs, larvae and adults, in considerable numbers (Muraleedharan & Ananthakrishnan, 1971).

TABLE 1. Gall thrips associations.

1. Gall species and one inquiline species:

| | |
|---|---|
| *Alocothrips hadrocerus* | *Maytenus senegalensis* |
| *Aeglothrips denticulus* | (India) |
| *Sphingothrips trachypogon* | *Disopyros maritima* |
| *Synergothrips prolatus* | (India) |
| *Austrothrips cochinchinensis* | *Calycopteris floribundus* |
| *Androthrips ramachandrai* | (India) |
| *Dixothrips onerosus* | *Terminalia chebula* |
| *Corycidothrips inquilinus* | (India) |
| *Aneurothrips priesneri* | *Cordia obliqua* |
| *Androthrips melastomae* | (India) |
| *Liothrips karnyi* | *Piper nigrum* |
| *Androthrips flavipes* | (India) |

2. Company galls involving more than 3 species in a gall:

| | |
|---|---|
| *Arrhenothrips dhumrapaksha* | *Ficus retusa* |
| *Crotonothrips dhirgavadana* | (India) |
| *Liothrips kannani* | |
| *Mesothrips bhimabahu* | |
| *Mesothrips apatelus* | |
| *Androthrips melastomae* | |
| *Haplothrips aculeatus* | |
| *Androthrips flavipes* | |
| *Mesandrothrips inquilinus* | |
| *Gynaikothrips hystrix* | *Ficus* sp. |
| *Gynaikothrips hopkinsoni* | (Samoa & Tonga) |
| *Dimorphothrips microchaetus* | |
| *D.solitus* | |
| *D.idoliceps* | |
| *Euoplothrips buxtoni* | |
| *E.incognitus* | |
| *E.uncinatus* | |
| *Mesothrips extensivus* | *Mallotus philippinensis* |
| *Liothrips brevisetosus* | (India) |
| *Liothrips bosei* | |
| *Liothrips flavitibia* | |
| *Liothrips mucronis* | |
| *Mesothrips malloti* | |
| *Liothrips emulatus* | *Schefflera* sp. |
| *Liothrips fragilis* | (India) |
| *Liothrips retusus* | |
| *Gynaikothrips schefflericola* | |
| *Sacothrips malvus* | *Geijera parviflora* |
| *S.ingens* | (Australia) |
| *S.galbus* | |
| *Moultonoides geijerae* | |
| *Choleothrips percnus* | |
| *Choleothrips geijerae* | |
| *Liothrips nuvosegnus* | *Conocephalus suaveolens* |
| *Liothrips racemosae* | (Java) |
| *Liothrips taurus* | |
| *Eugynothrips conocephal* | |
| *Eugynothrips persinula* | |
| *Liothrips fumipennis* | |
| *Aneurothrips punctipennis* | |

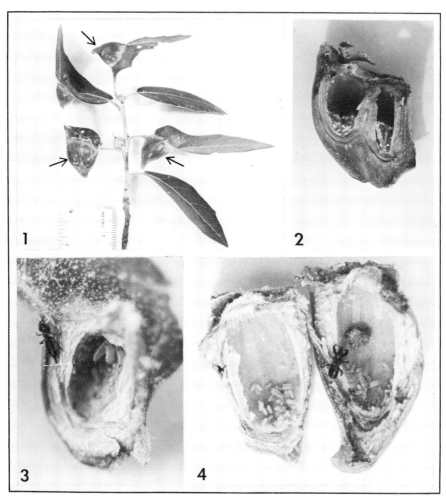

Plate 23. 1. Leaf galls on *Quercus* produced by *Olliffiella cristi-cola*; 2. Two fused galls opened to show gall makers at the bottom; 3. An open gall with an adult female *Torvothrips* and eggs; 4. An open gall with an adult female and several nymphs (Courtesy Prof. Michael Kosztarab).

## GALL FORM AND POPULATION TRENDS

Intraspacific variation is a frequent feature in thrips galls, adding to the complexity in organizational patterns, particularly in view of gall form being controlled by the developmental stage of the organ concerned. The time of gall initiation is very important in cecidogenesis. Structural diversities involve the total expression of galling effect, and incomplete or partial expression resulting in incomplete or

110

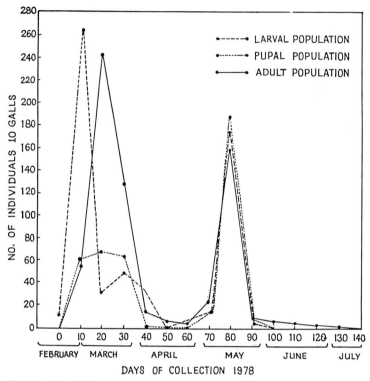

Fig.32. Population trends of *Aneurothrips priesneri* in galls of *Cordia* sp.

partial galls respectively, according as to whether they are induced at a very early stage or a later stage in leaf development. Gall initiation occurring during differentiation phase of the leaf results in the complete reorientation of the normal morphogenetic activity of the leaf. With the developing leaves having crossed the stage of 'determination', combined with a weak feeding impact due to small populations of thrips, an incomplete or partial morphogenetic reorientation results in partial galls (Raman *et al.*, 1977). Analysis of the total population trends of *Gynaikothrips flaviantennatus* in partial and complete galls revealed significant differences. The average population, over a period of 55 days in the case of complete galls was as high as 87%, while partial galls displayed the gall maker incidence to be as low as 13%, a feature also exhibited in both the larval and adult populations (Table 2).

The age of the gall and the involved thrips population are essential in interpreting the nature of tissue reactions which result in diverse organization patterns. The populations of thrips inclusive of larvae and adults in the complex galls appear to be 3-15 times more than that in the simpler galls. This is clearly indicated by the population build-up in such galls as *Casearia tomentosa* up to the 15th day of gall development, but declines with the age of the gall, the variability in populations per

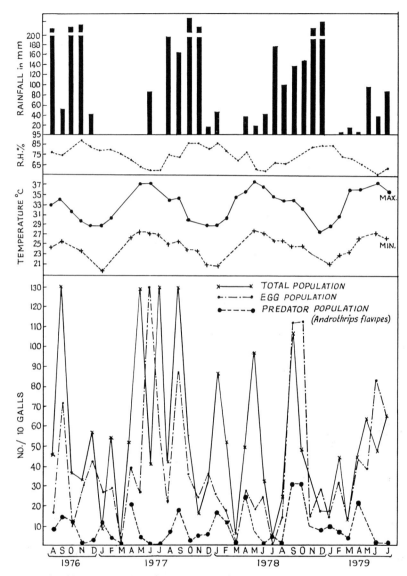

Fig.33. Population fluctuation of *Schedothrips orientalis*.

gall ranging from 2-65 individuals. The population of the gall maker has a decisive influence on the morphology of the galls. Therefore early infection by some organisms often result in complete or complex galls, while late infection coupled with population impact ends up in partial or incomplete galls (Ananthakrishnan, 1980; Raman, 1981).

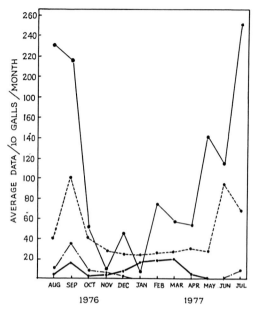

Fig.34. Population trends of *Schedothrips orientalis* and its parasite *Tetrastichus thripophonus* and inquiline predator *Androthrips flavipes*. •———• *Schedothrips orientalis* total population; •······•• *Schedothrips
orientalis* egg population; •—•—•—• *Tetrastichus thripophonus* population;
▬▬▬ *Androthrips flavipes* total population.


TABLE 2. Population trends of *Gynaikothrips flaviantennatus* in the
galls of *Casearia tomentosa*.

| Total population (%) | | Larval population (%) | | Adult population (%) | |
|---|---|---|---|---|---|
| Complete gall | partial gall | Complete gall | partial gall | Complete gall | partial gall |
| 86 | 14 | 76 | 24 | 82 | 18 |
| 79 | 21 | 100 | -- | 67 | 33 |
| 94 | 6 | 100 | -- | 83 | 17 |
| 97 | 3 | 97 | 3 | 64 | 36 |
| 85 | 15 | 56 | 44 | 87 | 13 |
| 91 | 9 | 99 | 1 | 62 | 38 |

## FACTORS INFLUENCING GALL THRIPS

Gall thrips complete their life-cycles usually within 30 days and this generally coincides with the monthly production of young leaves on host plants, so that emergence of adult thrips synchronises with the formation of young leaf buds (Varadarasan & Ananthakrishnan, 1981). Abiotic factors, principally heavy rainfall, have a distinct visible effect on gall thrips populations, but population fluctuations are generally brought about by biotic factors like the presence and the absence of young leaves, and predation by the anthocorid bug *Montandoniola moraguesi*, the predatory thrips *Androthrips flavipes* and hymenopteran parasites like *Tetrastichus thripophonus*. Taking the more simple, partial leaf fold gall on *Cordia obliqua* caused by *Aneurothrips priesneri*, it is seen that the individual gall has a life of 80 days, with the gall-maker population active up to 40 days. The population reaches the maximum of 110 in 10-30 days of gall development declining by the 40th day.

In *Aneurothrips*, restricted to the summer months (March to July) two generations were evident in about 130 days, each for approximately 50-60 days and separated by a gap of 10-20 days. The overall population was (a) high (210/10 galls) by the tenth day of population initiation (b) the adult populations (242/10 galls, and pupal 68/10 galls) reached the maximum in 20 days (c) by the 40th day the entire population started declining (d) the population was maintained at a lower level from 50th-60th day (e) increase in populations of all stages from 70th day with the peak by 80th day (172 larvae, 190 pupae and 160 adults/10 galls (f) population declined by 90th day with the adult population maintained at a low level (2-3/10 galls) till the 130th day (Fig. 32).

The periodicity of occurrence of the different species of gall thrips appear to vary considerably in the different species possibly due to the distinct correlation existing between the population abundance of gall thrips and the production of young leaves on the host plants. Accordingly the galls of *Pavetta hispidula* formed by *Teuchothrips longus*, of *Memecylon edule* by *Crotonothrips dantahasta* are mostly abundant for seven months in the year, while *Mimusops elengi* and the gall thrips *Arrhenothrips ramakrishnae* occur throughout the year. *Acacia leucophloea* galls by *Thilakothrips babuli* is highly seasonal, the rosette galls and the inflorescence galls occurring for about 3-5 months in a year. Galls of *Ventilago maderaspatana* induced by *Schedothrips orientalis* and *Casearia tomentosa* by *Gynaikothrips flaviantennatus* occur for about 6-8 and 4-9 months respectively (Fig. 33). Biotic factors having an important influence on the population of gall-making thrips, the number of predatory/parasites or the combined effects of both. In these six gall thrips, the inquiline predator, *A.flavipes*, the anthocorid bug, *M.moraguesi*, and the internal larval parasite, *T.thripophonus* act detrimentally on the populations at different periods. The presence of *A.flavipes* is found to be an important factor in population fluctuations both in *A.ramakrishnae* and *S.orientalis* (Fig 34). Besides, the population of *S.orientalis* is found to be influenced by *T.thripophonus*, abundant in November and February. Only the anthocorid bug appears to affect the population in *G.flaviantennatus*. This bug exhibits 2-3 peaks a year, each spread over 1-3 months.

The populations of *C.dantahasta* and *T.longus* in the galls of *M.edule* and *P.hispidula* respectively, observed for seven months for detailed stu-

114

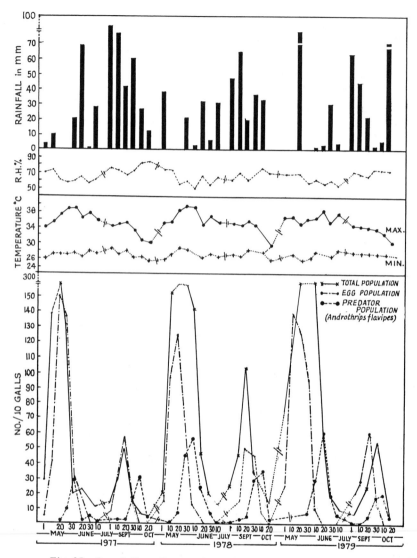

Fig.35. Population fluctuation of *Thilakothrips babuli*.

dies revealed their absence for five months and this coincided well with the absence of new leaf formation in *M.edule* and *P.hispidula*. The few stragglers found during this period have abundant fat bodies and appear to be in a temporary state of diapause. When such thrips are provided with young leaves, normally absent in that season, feeding and mating activities become evident and they reproduce normally. The population of *C.dantahasta* is affected by *A.flavipes* and that of *T.longus* by

*M.moraguesi.* Unlike all the other previously mentioned gall thrips, the population abundance of *T.babuli* is restricted to only three months -- two months in rosette galls and one in floret galls with 1-2 peaks in each habitat (Fig. 35). With maturation, the rosette gall begins to dry up, and thrips population also dwindles, leaving behind very few apterous adults. These adults remain within the dry galls and diapause. With *Acacia* sprouting flower buds, the apterous adults leave the diapausing site and migrate to the flowers to form floret galls, in which all polymorphic forms are established. Both in the rosette and floret galls, individuals of *T.babuli* are predated upon by *A.flavipes*, considerably decimating the population of the gall-maker (Varadarasan & Ananthakrishnan, 1981).

\* \* \* \* \*

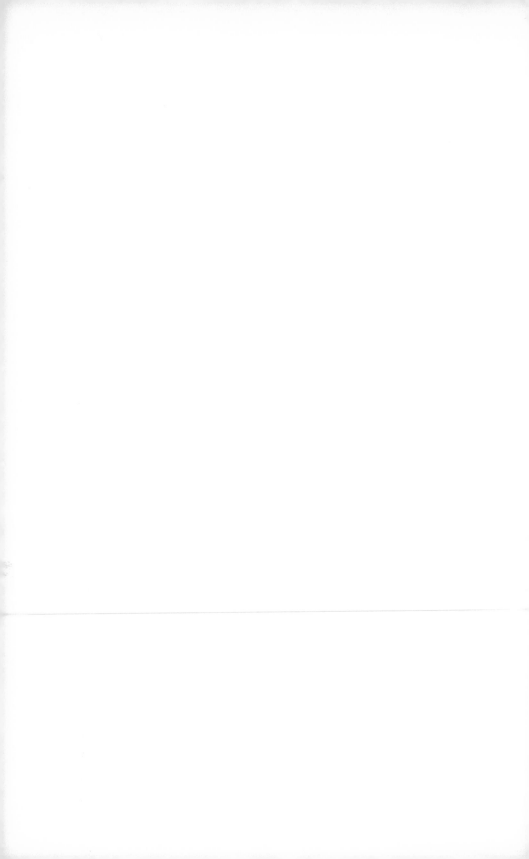

## ECOLOGY OF MYCOPHAGOUS THRIPS

Mycophagy among insects is widespread, many species inhabiting a variety of microhabitats particularly offered by dead-trees, the complexity of which forms an important factor governing the breeding pattern of the individuals inhabiting them. The cavernicolous quality of insects living spaces which dead trees offer, tend to restrict the number of insect species in general, but in so far as thrips are concerned there is a comparative richness of species both in terms of species numbers as well as of their abundance. As such dead trees besides offering excellent breeding sites of diverse insect species, are good examples of functional convergence, particularly indicating similarities of breeding structure (Hamilton, 1978). In his initial assessment of the evolution and diversity of insects living under bark, Hamilton suggests that the habitats lying immediately beneath the bark are extremely productive examples of wing polymorphism, of male haploidy, special breeding structures due to social or subsocial behaviour and of the development of certain types of sex-limited diversity. These appear to be very typical of mycophagous thrips as well, and several examples are discussed in this Chapter.

Tropical and subtropical regions of the world harbour a wealth of thrips species feeding entirely on fungal hyphae or their break-down products or spores, distributed in various habitats such as dead branches and leaves which form the litter above the soil particularly in forest areas, drying grass tussocks, subcortical regions of living and dead trees, polyporgous fungi, as well as in many other situations such as fungusinfested leaves of palms, dead or living, as also in their spathes and spadices. Species of *Strepterothrips*, such as *S.tuberculatus* have been recorded from birds' nests from Australia (Mound & Ward, 1977). They are mostly associated with early stages of decay and thrips are found in litter in the uppermost layers where the leaves are still entire. Species associated with fresh, dead twigs and branches are not only more abundant, but are among the largest and most spectacular as in species of *Dinothrips, Mecynothrips, Elaphrothrips*, and *Bactrothrips*.

Generally thrips are associated with the early stages of fungal infestation, especially before the wood becomes soft, waterlogged and ant-infested (Mound, 1974). Basically the fungus-feeding thrips involve the mycetobionts or mycetophiles (Graves, 1960; Graves & Graves, 1970) feeding on the mycelia as in phlaeothripines; and the sporophiles or spore feeding idolothripines. Transitional groups between the two categories also occur, *Polyphemothrips, Empresmothrips, Symphyothrips* being striking instances. By distribution they are known to occur in tropical rain forests and have been collected from leaf litter in the Australian rain forests, though they are more common in the wet tropics, being very abundant in the Western Ghats and forests of North Eastern India, not to mention the other tropical situations met with in South America and Africa. *Uzelothrips, Merothrips*, and *Erotidothrips* among the more primi-

tive members of the group, are associated with litter and dead twigs from
tropical forests. Species from leaf litter in India, Malaysia and Indo-
nesia are, however, comparatively few, involving species of the genera
*Mystrothrips, Uzelothrips, Phylladothrips, Plectrothrips*, and Urothripids, to
mention a few. But the richest source of leaf litter thrips has been
recorded from Trinidad, Eastern Australia, and Southern Brazil, and all
other tropical and subtropical areas with a diverse flora and a marked
variation in rainfall between the seasons of the year. It is of interest
that the rain forest leaf litter of Australia has only a few species,
although the rain forest litter of Solomon Islands and Trinidad has comparatively many more thrips (Mound, 1972). The highest concentration of
a single species of thrips so far recorded from leaf litter relates to
*Preeriella jacotia*, with 2500 individuals collected from leaf litter with
an RH range of 95-99% (Hartwig, 1978). This is surprising as thrips are
generally not met with in wet litter and under trees with large leaves,
though one rarely comes across stray individuals of *Azaleothrips amabilis*
in such leaves. Leaf litter produced by diverse large trees and shrub
flora involving smaller leaves, with perhaps an open cavity structure with
a large area of leaf surface exposed and bearing fungi, form a more
congenial habitat in which thrips move and feed. Leaf litter is a semi-
permanent habitat forming a more or less extensive as well as a uniform
habitat in forests, but optimum conditions are patchy and transitory.

Many species of thrips are common in relatively dry areas, even on
rocky, exposed places where litter is a thin and discontinuous layer such
as those formed by leaves of eucalyptus trees. *Idolothrips spectrum* of
Australia is a typical example of a species occurring in dead eucalyptus
leaves. No competitive exclusion between species exists, thereby
accounting for their widespread distribution. Unlike phytophagous species which are limited by the range of host-plants, the mycophagous species enjoy a continuous habitat. This is especially so in the leaf
litter habitat where the ease with which the individuals intermingle is
likely to permit considerable gene flow between populations of incipient species. At the same time the relatively weak constancy of the leaf litter habitat is also likely to reduce the rates of speciation and increase chances of
survival of relic species (Mound & O'Neill, 1974). Both excess of food
resources and an increase in the available niches appear to be the major
causes of abundance, though as Mound (1976, 1977) puts it, species diversity
is very great in leaf litter habitat, populations are extensive and relatively
dense. An interesting aspect is that the quality and quantity of food
available vary with season and weather, because the occurrence of the fungal
hyphae or their break-down products or spores on which the feeding occurs,
depends on environmental factors. Mycophagous species generally derive their
sterol requirements from ergosterol occurring in these fungi that are essential for their growth and development. Species like *Tiarothrips subramanii*,
feed on a wide range of fungi occurring on a single host *Borassus flabellifer*,
and the availability of an equally wide range of mycosterols from these fungi
possibly enable sizable populations to survive over long periods of time
(Plate 24).

Examination of the gut content of sporophagous species such as
*Tiarothrips subramanii* revealed their relative preference for fungal spores
in terms of their abundance. Analysis of the gut contents of *Tiarothrips*
fed on a complex of fungi revealed the presence of large numbers of

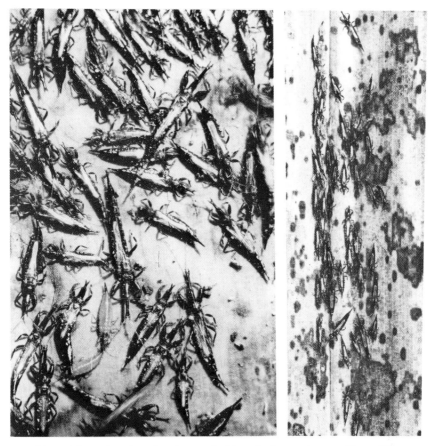

Plate 24. - A natural colony of *Tiarothrips subramanii* on *Borassus flabellifer* (right) and a portion of the colony (enlarged).

spores of *Anthostomella consanguinea*. Larvae fed on different fungi showed that *Anthostomella phoenicicola* was preferred by the first and second larval stages. The rate of development was equally high when reared on *A.phoenicicola* and *A.consanguinea*.

The percentage of adult emergence was however high when reared on *A.phoenicicola*, comparatively low on *A.consanguinea*, and very low on *Pestalotia algeriensis* and *Melanographium citri*, indicating the influence of fungal food over the rate of development (Ananthakrishnan *et al.*, 1983) (Plate 25 & 26). It is interesting that many species have inherited the capacity to react to fluctuations in the environment by varying body structure as well as population size. The amount of fungal food available is also a crucial factor. Observations on the feeding sites, fungal resource utilization, feeding range and dispersal in *Loyolaia indica* on different hosts during different seasons revealed

120

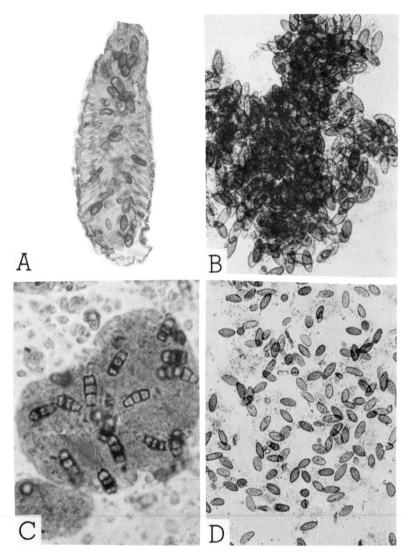

Plate 25. Showing spores fed by *Tiarothrips subramanii*. A - Portion
of foregut with spores, B - *Anthostomella consanguinea* mass from foregut,
C - *Pestalotia* sp. from gut of *Elaphrothrips denticollis*,
D - *A.consanguinea*, a few spores isolated.

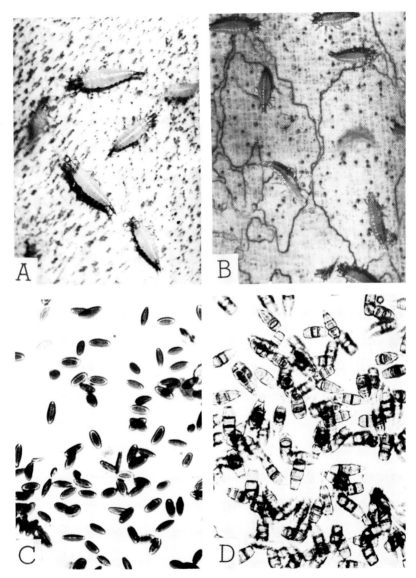

Plate 26. A - Larvae of *Tiarothrips subramanii* feeding on *Melanographium citri*. B - Immature stages of *T.subramanii* feeding on spores of *Anthostomella phoenicicola*. C,D - A portion of the spores from the gut of *Tiarothrips subramanii*. C - *Anthostomella phoenicicola*, D - *Pestalotia* sp.

that dispersal is facultative, being triggered by abiotic factors
(Anathakrishnan & Suresh, 1983) (in press) (Plate 27). Table 1 provides
some examples of fungal associates of some mycetophagous and sporophagous
thrips.

TABLE 1. The fungal associates of some mycetophagous and sporophagous thrips.

| Thrips species | Fungal species | Group of Fungi | Fungal hosts |
|---|---|---|---|
| *Merothrips morgani* | *Polyporus gilvus* | | |
| | *P.adustus* | Basidiomycetes | Under bark |
| | *P.versicolor* | (woody | (Graves & |
| | | polyporaceae) | Graves, 1970) |
| | *Ganoderma tsugae* | | |
| *Ecacanthothrips tibialis* | *Agaricostilbum palmicola* | Hyphomycetes | Dry petioles of *Cocos nucifera* |
| | *Torula* sp. | | |
| | *Drechslera* sp. | | |
| *Hoplandrothrips flavipes* | *Lasipodiplodia theobromae* | Coleomycetes | Dead twigs and bark of trees as well as |
| | *Pestalotia* sp. | | petioles and leaves of |
| | *Aspergillus* sp. | | coconut and Areca |
| | *Tetraploa* sp. | | |
| *Hoplothrips augusticeps* | *Ganoderma applanatum* | Woody polyporaceae | Dead bark (Graves & Graves, 1970) |
| | *Polyporus gilvus* | Basidiomycetes | |
| | *Fomes fomentarius* | | |
| | *F.fraxinophilus* | | |
| *Hoplothrips beechae* | *Ganoderma applanatum* | Woody polyporaceae | Dead bark (Graves & Graves, 1970) |
| | *Polyporus hirsutus* | Basidiomycetes | |
| *Hoplothrips fungosus* | Polyporoid fungi | Basidiomycetes | Dead wood |
| *Polyphemothrips indicus* | *Anthostomella consanguinea* | Ascomycetes | Dry leaves of *Borassus flabellifer* |
| *Phthirothrips morgani* | *Stereum fasciatum* | Woody polyporaceae | Dead bark (Graves & Graves, 1970) |
| | *Polyporus paragamenus* | Basidiomycetes | |

| | | | |
|---|---|---|---|
| *Bactridothrips idolomorphus* | *Pestalotia* sp. | Coelomycetes | Dry leaves of *Shorea robusta* |
| *Dinothrips sumatrensis* | *Lasiodiplodia theobromae* | Coelomycetes | Dry barks of *Mallotus albus* |
| *Elaphrothrips denticollis* | *Phomopsis tectonae* | Coelomycetes | Dry leaves of *Tectona grandis* |
| *Elaphrothrips procer* | *Pestalotia* sp. | Coelomycetes | Dry twigs and leaves of *Zizyphus oenoplia* |
| *Loyolia indica* | *Lojkania cynodontifolii* | Ascomycetes | Dry leaves & leaf sheaths of *Cynodon dactylon* |
| *Mecynothrips simplex* | *Pestalotia* sp. | Coelomycetes | Dry leaves of *Areca catechu* |
| *Neothrips indicus* | *Anthostomella sphaeroidea* | Ascomycetes | Decaying scape of *Agave americana* |
| *Priesneriana kabandha* | *Cytospora* sp. | Coelomycetes | Dead wood & bark crevices of *Eucalyptus globulus* |
| *Tiarothrips subramanii* | *Anthostomella consanguinea* | Ascomycetes | Dry leaves of *Borassus flabellifer* |
| | *Anthostomella phoenicicola* | Ascomycetes | |
| | *Anthostomella sepelibilis* | Ascomycetes | |
| | *Pestalotia algeriensis* | Coelomycetes | |
| | *Melanographium citri* | Hyphomycetes | |
| | *Alternaria* sp. | Hyphomycetes | |

The subcortical regions of dead and fallen trees, and sometimes of living trees, as well as dead twigs and branches harbour thrips species-complexes the composition of which varies in terms of their geographical distribution. In general, it may be mentioned that more species of such genera as *Hoplandrothrips*, *Adraneothrips*, *Hoplothrips*, *Elaphrothrips*, *Apelaunothrips* and *Nesothrips* are very characteristic of such habitats. An important aspect is that rotting trees tend to impose subdivisions, so that if populations are divisible into many 'quasi-isolated demes' (Hamilton, 1978) the species are able to make best, rapid evolutionary advances. The condition of the bark, the degree of decay, as well as the state of invasion by fungi are of course essential factors, with very often a series of fungi attacking in succession the dead leaves or branches, enabling a continuity in the availability of mycelia or spores. Pit-trap studies using coconut spathes and petioles resulted in the presence of such fungi as *Torula* sp., *Agaricostilbum palmicola*, *Dreschlera* sp., and species of *Aspergillus*. Correlated with their abundance, myce-tophilous species like *Azaleothrips amabilis*, *Hoplandrothrips flavipes* and *Ecacanthothrips tibialis* make their appearance. A further feature of dead tree complexes is that many species tend to readily mate within

124

Plate 27. Seasonal cycle of *Loyolaia indica* on different grasses –
1. Macropterous female, 2. Cycle, 3. Apterous female.

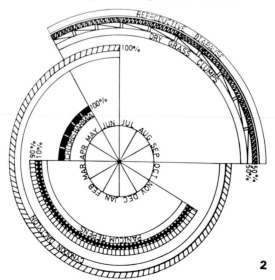

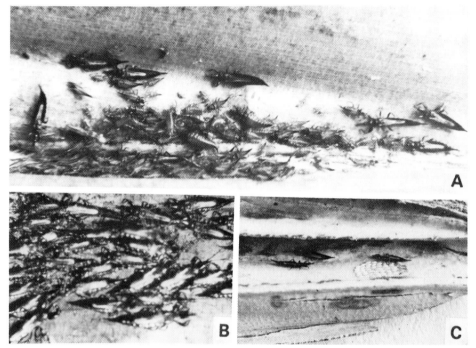

Plate 28. A - A colony of *Tiarothrips subramanii* with oedymerous males around the aggregation of nymphs; B - A portion of the colony of *Tiarothrips subramanii* adults (enlarged); C - *Tiarothrips subramanii* female, with a batch of eggs.

the habitat improving the potential for increase and colonization, contributing to the development of subsocial behaviour as in species of *Tiarothrips*, *Dinothrips*, etc. More or less connected with this subsocial behaviour or subsociality is the development of numerous sex-limited morphs reflecting particularly the role of the males (Hamilton, 1978). The aggregating tendency in species such as *Priesneriana kabandha* beneath the bark of eucalyptus, *Tiarothrips subramanii* on the drying leaves of *Borassus flabellifer* in clusters of 60-70 and 15-42 individuals respectively, with their oedymerous males often adopting defensive postures are typical instances of such subsocial behaviour in mycophagous thrips - a feature equally common in species of *Ecacanthothrips*, *Dinothrips*, and *Diceratothrips* (Plate 28).

The association of thrips with fungi is not restricted to the tubiliferous thrips alone as indicated earlier, but even the more primitive terebrantians, *Uzelothrips* and merothripids, are known to be mycophagous. Many Terebrantia are known to feed on and disseminate spores; the wheat rust, *Puccinia graminis* is spread by *Euphysothrips minozzi* and records of the extension of the feeding habits of this species on *Uromyces appendiculater* infesting *Dolichos lablab*, *Puccinia pennisetum* on *Pennisetum typhoides*, on *Oidiopsis faurica* and *Melanospora euphorbiae* infesting *Euphorbia geniculata* are now known (David *et al.*, 1973). *Megaphysothrips subramanii* associated with the coffee leaf rust, *Chaetanaphothrips signi-pennis* on banana rusts are further examples. Thrips association with mosses, lichens, and ferns has been briefly discussed earlier. It would be difficult to visualize the evolution of spore-feeding in Thysanoptera, since the relatively better evolved tubuliferan species like *Lissothrips muscorum* occur on mosses; species of *Bournierothrips* are on record feeding on mosses in West Africa, and species of *Nanothrips* are known to be asociated with the lichen-infested twigs. Ferns have provided suf-ficient instances of thrips feeding on spores, such as *Indusiothrips seshadrii*, *Scirtothrips pteridicola* etc. The greater morphological complexity of the host plant offers greater diversity of potential niches, and this partially accounts for the decreasing number of species associated with different growth forms. Considering this, the most important morphological difference between angiosperms and ferns is the lack of complex reproductive structures in ferns, while in the angiosperms these portions of the plant represent a number of habitats not available to insects utilising ferns. Further, when ferns were reaching their height during late carboniferous and early Permian periods, many of the modern groups of phytophagous insects began to appear and hence many took to angiosperms (Hendrix, 1980).

The association of thrips with polyporous fungi is equally of interest. Graves and Graves (1970) have recorded eleven species asso-ciated with the sporocarps of woody shelf-fungi like *Polyporus, Gano-derma, Stereum* etc. Several species of *Hoplothrips* inhabit these fungi and hundreds of individuals of *Hoplothrips fungosus* have been recorded from polyporoid fungi from Madras.

*Merothrips morgani* inhabits *Polyporus gilvus* which is the larval host of this species, as also *P.adustus, P.versicolor,* and *Ganoderma tsu-gae* in North America. *Hoplothrips angusticeps* has been known to occur in large numbers in *Ganoderma applanatum, Polyporus gilvus, Fomes fomen-tarius, F.fraxinophilus* etc., and it is confirmed that this species lives and breeds in woody members of Polyporaceae. Aggregations of *Hoplothrips beachae* involving both adults and immatures were observed on *Ganoderma applanatum* (Graves, 1960; Graves & Graves, 1970).

## PROBLEMS OF STRUCTURAL PATTERNS

The various dead tree habitats offer productive examples of wing polymorphism, very well evident in several species of such genera as *Allothrips, Apelaunothrips, Loyolaia, Priesneriana, Hoplothrips, Nanothrips, Nesothrips* etc. Weak wing structure seen in some species appear to be functional adaptations to leaf litter habitat. The occurrence of dealates in many species occupying some of these habitats appear to be adaptations to a situation in which wings are a handicap and in many instances flattening of the body goes hand in hand with winglessness; this is very typical of subcortical situations. Further, winglessness in polymorphic species tending to be gregarious, such as in *Priesneriana kabandha*, would be an additional device for greater and more effective fecundity, and a consequent increase in population size, and this often is the case with subcortical polymorphism. A further feature in such species wherein wing polymorphism occurs in individuals of a population, is the occurrence of structural anomalies associated with

Plate 29. Oedymere and Gynaecoid males of *Hoplothrips fungosus*.

winged as well as wingless conditions. In particular, many species of *Hoplothrips* such as *H.fungosus*, *H.bradleyi*, *H.orientalis* etc., show this phenomenon to a remarkable degree (Plate 29). Besides the reduction in the ommatidial number and lack of ocelli in apterous forms, the form of the head itself may be variable, developing horn-like projections below the eyes and associated modifications in the thorax, as in *H.mutabilis* (Hood, 1955).

The problem of structural patterns has fascinated biologists for a long time, particularly the possible mechanisms by which new patterns involving origin of neomorphs could arise during morphogenesis. Thrips provide the best examples of extreme intraspecific diversity involving quite often a complicated array of characters which provide a 'release mechanism' enhancing the variability of the species.

Sex-limited polymorphism, besides wing polymorphism is a common feature met with in several mycophagous species, and in view of the co-existence of different morphs in the same population, the definition of polymorphism as adopted by Richards (1960) appears convincing: 'one or more sexes of the species occurring in two or more forms which are normally sharply distinct to be recognizable without morphometric analysis'. As indicated earlier, when alary polymorphism exists in species showing sex-limited diversity, further complications often arise.

Variations are magnified to a very large extent by the high incidence of heterogony or allomorphosis or absolute size allometry of
adults, making the morphological definition of the species very difficult. A finely intergraded series is more often noticeable in populations of such species and the two extremes are often referred to as the
minor or gynaecoid males and the major or oedymerous males. Oedymerism
as defined earlier (Ananthakrishnan, 1968a,b, 1969) involves the development of bizarre forms with strikingly enlarged parts affecting mostly the
structure and armature of the forelegs and incident changes in thoracic
structure, while gynaecoidism results in opposite traits, with weakly
developed forelegs having armature highly reduced or wanting and
resembling the females in general make-up. The patterns of diversity
differ in the males of different species or species complexes. Two closely allied species may possess an almost similar structure among the
females, but the patterns of oedymerism among the males may vary, as is
typical of the members of the *Gastrothrips-Nesothrips* complex
(Ananthakrishnan, 1973). Many species show very simple patterns
involving just an enlargement of the forelegs without any associated
structural complications of other regions in so far as the expression or
suppression of features in the oedymerous and gynaecoid individuals are
concerned. When, however, oedymerous traits are coupled with the development of additional features expressed by the individuals, the patterns
are referred to as multiple or polyphasic. Multiple or polyphasic patterns, therefore, involve not only pronounced development of several
parts, varying with species or species groups, but also result in the
suppression of characteristics at the level of the gynaecoids. The
lateral mesothoracic fork in *Dinothrips sumatrensis*, the peg-like process
in *D.longicaudus*, the pendulous coxal prolongations in *Gastrothrips anolis*, the median tongue-like process of the metasternum in *G.falcatus*, the
antero-lateral pronotal horns of *Mecynothrips wallacei* are among the
large number of such expressions in oedymerous males (Ananthakrishnan,
1973). There could be no better examples of patterns involving multipli-
city of features in the transition from gynaecoidism to oedymerism as in
*Ecacanthothrips tibialis* and *Tiarothrips subramanii*. *Ecacanthothrips
tibialis* shows a profound gap between the gynaecoid and oedymerous forms,
the gynaecoids being exceedingly feeble in general make-up, lacking a
strong pronotum, cheek setae, femora and teeth, weak tarsal tooth and
absence of coxal prolongation. Further, they develop tibial tubercles
beyond the middle of foretibia, a feature lacking in normal and oedymerous males; the outer margin of the forefemora at the base, tends to be
clearly concave and is fringed with a cluster of fine hairs. This con-
cavity becomes progressively reduced, along with the size and number of
the fringing hairs as we proceed down the series to the gynaecoid. In
*Tiarothrips* the third antennal segment, the anteocular head process and
the forefemora keep pace with other in such a way that the head process
passes from a weak, straight-sided condition to an almost monstrous proportion double the head length and strongly corrugated, with asymmetrical
sides strongly armed with long setae (Plate 30). Thus in *T.subramanii*
three phases in growth patterns could be recognized: (a) 3rd antennal
segment weak, sides not corrugate, without strong setae at apex, head

---

Plate 30. Gynaecoid and Oedymerous males of - 1,2. *Tiarothrips subramanii*; 3,4. *Ecacanthothrips tibialis*.

production shorter than head, cheek setae weak, forefemora weak as also foretarsal tooth, (b) 3rd antennal segment moderately long, weakly sinuate margins, better armature of spines at apex; head production almost as long as the head, forefemora wider, and foretarsal tooth more prominent, and (c) 3rd antennal segment very long, sides very strongly and asymmetrically sinuate and corrugate, with deep concavities, apical armature very strong; head production longer than the head, forefemora much wider, foretarsal tooth very strong and long. Many more such examples are available when one examines a long series of individuals within large populations and Ananthakrishnan (1973) has vividly outlined the diverse patterns.

An essential aspect of studies dealing with sex-limited diversities indicated earlier relates to the magnification of variations by a high incidence of allometry or relative growth. As growth rates form a part of the general organization of an insect, changes in the rate of growth of one part of the body is invariably associated with similar changes in the neighbouring part. For this purpose, the number of individuals in a population is a very important measure of diversity and when the form and abundance are known, it enables statistical interpretation of the growth rates of various parts of the body in different morphs.

An analysis of the various diversity patterns would indicate that intraspecific diversity enables a combination of resources scattered in time and space to provide a composite niche for a species and enables the species to put a number of evolutionary opportunities together to make a larger package (Southwood, 1978). Since phenotypic flexibility is a characteristic feature of mycophagous species populations, it may be concluded that all characters of the individuals of a species are highly polygenic and all genotypes tend to vary phenotypically, and natural selection tends to act as on the extreme phenotypes. Both pleiotropy and polygeny bring about a network of interactions resulting in considerable variations in the phenotype. Adaptive strategies are very evident in the extreme forms, where the normal process of selection in favour of hetero-zygotes is slowed down allowing the extreme phenotypes to express their variants resulting in a pool of striking morphs. Taking into con-sideration, the diverse ways in which new characteristics appear and disappear in the extreme phenotypes, coupled with the timing of their expression, it would appear that the degree of the penetrant effect of genes concerned may also be primarily responsible for the varying effects. Further, the possibility of the extreme forms possessing a selective advantage indicates that there should be a mechanism which would continually act towards establishing an equilibrium of selective advantages of the two extremes leading to a persistent dimorphism (Gadgil, 1972).

* * * * *

## THRIPS AND POLLINATION ECOLOGY

Pollination ecology or anthecology deals with the dynamics of pollen transfer mechanisms and recent researches in this field incorporating studies of insect behaviour in relation fo flower-insect adaptation have added significantly to our knowledge on pollination. While many Hymenoptera and Lepidoptera are well-known pollinators, the role of thrips in pollination was established in the early part of this century by Shaw (1914) and Annand (1926) and has come to be better recognized in recent years. The habits of thrips appear very conducive to cross-pollination and they are able to carry pollen grains of variety of flowers by flight in sufficient quantities, to be of considerable use in pollination. The ability of thrips to carry pollen grains from the anther to the stigma naturally depends on the size, viscosity of the pollen grains, attractiveness of the flowers as well as the number and species of thrips present. The number of individuals present in the flower as well as the amount of pollen grains per insect would determine the total amount of pollen that they carry. The bulk of the pollen grains is generally carried on the thoracic and abdominal setae as well as on the wing setae, fringes and antennae. As such species with well-developed setae such as those of *Frankliniella* are more efficient carriers of pollen. The maximum number of pollen grains carried is around 200 per thrips in *Frankliniella schultzei* inhabiting Compositae flowers (Ananthakrishnan 1982). Available information indicates that *Frankliniella tritici* carries as many as 76 pollen grains in lupines and varying in number from 1-20 in the same thrips species in flowers of alfalfa, plums and daisy (Annand, 1926; Lewis, 1973). *Thrips tabaci* has been known to carry as many as 140 pollen grains of sugar beet. Involvement of *Frankliniella parvula* in the pollination of *Theobroma cacao* (Billes, 1941), *Frankliniella occidentalis* of beans and onion (Carlson, 1964) and species of *Taeniothrips* of *Calluna* and *Erica* flowers (Hagerup, 1950; Hagerup & Hagerup, 1953) has been well established. *F.occidentalis* by penetrating a flower bud of *Phaseolus vulgaris* before it opens can pollinate it earlier (Mackie & Smith, 1935; Lewis, 1973). Aspects relating to the petal colour change in *Lantana camara* and *Wedelia chinensis*, an incidental effect of thrips pollination, have been discussed by Mathur & Mohan Ram (1978) and Ananthakrishnan *et al* (1981).

An aspect of interest relates to Sabah Oil palm pollination by thrips in the wet season and the presence of *Thrips hawaiiensis* in the flowers of older palms is associated with the acceptable levels of pollination which does not occur in young palms (Syed, 1979). A low population inside the young palm is apparently due to the few male inflorescences. *Thrips hawaiiensis* makes its appearance as soon as the male flowers open and around 800 larvae were extracted from each spikelet. The population of this species in the male inflorescence was higher than that of female flowers and each male inflorescence harboured a maximum of 1000 individuals per spikelet. The very high density on male inflorescences referred to as 'saturation level' also appears to be an effective factor for pollination. Syed (1978) indicated the saturation level between 25 and 33 adults per cm length of male spikelets. As an adaptation to pollination, it is found that *Thrips hawaiiensis* visits female flowers after visiting male flowers, a feature revealed by the fresh pollen grains occurring on them.

Pollen movement in dioecious individuals of *Arisaema triphyllum* was assessed on the basis of the density of the pollen donor, impact of thrips in transporting the pollen, the density of the females to individual females and to the distance between the pollen donor and the pollen acceptor (Rust, 1980). The movement of pollen in *A.triphyllum* is limited to the dispersal of the pollinating insect, *Heterothrips arisaemae* whose population varied with the average of 10 thrips per male flower and 0.4 in a female flower. An analysis of the distribution pattern of thrips in female flowers showed the poisson type of distribution with only 45% chances of a female flower being visited by one or more thrips. While studying the phenomenon of thrips population in terms of seed production, it was found that the density of the male plants as well as the distance between male and female plants showed marked effect on seed production. The mean distance between male and female plants and average density of the male plants are 47.3 + 7.1 cm and 1.5 $\pm$ 0.1 per 0.25 m$^2$ respectively. Observations of Rust (1980) indicated that as the distance increases between the male and female plant, the percentage of female producing seeds will decline and when the density of male plant increases, there will be a significant increase in the production of seeds.

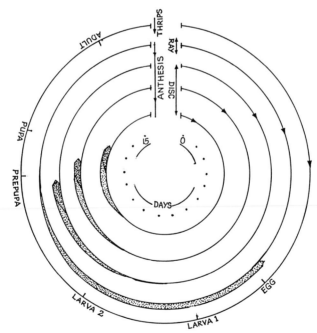

Fig.36. Phenology of *Wedelia chinensis* in relation to the biology of *Microcephalothrips abdominalis*.

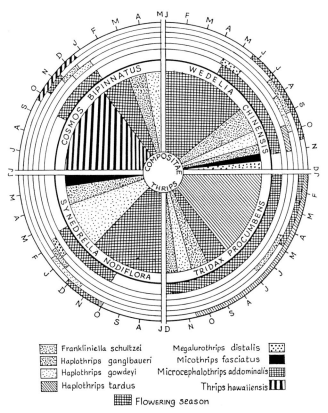

Frankliniella schultzei    Megalurothrips distalis
Haplothrips ganglbaueri    Micothrips fasciatus
Haplothrips gowdeyi    Microcephalothrips addominalis
Haplothrips tardus    Thrips hawaiiensis
Flowering season

Fig.37. Seasonal succession of thrips in four species of Compositae in relation to pollination.

## HOST PLANT-THRIPS PROFILES

The adaptive significance in terms of the pollinator and flower appears impressive in view of the strategies such as is evident in species like *Microcepalothrips abdominalis* which has a 9-12 days life cycle, its oviposition coinciding with the emergence of the ray petals of *Wedelia chinensis* in its late bud stage, so that as the larvae emerge from eggs, anthesis and nectar production get synchronized (Fig. 36). Synchronization in terms of flowering periodicity and phenology of the pollinating thrips appears to be controlled by the population build-up of thrips, eventually leading to migration. This is reflected by studies on thrips pollination of Compositae such as *Tridax procumbens*, *Wedelia chinensis*, *Synedrella nodiflora*, *Vernonia cinerea*, *Ageratum conyzoides*, *Cosmos bipinnatus* etc., which reveal two fundamental aspects: (a) species packing, species dominance and species succession on the one hand and, (b) population build-up of the different species of thrips on the other. Figure 37 illustrates the nature of species packing as well as their relative dominance in four different composite hosts, alongside

134

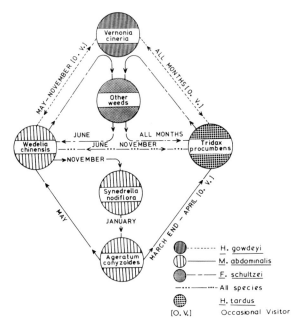

Fig.38. Migratory trends in different species of thrips infesting five species of Compositae.

with the succession of flowering season. Observations on species-packing in *T.procumbens* and *W.chinensis* revealed that these two species of flowers are being visited by *Haplothrips tardus*, *Haplothrips gowdeyi*, *Frankliniella schultzei* and *Microcephalothrips abdominalis*. Fluctuations in species-packing was found in both the cases, sometimes with 2 or 3 species in a capitulum. However, *M.abdominalis* was always the dominant species in *Wedelia*, and *H.tardus* in *Tridax*. When all the four species happen to be there in a capitulum, they showed a peculiar behavioural pattern so that terebrantians which are smaller did not enter a floret, while species of *Haplothrips* which are larger remained inside. Considering the dominance of populations of the invading species in a flower, *M.abdominalis* seemed to show preference for *Wedelia*, *Synedrella* and *Ageratum* and *H.tardus* for *Tridax* and *H.gowdeyi* for *Vernonia*.

Abundance of anthophilous thrips population is mainly determined by (i) the flowering season of the host plants, (ii) the effect of abiotic factors like temperature, rainfall and relative humidity, and (iii) the influence of predators. *M.abdominalis* was found dominant in *Wedelia* from May to November, its maximum population being in the month of August (900 thrips/50 heads), probably due to the availability of a large number of flowers as well as less rainfall (5 mm) and optimum temperature (30°C). The sudden fall in *M.abdominalis* and *F.schultzei* populations in the month of November in *Wedelia* is related to the termination of the flowering season and also the predatory efficiency of the anthocorid bug *Orius indicus*. As soon as the flowering season of *Wedelia* terminated, *Synedrella* started blooming sequentially, followed by *Ageratum*. The continuous availability of different host plants possibly prevented the complete decline of thrips populations, that resulted in maintaining their number almost constantly throughout the year. Fig. 38 shows the migratory trends of four anthophilous thrips species in their respective host plants. Migration of different thrips species to diverse host-plants was observed during off-seasons of flowering, and this sort of a migration between flowers of different species indicates that migration mainly depends on floral availability in different seasons, providing shelter and food towards build-up of their population (Ananthakrishnan et al., 1981).

This continuous build-up of thrips population in a flower leads to inter-, intraspecific competitions among thrips species which bring about migration, ultimately enhancing the possibilities of cross-pollination. Effective cross-pollination mainly depends on (i) the blooming time of the flowers, (ii) amount of food reward (nectar/pollen) for the pollinator, and (iii) structures facilitating access to the flowers and food. These facilities are very clearly evident in the hosts referred to, with a characteristic synchronization in the relative abundance of thrips as well as the species packing in the capitula of the plants studied. Incidentally, a limitation of the food reward from the flower to the forager encourages them to visit other plants of the same species. The species living in the heterogamous heads of Compositae with solitary inflorescences, seem to spend more energy for their visit to other flowers where the food reward is high. In contrast, thrips inhabiting homogamous capitula spend lesser energy for their migration due to corymbose arrangement of the heads, where the nectar availability is also less (Gopinathan et al., 1981). Thus, a balance as visualized by Heinrich and Raven (1972), exists between the nectar/pollen availability and the incidental calorific reward of a flower on the one hand, and the energy expenditure by the pollinator on the other.

Frequent movements of different species of adults and larvae of *M.abdominalis*, *F.schultzei*, *H.tardus* and *H.gowdeyi* from floret to floret were observed in their respective host plants such as *W.chinensis*, *T.procumbens* and *V.cineria*. The agile movement of *F.schultzei* involving frequent spreading and shaking of wings caused the pollen grains to fall on the stigmas. Pollen grains carried by *Haplothrips* sp. on the abdominal region, particularly at the region of the anal setae, rub against the stigmatic surface, owing to the large body size as compared with that of *M.abdominalis* and *F.schultzei*; this process is further facilitated by the peculiar backward movements of *H.tardus*. The frequent combing of the body surface with its hind legs enables shedding of pollen grains on the stigmatic surface when the insect lands on the stigma. *H.tardus* has been observed to migrate to the ray florets after visiting the disc florets, thereby pollinating ray florets to a certain extent. Table 1 provides a comparative picture of the pollen carrying efficiency of larvae and adults of different species of thrips inhabiting the Compositae flowers (Ananthakrishnan et al., 1981).

Involvement of *Thrips hawaiiensis* along with the other foraging insects such as bees and butterflies in the pollination of *Cosmos bipin-*

*natus* revealed that the rate of seed-setting was 50-65% in the thrips pollinated flowers, whereas 70-90% of seeds were obtained in the natural condition where the pollination activity was contributed by a combined effort of thrips, bees and butterflies. Thrips are generally considered as pure pollinators due to the presence of pollen grains of only one plant species alone and hence categorized as a homogenous type, whereas the bees and butterflies are the heterogenous type since they also carry other pollen grains (Varatharajan *et al.*, 1982).

TABLE 1. Pollen loads of some thrips species infesting some Compositae.

| | Number of pollen grains carried by each thrips | | | | | | | | | |
| | Heterogamous heads | | | | | | Homogamous heads | | | |
| | *Wedelia chinensis* | | *Tridax procumbens* | | *Cosmos bipinnatus* | | *Ageratum conyzoides* | | *Vernonia cineria* | |
| | Min | Max | Min | Max | Min | Max | Min | Max | Min | Max |
|---|---|---|---|---|---|---|---|---|---|---|
| *Frankliniella* | | | | | | | | | | |
| *schultzei* (Larva) | 120 | 180 | 150 | 200 | – | – | – | – | .. | .. |
| *F.schultzei* (Larva) | 90 | 130 | 125 | 170 | – | – | – | – | – | – |
| *Megalurothrips* | | | | | | | | | | |
| *distalis* | 90 | 150 | – | – | – | – | – | – | – | – |
| *M.distalis* (Larva) | 60 | 110 | – | – | – | – | – | – | – | – |
| *Micothrips fasciatus* | 30 | 55 | – | – | – | – | – | – | – | – |
| *M.fasciatus* (Larva) | 25 | 40 | – | – | – | – | – | – | – | – |
| *Microcephalothrips* | | | | | | | | | | |
| *abdominalis* | 35 | 60 | 40 | 75 | 65 | 125 | 32 | 56 | – | – |
| *M.abdominalis* | | | | | | | | | | |
| (Larva) | 30 | 45 | 25 | 52 | 45 | 80 | 55 | 85 | – | – |
| *Thrips hawaiiensis* | – | – | – | – | 90 | 160 | – | – | – | – |
| *T.hawaiiensis* | | | | | | | | | | |
| (Larva) | – | – | – | – | 50 | 100 | – | – | – | – |
| *Haplothrips gowdeyi* | 90 | 120 | 125 | 180 | – | – | – | – | 40 | 65 |
| *H.gowdeyi* (Larva) | 70 | 110 | 90 | 140 | – | – | – | – | 70 | 90 |
| *Haplothrips tardus* | 90 | 140 | 120 | 160 | – | – | – | – | – | – |
| *H.tardus* (Larva) | 70 | 100 | 80 | 120 | – | – | – | – | – | – |

Flower-Insect coadaptation is a continuing process since the dynamics of pollen transfer mechanisms are closely related to the behavioural characteristics of the pollinators. In this context an analysis of the "adaptation spectrum" of thrips would involve aspects such as availability of pollen/nectar as food, stigmatic exudations, (generally absent in Compositae), nectarine exudations through minute stomatal pores adjacent to the stylar base, favourable microenvironment within the corolla tube providing suitable oviposition sites enabling the emerging larvae to become dusted with pollen in their upward and downward movements within the tube, the architecture of the pollen-wall coupled with the setal arrangements on the body of thrips, and the synchronization of anthesis and nectar secretion. Studies on the floral stomata showed that they are arranged in specific patterns around the nectaries at the stylar base of the disc florets. The number of stomata and the size of the nectary will vary from species to species. Regarding the functional importance of these floral stomata in relation to the foraging behavior of the pollinatory organisms, it is clearly evident that larger the floret, the greater the number of stomata, resulting in the regulation or attraction of more of insect visitors, diversified qualitatively and quantitatively to achieve the target function of pollination (Gopinathan & Varatharajan, 1982).

\* \* \* \* \*

## THRIPS-HOST PLANT INTERACTIONS

Phytophagous insects appear to have kept pace with the colonization of plant communities, leading often to the selection of individuals adapted to a range of different host plants. The favoured host plant is not only "fed on, but lived on" (Kennedy, 1953) enabling a near perfect symbiotic relationship. In time, therefore, both the host plants and the insect species evolved diverse mechanisms enabling their survival. The choice of a host plant by a phytophagous species and its ability to break down plant resistance depend on the physiological state of both partners. Successful interaction of an insect with its host plant also appears to be dependent on a complex set of environmental, visual, tactile and chemical factors which often tend to appreciably influence the behaviour and physiology of insects. Modification of any of these factors equally influence the suitability or otherwise of any plant as a host for an insect. Plants, besides considerably increasing both the amount of diversity of living space available to insects, also offer microenvironments essential for a variety of functions involving courtship, aggregation etc. (Eastop, 1981). Further, insects are generally believed to be more temperature-dependent than plants, so that climatic changes tend to result in varying rates of development, leading to variations in the degree of intensity of insect infestation from year to year. Species-area relationships also form a vital factor for phytophagous insects and plant taxa begin to accumulate pest species on introduction in a new area (Southwood, 1961). Though resistance to insects is a natural property of plants, climatic factors and natural enemies also serve to restrain them, and changes in the host plant environment may also produce effective resistance against insect attacks (van Emden, 1965). All the same, to be successful, environmental versatility on the part of insects is an essential aspect, so that in the process they tend to develop structural, physiological and behavioural characteristics, which enable them to behave differently in diverse habitats, at different periods of their development and under varying environmental conditions.

## MONOPHAGY, OLIGOPHAGY, AND POLYPHAGY

Food specialization of phytophagous insects is often the cause for host plant specificity. These "kaleidoscopic patterns" of feeding behaviour (Dethier, 1954) tend to reflect the diverse ways in which different species respond to such changes as aging, water stress, concentration of nutrients and so on taking place within the plant. Some plants exposed to insect attacks for long periods would in the course of time develop resistance factors to a greater degree than others. Alternately, the tendency for insects to become polyphagous is also possible and as plants evolve, feeding preferences may change to accommodate plant changes resulting in monophagous and polyphagous species (Dethier, 1954). Sometimes a species is considered to be strictly monophagous just because its host plant genus is represented by a single autochthonic species in a given locality; yet the species in question is known to behave as an oligophage when found in some other localities. It is to incorporate this feature that the notion of monophagy was extended to include certain kinds of restricted oligophagy (Nowakowski, 1962). It is also believed that monophagy should have secondarily originated from polyphagy. Many polyphagous or oligophagous species of thrips have been separated into monophagous races. From such races, monophagous species must have been derived by isolation and mutation so that both mono-, and polyphagy seem to have alternated in the course of evolution of these insects (Takahashi, 1938). To elaborate further, it is presumed that the geno-type of several polyphagous species is made up of many stabilized gene complexes from which special strains characterized by a different fre-quency of genes may be selected. Mixing of these strains with those of other segments of the population is prevented by spatial isolation, so that the possibility exists that from a single polyphagous population, separate groups characterized by different feeding habits could have ari-sen (Dethier, 1954). Apart from strict monophagy or euphagy involving feeding on a specific host plant, as in the case of many gall thrips, monophagous species also include species feeding on plants belonging to a single genus or subgenus. Very strict monophagism occurs in such species as *Stannardiana variegata* feeding on *Euphorbia antequorum*, *Taeniothrips claratris* on *Clitoria ternatea*, *Isothrips orientalis* on jasmine, *Haplo-thrips yuccae* on *Yucca* etc.; sometimes they may be xenophagous, occur-ring on a non-specific plant. Oliogophagy is more common that monophagy, the individuals feeding on related plants generally confined to the same natural order of plants or of closely allied ones. *Euryaplothrips crassus*, *Microcephalothrips abdominalis*, *Taeniothrips simplex*, *Panchaeotothrips indicus* feeding on species of Amarantaceae, Com-positae, Liliaceae and Marantaceae, respectively, are typical instances of this category. Typical polyphagous species occurring on a wide range of host plants, viz., species restricted to plants serving for the rearing of larvae, are met with in many species of the genera, *Thrips*, *Taeniothrips*, *Megalurothrips*, *Sericothrips*, *Anaphothrips*, *Frankliniella*, *Haplothrips*, to mention a few. Polyphagy in a species is not always accompanied by its common occurrence or at any rate by its uniform distribution on the host plants. Polyphagy appears to have ecological implications as it tends to prevent overexploitation of preferred plant species, enabling a more even feeding pressure on available resources. A polyphagous species by virtue of its catholicity in feeding is fre-quently able to occupy widely different ecological niches and geographic ranges (Dethier, 1954). However, in some cases alternate hosts serve only to provide water, sugar and other compounds just to keep the insects alive, but do not sustain reproduction. This is clearly evident in thrips and other insects passing the dry season as active adults in reproductive diapause so that during the dry season their host specifi-city decreases. But such alternate hosts in which they do not repro-duce appear to strongly influence the insect's fitness when it locates the primary host (Janzen, 1973). Different segments of a population could become restricted to special groups of plants merely by extending their range into areas where one species of plant happens to grow more abundantly to the virtual exclusion of the other. Alternately, discon-tinuity in plant ranges could result in one segment of a population occupying a different plant community from the other. As indicated earlier, this isolation would possibly assist in the differentiation of distinct generic frequencies in the two segments of the population of the concerned species. Sometimes the rate of development of an insect on

different plants with varying distribution might also vary sufficiently to
isolate adults temporarily. Host alteration in most cases has also the
advantage of escape from egg predation and possible interspecific competition (Stiling, 1980).

There is a close association of different species of thrips with
individual plant species as in aphids, so that we have the chillies-
thrips, onion-thrips, cardamom-thrips, rice-thrips, cassava-thrips,
grapevine-thrips, gladiolus-thrips, marijuana-thrips, etc., to cite just a
few instances. Heterogeneity in the botanical world would also appear
responsible for the non-acceptance of all plants as hosts, so that there
is a high taxonomic selectivity. There are exclusive feeders on
Poaceae (*Chirothrips* spp.), Compositae (*Microcephalothrips
abdominalis*), Amarantaceae (*Euryaplothrips crassus*), Euphorbiaceae
(*Stannardiana variegata*), and Marantaceae (*Panchaetothrips indicus*).
This feature is equally true of gall thrips as well, where species
belonging to particular genera are known to inhabit plants of specific
natural orders. In other words, it is possible to visualize the development of a parallel evolution in terms of thrips generic complexes associated with specific plant generic complexes. Gall induction by species
of *Crotonothrips* on Melastomaceae, of *Gynaikothrips* on Moraceae, of
*Liothrips* on Araliaciae and Piperaceae are some typical instances.

## FEEDING PREFERENCES AND ASSOCIATED STRATEGIES

It is the host plants which play a critical role in determining thrips
numbers, as of other insects and life history strategy is dictated by the
habitat or area accessible to the feeding stages. The plant species, it
must be realized, is not a homogeneous entity, but a heterogeneous one
with its "microchemical environment changing in time and space with
changing conditions of growth, climate and soil" (Dethier, 1954). Various parts of even a leaf produce significant differences in terms of
nutrient concentration and hence of reproductive success, and as such
the individual leaf is often considered as a heterogeneous habitat forming the smallest resource unit (Witham, 1980). Fresh young leaves, for
instance, after pruning become more acceptable for insects, in view of
their life-cycles, and increased egg production when reared on plants
containing high amino nitrogen. As such, the condition of the host plant
is a major factor in determining population density. The terms predic-
table, unpredictable and ephemeral habitats have been used with reference
to varying flushes of foliage in temporary vegetation, growth of vegetation in semi-arid areas with erratic rainfall and for habitats that are
relatively early in any natural recolonization succession. This implies
that the length of time the specific habitat remains suitable for
breeding and build-up of population is important (Southwood, 1977).
Southwood has further shown how "ecological strategies" of a species are
evolved in response to the habitat, as expressed through the
"reproductive success matrix", which implies that individuals of a species in time and space tend to evolve such strategies as would maximize
the numbers of their descendants to their habitat.

Evolution of feeding preferences appears to be interlinked with the
diversification of higher plants and the specialization of food with a
certain nutritional composition, as well as the appearance in plants of
toxic substances, accelerated the development of a sensory system

(Dethier, 1954). The leaf surface offers an environment for insects and both the physical as well as chemical factors of the leaf surfaces may be involved in food selection. The stomata and the trichomes and the complex chemical environment offered by the leaf surface appear important components in host selection, and recognition of the plant before the cuticle is pierced avoids the possibility of ingesting noxious substances even in small amounts (Chapman, 1977). Ananthakrishnan (1952) indicates the relationship between stomatal frequency and infestation factor in *Retithrips syriacus* feeding on a number of host plants. Maxillary and labial tactile receptors may also be involved in detecting the textural differences in leaves like smoothness from pubescence, young from old, etc. The preferences shown by the cassava thrips, *Frankliniella* sp., and *Corynothrips stenoapterous* to leaves with few or no hairs and the strong relationship between number of hairs per leaf lobe and degree of resistance, are good examples. The number of hairs per leaf lobe increased when leaves expanded and particularly after flowering, the number of hairs/leaf lobe decreased and thrips resistance also decreased (Schoonhoven, 1974). Tactile receptors appear to monitor the consistency of leaves or portions of leaves, as is evident by the exploitation of particular feeding sites on leaves such as that of cashew and cocoa by the cocoa thrips *Selenothrips rubrocinctus*. The longer hairs on the maxillary palps may serve as tactile probes and may be mechanisms to maintain feeding specificity. While this may be true of many phytophagous thrips, sufficient information is not available as regards the sensory mechanisms involved in thrips feeding. Nevertheless, it is not difficult to presume that in view of the labium and the hypopharynx of thrips mouthcone being pressed on to the feeding surface, the role of contact chemoreceptors would appear important, along with the role of olfaction in food selection behaviour. The distribution of the sensory setae on the maxillary and labial palps and on the labium also seem to differ within species and among species. For a proper appreciation of the feeding preferences of thrips, one has to take into consideration the tremendous diversity in the organization of the mouth cone both in the Tubulifera and the Terebrantia. In most Terebrantia the mouth cone is reasonably or moderately long and broadly rounded, with the stylets always confined to the mouth cone; in *Asprothrips*, *Pseudodendrothrips*, *Leucothrips* it is very much shorter, while it is very long and narrow in *Perissothrips*, *Rhinothripiella* and *Oxyrrhinothrips*, with the maxillary and labial palpi also elongate. The maximum diversity is met with among the Tubulifera, where the mouth cone could be very short and broad, with the stylets almost confined to the mouth cone as in *Bamboosiella* and *Antillothrips*, elongate, narrow and biconcave as in *Calamothrips* and some species of *Liophlaeothrips*, and elongate and broadly rounded as in *Rhynchothrips*. In general, those species with very short mouth cones appear restricted feeders. Unusually long, sometimes highly convoluted maxillary stylets occur in the *Casuarina* chlorophyll - feeding species of the genera *Adrothrips*, *Akthetothrips*, *Heligmothrips* and *Xyelothrips*. Mound (1970) suggests that these convoluted stylets are apparently adapted for insertion into the furrows which may be 100-200 um deep.

An assessment of thrips-host plant interactions, which is generally also the case with other phytophagous insect species, involves consideration of the following aspects:

      A. The stage of development of the host plant and time of attack.

B. Source of infestation and build-up of thrips population in plants.

C. Host plant strategies and regulation of thrips populations.

D. Host-plant responses in terms of gall formation and co-evolution of thrips host-plant species and plant families.

## SOURCE OF INFESTATION AND BUILD-UP OF THRIPS ON HOST PLANTS

Thrips build-up in the weeds in and around the cultivated fields or overwintering in nearby weeds and subsequent migration to the crops, often aided by the prevailing wind, with a heavier infestation on the windward than the leeward side, is a common phenomenon. The economic injury level can vary from area to area, and season to season depending upon local conditions, a feature well-documented in the case of soybean, cotton and chillies thrips. The margins of soyabean fields closely interface with vegetational zones proximal to the fields and many species can subsist in these zones prior to the emergence of soyabean seedlings, and from there spread into the soyabean fields early in the growing season. This is due to what is generally termed at the "edge effect" resulting in the occurrence of higher number of species in the margins of fields, which is an ecotone where two environments meet (Irwin & Price, 1976). Analysis of the build-up of pests, including thrips in cultivated cereal, pulse or millet fields, clearly indicates the important role of weeds in and around the fields, so that infestation results from the segregation of a few local species associated with related wild plants and their adaptation to the crop, which often presents very similar, but vastly improved conditions for existence (Uvarov, 1964; Ananthakrishnan, 1980). In spite of their continued migration to the crops, these weeds or wild plants still continue to serve as reservoirs from which there is a replenishment of the species, whenever populations tend to become dense due to artificial control methods. A good example is the chilli thrips, *Scirtothrips dorsalis* which continues to plague the chilli-growing tracts of India, in view of the excessive build-up of populations in the surrounding vegetation, which with their luxuriant growth acts as a reservoir of this thrips. It would, therefore, appear very necessary to study the population fluctuations of pest species both within the crop as well as in the weeds or wild vegetation around, in any attempt to understand their source of infestation and pest status, before adopting control measures.

Migration, whether of short or long duration, enables a species to keep pace with the changes in the location of its habitat. They are, therefore, of primary evolutionary importance, ensuring that insects leave either temporary habitats (flowers and annual plants), or permanent habitats (trees, woody shrubs, bark etc.) which tend to become unsuitable for breeding in the course of time (Johnson, 1968). Thrips tend to be evenly distributed up to 30 feet (Korting, 1931) and there is a close relationship between catch and flight. Lewis (1961) in England has estimated the total number of thrips caught, in terms of species as well as numbers of thrips in permanent and temporary habitats, with as many as 13-9744 in the former and with very negligible numbers in the latter.

Habitat unfavourability is generally assessed in terms of food shortage
and climatic extremes and insects must be highly adaptable to be successful pests and a mobile population is one of their adaptive traits
(Taylor, 1970). The cereal thrips, *Limothrips cerealium* and *L.denti-
cornis* hibernate in grass and bark as adult winged females, and during
spring they emerge on warm days, fly upwards and become wind-borne
(Lewis, 1963). Migrants could be considered as "r" strategists as they
are successful in moving from one habitat to another, in spite of heavy
mortality, doing so at a stage where their reproductive potential is high
(Kennedy, 1974). A living hedge, for instance, is both a wind-break and
a habitat so that the pattern of distribution is often more complicated
than near a simple wind-break, because populations of insects like
*Limothrips* spp. may spread from hibernating, breeding and feeding sites
(Lewis, 1969). Another aspect of colonization that influences species
composition is the proximity of potential colonists to areas of colonization. Species like *Sericothrips variabilis* which are early colonists are
reported to drift in on jet winds and currents from as far as hundreds of
miles away, drifting northward from warmer climates (Irwin & Price,
1976).

Thrips are known to be among the well-known migratory groups of
insects. Available information on the flight periodicities and aerial
densities of thrips is principally due to the investigations of Lewis
(1965). Many Thysanoptera like *Zaniothrips ricini* after emergence from
the soil and other hiding places, migrate over short distances in search
of host plants. They are weak fliers, voluntarily launching into the air
and invariably get drifted by wind currents. Olfactory and visual responses enable them to land at the selected sites only in lighter winds.
Mass flights in suitable weather are observed in macropterous individuals
and the common ones involved in such flights are females of thrips inhabiting grass and cereals, which not only provide uniform breeding sites
over large areas, but are also widely distributed and ensure survival.
If sufficient food is available, such movements are restricted, only a
shortage of food followed by rising temperature, inducing them to
migrate. Most mass flights occurred in sunny, settled weather and the
suggested metereological criteria for flight are (1) no rain or drizzle
during the day (2) maximum temperature of at least 20°C, (3) mean
temperature more than that of the previous day, (4) at least one hour
sunshine and (5) dew-point in the range of 5-15°C (Lewis & Hurst, 1966).
Density appears to decrease with height and thrips have been known to
prefer flying at heights of more than one metre up to 14.6 m. Aeiral
densities as large as 60,000 thrips per 10 cu ft were recorded by Lewis
(1965), the density of all species decreasing with height, but the
rapidity of the decrease differed with species (Lewis, 1959).

By using suction traps to sample a constant volume of air, the true
density of thrips in the air has been estimated and studied and the
correct proportions of different species at various heights determined.
During summer many migrate from host to host for oviposition and aerial
populations appear to be very high during this time. Thrips in flight
contain individuals in all stages of ovarian development, viz., old,
maturing and laying females. Lewis (1959) arbitrarily divided the life-
cycle of *Limothrips cerealium* into six stages, viz., emergence from
winter-quarters, development of the ovary and commencement of extensive
oviposition, movement to fresh host plants and appearance of new genera-

tions and death of old females, development of new generation on cereals, movement from cereals, and hibernation. Immature females readily take to flight, get dispersed widely, while the gravid females are seen to fly around and between the hosts, unless they are accidentally drifted by strong winds. Dry winds are also known to destroy thrips in considerable numbers within a short time by desiccation and these winds appear responsible for the sudden decrease in the population of *Thrips tabaci* (Priesner, 1960). Incidentally infestation of the coffee thrips *Diarthrothrips coffeae* in Africa has been reported to be more on trees growing on the leeward side of slopes and of windbreaks where temperature is higher. Most cases of outbreaks followed prolonged dry seasons and continuous heat, with most of these occurring during drought and ending soon after onset of heavy rains. Severe outbreaks occurred when the temperature rose above 18°C (Le Pelley, 1968). Wind-breaks are also known to affect the patterns of distribution of thrips, as of other insects, the shelter produced by wind-breaks and wind speed, playing an important role (Lewis, 1970). Wind-breaks increase the numbers of insects in the air near them and on adjacent crops by creating 'wind-shadows' in which airborne insects accumulate and they provide feeding and breeding sites from which they can spread and affect the local populations. Whenever insects originate in a living wind-break, the patterns of infestation will differ (Lewis, 1968).

Temperature has considerable influence in the proportion of thrips emerging and attaining flight condition and this is very well illustrated by *Limothrips cerealium* emerging from hibernation in bark. Emergence and take-off in this species is influenced by the temperature of the bark and air immediately above it. With sunshine striking the bark and consequent increase in temperature and light intensity, the emerging of thrips becomes active, orienting upwards, downwards or horizontally within a few minutes of emergence. Emergence was quicker at 25°c than at lower temperatures. During hibernation many thrips appear to lose their ability to fly and regain their flight ability only after passing through a flight maturation period that is temperature-dependent. At 25°C, 20°C and 15°C respectively, 611, 641, and 254 thrips emerged and the duration of emergence at these temperatures were 10, 14, and 28 days respectively (Lewis, 1963). It would, therefore, be evident that thrips as in the case of other insects reach a new habitat after a successful migration, which implies that the principal evolutionary advantage of such movements enables a species to keep pace with the location of its habitats and this appears to be true with species associated with temporary habitats (Southwood, 1962). Though weak flyers, thrips are carried by air current leading to effective dispersal. As a result of trapping airborne thrips to determine the effectiveness of migration in terms of abundance according to habitat, Lewis (1961) concluded that the mean catch per species was high in those species with temporary habitats.

It would be useful to discuss a few well-known examples of thrips infesting cultivated fields and the need to recognize the crop and the vegetation around as a unit. Considering the population build-up in productive cabbage fields in the United States of America, it is evident that *Frankliniella tritici*, *F.exigua* and *F.tenuicornis* have seriously damaged maturing fresh market cabbage, the thrips apparently migrating from alfalfa and winter wheat where they had attained great numbers, the crop losses ranging from 36 to 39%. *Thrips tabaci* is potentially a serious pest of cabbage and the common use of alfalfa and winter wheat in crop rotation in areas where cabbage is grown, aggravates the incidence of this pest species (Wolfenberger, 1964). *F.tritici*, though feeding on a large number of hosts, has a decided preference for plants belonging to the grass, legume and rose families, as also for forage crops like alfalfa and vetch influencing the population build-up and seriously damaging cotton. *Frankliniella fusca* has been reported as causing a reduction of leaf surface of seedling cotton plants by 50% or more and height approximately by 20% by the time the plants are six weeks old. *Thrips tabaci* is known to be predominant in seedling cotton and though only 10% of the total number of adult thrips taken from cotton during the first six weeks of growth were *Frankliniella* sp., a reversal of species predominance occurred subsequently with the flower thrips attaining 80% of the total number (Hightower & Martin, 1956). Adults of overwintering *Stenchaetothrips biformis* emerges in mid April, laid eggs on *Leersia japonica* and other grasses where the first generation live and during early may, they migrate and colonized into paddy fields in China (Anonymous, 1976). There is a clear relationship between thrips damage and developing stage of rice plants and with the development of the double cropping system of rice cultivation and with extensive planting of early rice, thrips populations have been on the increase. Incidentally, taking the case of the rice thrips in India, of the several species of weeds recorded from paddy fields in southern India, the species *Echinochloa crusgalli*, *Cyperus iria*, *C.rotundus* and *C.difformis* appear dominant in view of their heavier density per sq. metre and their harbouring large populations of *Haplothrips ganglbaueri*. Further, in view of their flowering earlier than the paddy plants, heavy populations of thrips are built up, enabling subsequent migration to the crop, resulting in considerable chaffiness of grains (Anathakrishnan, 1977; Anathakrishnan & Kandasamy, 1977). The role of such weeds in relation to the infestation of *Stenchaetothrips biformis*, in the nursery stage appears equally significant. Ananthakrishnan and Thirumalai (1977), and Anathakrishnan and Daniel (1981) have further indicated the role of the weed *Chloris barbata* as the alternate host of *Chirothrips mexicanus* and *Exothrips haemavarna* damaging young ear-heads of *Pennisetum typhoides*, the former in particular, building up their population both by sexual reproduction and arrhenotokous parthenogenesis. A standing example of the interaction of thrips species in crop communities is seen in the mixed cropping system where cotton, chillies and onion and to a limited extent tomatoes are cultivated. The three major pest species, *Thrips tabaci*, the onion thrips, *Scirtothrips dorsalis*, the chillies thrips and *Frankliniella schultzei* infesting these crops, are very highly polyphagous and are maintained in considerable numbers in various weeds and other wild vegetation. While chillies and onion are mostly unattacked by other species, there occurs a concentrated infestation on the cotton seedlings (Ananthakrishnan, 1980a).

In general, the population build-up of thrips follows certain pathways, as has been well illustrated in the case of *Thrips nigripilosus* on Pyrethrum (Bullock, 1965) and *Limothrips cerealium* (Lewis, 1961) involving (a) initial period of rapid increase, having colonized from other areas (b) a protracted period of more or less arithmetic increase (c) a period of accelerated increase (d) a final period of very rapid acceleration perhaps due to a response to favourable climatic conditions. In cowpea crops in Nigeria where the flowers are heavily infested with *Megalurothrips sjostedti*, immigrant population of adults mainly from alternate host plants augment infestation of thrips. Such alternate hosts as *Phaseolus vulgaris*, *Glyricidia* sp., *Caesalpinia* sp., *Crotalaria juncea*, and *Vigna triloba* probably play a major role in the production dynamics of this species. The population build-up on cowpea within 12-34 days was correlated with the cumulative numbers of flowers on the plant and was related in particular to the flowering duration pattern. *Centrosoma* is a perennial cover legume pasture and hedge crop in which flowering occurs intermittently for many months in the year. Peak populations in both cowpea and *Centrosoma* were influenced mainly by the flowering cycles and pollen abundance. Studies on the population dynamics also indicated that M.sjostedti were maintained at low levels in *Centrosoma* throughout the year, whereas they exploded twice to thrice their peak size on *Centrosoma* where they infest cowpea crops (Taylor, 1974).

## STAGE OF DEVELOPMENT AND INSECT ATTACK

Areas of active cell division and growth in plants are favourite feeding sites, often with sufficient concentration of sugars and amino compounds. In general, there are two critical stages one immediately after germination and the other at the inflorescence stage (Bardner & Fletcher, 1965). The time of attack may greatly affect the distribution of insects on the plants, as for instance *Frankliniella schultzei* which normally infests flowers, attacks leaves if flowering is delayed. Gall thrips in particular, prefer undifferentiated tissues. Diversion of the plant resources to the galls restricts the development of normal tissues.

The tobacco thrips *Frankliniella fusca* attacks seedling cotton as soon as it breaks through the soil and one or more generations develop during the following month to six weeks before they leave cotton. Maximum populations usually develop approximately one month after the seedling plants have emerged from the soil (Newsom *et al.*, 1953). A high percentage of seedling cotton are malformed and stunted through attack by the species *Frankliniella tritici*, *Sercothrips variabilis*, and *Frankliniella fusca*, there being 14-620 thrips/plant. Thrips-injured cotton is recognized early by the occurrence of two or more main branches and sometimes with excessive branching of vegetative branches. In the case of the lily thrips *Liothrips vaneeckei* bulbs are heavily infested, attacking first the scale surfaces which become flabby and paper-like and a typical colony of 50 individuals clustered upon the innerside of the bulb scales (Hodson, 1935). In irrigated vineyards *Drepanothrips reuteri* attacks leaves in all positions, but then the first, third and sixth had considerably higher numbers and these provided food and oviposition sites, so that vines that continuously produced new vegetation had the capacity to support a large number of thrips (Yokoyama, 1977) and adults emerged from hibernation with the opening of buds. Such spatial patterns are very evident in soyabean fields where two species, *Frankliniella tritici* and *Sericothrips variabilis* appear dominant. All stages of *F.tritici* appear concentrated in terminal buds and blossoms. Adults of *Sericothrips variabilis* were found most commonly on the uppermost fully expanded trifoliate or the one immediately below it. Larvae of *S.variabilis* were generally concentrated on the third to sixth trifoliate below the terminal (Irwin *et al.*, 1979).

Seven species of thrips occupy various parts of the castor plant in Madras. *Toxothrips ricinus*, a highly host specific species occurs in almost all seasons, the adults and larvae being found inside the bract which covers the young buds, the occurrence of the species being highly restricted to this niche. *Scirtothrips dorsalis* occurs on the dorsal and ventral sides of the tender leaves of first and the second nodes. Rarely the adults occur on the leaves of III and IV nodes, mainly occupying the ventral side of leaves. Larval population is mostly restricted to the leaves found on first and second nodes. *Retithrips syriacus*, another polyphagous species occurs mostly on the leaves of third node onwards. Comparatively large numbers are seen on fourth and fifth nodal leaves. The adult and immature forms of this species occur both on the dorsal and ventral sides of the foliage. Along with the population of *Retithrips syriacus*, on the third to sixth nodal leaves, comparatively low populations of *Rhipiphorothrips cruentatus* and *Astrothrips tumiceps* also occur. *Zaniothrips ricini* inhabits the leaves of fourth to sixth nodes. The weed *Achyranthes aspera*, very common in groundnut fields harbours four species of thrips, viz., *Chiridothrips indicus*, *Frankliniella schultzei*, *Ayyaria chaetophora* and *Caliothrips indicus*. *Chiridothrips indicus* is restricted only to the inflorescence and an average number of 60 thrips can be collected from a single inflorescence. *F.schultzei* occupies the first nodal leaves, while adults and larvae of *Caliothrips indicus* occur on the third and fourth nodal leaves of both flowering and non-flowering plants. Gravid females of *Caliothrips indicus* tend to select the second nodal leaves for egg-laying (Ananthakrishnan, et al. (1982)

As leaves provide the majority of the plant surface for insects to inhabit, the index of habitat space is composed of leaf number and leaf area/width components (Price, 1976) and space, food and shelter increase with them. In grasses the vertical height of vegetation explains the increased variation in the richness of species than grass biomass. Taller grasses may allow for further resource partioning along a vertical gradient. Most niche separation among feeders appears attributable to partioning of the grass system (Tallamy & Danno, 1979).

It is interesting to note that *Scirtothrips citri* is common on leaves of all ages, while its ecological analogue elsewhere, *Pseudothrips inaequalis* is restricted to very young leaves. But this species was known to undergo what has been called on 'ecological release' in an island, attracting old leaves and increasing in population size greatly, resulting in an 'ephemeral population explosion' (Simberloff, 1978).

Like other phytophagous insects, thrips prefer young or growing tissues to mature parts of the plants, as the concentration of soluble amino acids and amides in the sap is high rendering the plants more nutritious (Kennedy, 1958). In the case of cocoa thrips, *Selenothrips rubrocinctus*, only leaf tissues within certain limits of maturity seem acceptable, since they appear to have the ability to recognize the condition of retardation of protein synthesis in the leaf resulting in high proportion of nitrogen compounds. There also appears to be a significant correlation between leaf amino nitrogen and *Selenothrips* attack which occurs on leaves of later wet season flushes, reaching a peak shortly after they have hardened. An upper physiological age limit has been recognized over which a leaf is suitable for colonization. Very young flaccid leaf tissue is not acceptable. Aging generally implies increased transport of nitrogen compounds and in the absence of predators the curve for cocoa thrips abundance generally follows that for the aging of the leaf. Diminishing of leaf moisture appears favourable to thrips attack (Fennah, 1963). Though *Selenothrips* can multiply at lower day-time humidities, increased humidity does not interfere very much with their multiplication.

## HOST PLANT STRATEGIES

Total, partial and non-preference mechanisms in plants to phytophagous insects in general and thrips in particular, appear to be associated with several factors, which may exert a positive influence on host plant acceptance. These factors tend to evoke an aggregating response when in lower concentrations and feeding inhibition or host avoidance reactions in higher concentrations. The overall concentrations of free amino acids in plants are extremely variable depending on age, species, variety, part of plant and a large number of environmental conditions. The amino acid composition is equally variable, affecting the feeding behaviour of insects like thrips and aphids and other phytophagous species. Free amino acids are one among the many metabolic products occurring in plants which help to maintain and sustain feeding. Lower concentrations of varying essential free amino acids may also influence the degree of acceptance of plants by thrips and should all of them occur in the proportion needed as in *Vitis vinifera*, heavy aggregation of *Rhipiphorothrips cruentatus* and to some extent of *Retithrips syriacus* often result in heavy tissue damage (Ananthakrishnan & Muraleedharan, 1972). Synergistic action of free aminoacids with other compounds such as sucrose and other sugars etc., has also been reported as causing feeding stimulation (Dethier, 1966). Remarkable accumulation of free amino acids in chlorotic leaves where the total free amino acids increase by 4.1 times as compared to healthy leaves, and the appearance of considerable amounts of arginine and amides such as aspargine and glutamine has been known to stimulate feeding of jassids (Sogawa, 1971).

Though plant resistance to insects has been explained on the basis of three fundamental mechanisms, viz., non-preference, antibiosis and tolerance (Painter, 1951), the subsequent discovery of allelophathic relationships between plants and insects, have indicated that such relationships appear to be mostly due to the presence of allomones or their absence, or the presence in only sub-optimal levels of kairomones (Kogan, 1976; Beck, 1965). Viewed in this context, tolerance involves an adaptive mechanism for the survival of a plant against herbivore pressure. Antibiosis involves such features of plants which adversely affect the metabolism of a phytophagous insect and this is clearly evident in the slower development of several species of thrips on such resistant plants. While non-preference implies that the host is undesirable and needs to be avoided by the feeding insect, the term *antixenosis* or *antixenotic* factors is suggested to imply that due to certain causal factors in the host plant, the insect is kept away and it avoids the host (Kogan & Ortman, 1978). Species like *Megalurothrips sjostedti* heavily infest cowpea flowers and the plant is known to react be releasing ethylene, and this release by *Vigna unguiculata* peduncles, provides a basis for thrips resistance screening with ethephon, a synthetic growth regulator (Wien & Roesingh, 1980). The resistance of crop plants can also be affected by the conditions under which they are grown. Preferences of thrips and other insects for a particular plant may depend on age, height and whether or not it is previously infested. In addition, the suitability of a plant for growth, survival and reproduction of thrips, the degree of antibiosis may be equally affected by water stress, fertilizers, etc.

The species *Frankliniella williamsi* and *Corynothrips stenoapterus* are dry season pests of cassava in tropical America and yield losses due to thrips attack in this area ranged from 8-15% in susceptible varieties and 11% in varieties with intermediate resistance. As regards the possible nature of the resistance, a strong relationship between the number of hairs on the leaf lobe and degree of resistance was found and there was no correlation with leaf hydrogen cyanide content (Schoonhoven, 1974). Leaves of susceptible clones had few or no hairs, while resistant varieties had many. The total number of hairs per leaf lobe increased when leaves expanded and the number of hairs on unexpanded leaves of plants of different ages appeared constant until flowering. After flowering the number of hairs/leaf lobes decreased and thrips resistance also decreased. No relationship could be established between thrips resistance and leaf cyanide content and as indicated in Table 1, the hairiness of unexpanded leaves was closely related to plant damage and degree of resistance.

TABLE 1. Relation between leaf cyanide content and hairiness of leaf lobe in Cassava.

| Average No. of thrips terminal bud | Average No. of hairs/leaf lobe | Leaf cyanide PPm. |
|---|---|---|
| 0.7 | 752 | 21,540 |
| 1.2 | 942 | 5,273 |
| 1.6 | 928 | 58 |
| 3.8 | 894 | 65 |
| 4.4 | 925 | 618 |

(after Schoonhoven, 1974)

Similarly, studies on the relative resistance of *Gossypium hirsutum* to thrips injury, showed that pubescence was associated with a high level of resistance to thrips. Other morphological traits lira-leaf shape, red plant colour, glandless, nectariless, smooth leaf did not provide the plant with resistance. Significantly less leaf area damage occurred on a pubescent cultivar (Quissenberry & Rummel, 1979). The rise of pubescent cotton cultivator might significantly reduce the amount of insecticide applied for thrips control. Among the two cultivated species of cotton in southern India, desi cotton (*G.arboreum*) appears to be resistant to thrips, while Cambodia cotton (*G.hirsutum*) has been found susceptible (Annappan & Aaron, 1965).

It is well-known that *Thrips tabaci* is a serious pest of onions all over the world and of the many varieties tested, white persian was found outstanding in its resistance showing comparatively little injury. The shape of leaves, angle of divergence of the two innermost leaves and the distance apart of the leaf blades on the sheath column appeared important. The leaves of the flattened variety enable the two opposite leaves to become pressed protecting the larvae; the leaves of the Persian variety are circular in cross section, reducing protection to a minimum. The wide angle between the two innermost emerged leaves in young plants serves to restrict the populations and the greater vertical distance between the leaf blades prevents accumulation of thrips in the sheaths.

Significant information is available regarding host relations of *Selenothrips rubrocinctus*, a very serious pest of cocoa and cashew. In cocoa the first leaves are unlikely to suffer and as leaves grow older, potash and nitrogen become progressively withdrawn, but metals like iron and zinc do not appear to be lost and the leaves pass through peak constructional activities. The relationship between the rate of protein synthesis only changes in favour of protein hydrolysis as months pass. At the same time moisture content is heaviest in old leaves, their cell walls are tough, and they lose a substantial part of their nitrogen. These changes result in their immunity from thrips attack. Where specific nutrients are unavailable in the leaf, a direct retardation of protein hydrolysis occurs. Depletion of potash leads to an imbalance and with an unduly high level of moisture under certain conditions and reduction in hormonal level of apical buds, the branches become forked, thin, and short resulting in a condition termed the 'stag-head' and this condition appeared physiologically predisposed to thrips attack. Thrips are presumed to be able to recognize this condition when protein synthesis becomes retarded and with an increase of nitrogen compounds they appear more conductive to multiplication. Detachment of leaves result in an upsurge of amino nitrogen in the leaf cells simultaneously with wilting, and this condition also appears highly attractive for thrips (Fennah, 1963; Entwistle, 1972).

The morphological complexity of the host plant also appears to be an important factor. Lawton and Schroder (1977) indicate that, in general, woody shrubs support insect faunas equal to herbaceous perennials, but these faunas are numerically more than those for weeds and other annuals, which, in turn, are more abundant than the fauna inhabiting monocotyledons. It has further been suggested that greater morphological complexity of the host plant offers greater diversity of the potential niches. The number and nature of these modifications greatly influence the possibility of successful host plant switching (Southwood, 1973). Taking the distribution of thrips on ferns, available records indicate that very few species like *Indusiothrips seshadrii*, *Monilothrips kempi*, *Scirtothrips pteridicola* in India and *Haplothrips rosai* and *Karnyothrips doliicornis* in Hawaii are specific to ferns. The most important morphological difference between angiosperms and ferns appears to be the lack of complex reproductive structures in ferns. These structures in the case of angiosperms represent a number of habitats not available for insects infesting ferns, thereby reducing the total number of species on any one form (Hendrix, 1980). One of the reasons attributed to this is that while ferns were reaching their climax during carboniferous and early permian periods, many of the modern groups of phytophagous insects like the hemipteroid groups including Thysanoptera had just begun to appear. Apart fom this the degree of monophagism of insects feeding on ferns is an important aspect in view of the biochemical simplicity of ferns.

Besides breeding for resistant varieties, environmental modification of the plants appear to provide sufficient scope for producing plants with sufficient resistance to pest attack through making the plant less readily selected or accepted by the host; by selecting for physical and chemical parameters through making the plant resistant to the initial attack by the pest, particularly where this attack is by the young stages and by reducing the nutritional quality of the plant for the pest, the rate of increase of the pest population could be limited (van Emden, 1965).

## GALL FORMATION AND HOST PLANT RESPONSES

Gall-formation involves recanalization and reorientation of plant development resulting in simple or bizarre abnormal structures within which generally, thrips and other insects live, feed and breed. Galling generally involves the ingestion of the plant material by the insects, its concentration or modification in the insect, and the injection of the newly processed material back into the host tissue. Only when a specific insect feeds on a specific part of a specific plant, will the mixture that is reinjected have the requisite constituents at the appropriate concentration to elicit a 'gall' response. The gross modifications during galling are generally localized to the immediate neighbourhood of the feeding area of the host, which results from a change in metabolism in response to the stimulus from the insect. This manifests itself largely due to the association being highly species-specific and these effects cannot be mimicked by an artificial injury of host-tissue. As a result of the association, the insect induces an altered cellular and metabolic environment around the feeding area, culminating in a highly characteristic type of differentiation pattern within the host-tissue. Frequently, the effects of galling extend beyond the attacked organ although the extent of these effects will vary with the power of the gall to act as efficient metabolic sinks.

Response patterns involving a spectrum of types seem to be a complex phenomenon conditioned not only by a number of physiological factors, but also by the status of the organisms involved in the interaction, viz., the gall-insect and the host plant. Such responses indicate the formation of galls to be time-bound responses relating to actual time of initiation of the gall and the thrips population, often resulting in 'complete' and 'incomplete' types (Ananthakrishnan, 1980).

Occurrence of large quantities of defence substances such as tannins, particularly in many thrips galls, suggest that gall formation may, in some cases, be due to an interaction between offensive stimuli of the insects and the defensive response of plants (Rosenthal & Janzen, 1978). Janzen (1977) suggests that the formation of phenolic substances is under the control of gall-making insects and these substances protect the gall-making insects from other herbivorous predators. At one extreme, they protect the plant against the 'non-adapted' gall makers, and at the other they have a great negative effect in plant fitness in the wake of being attacked by the gall-makers. Lignin and Tannin probably represent important classes of quantitative defensive substances reducing the digestibility of plant carbohydrates and proteins. Tannin reduces both the nutritional availability of soluble plant proteins and polysaccharides.

        Diverse strategies have been adopted by insects in colonizing plants
and evolving a pattern of insect biomass distribution, that is compatible
with resource availability and stability (Mattson, 1977).  Normally, a
balance must evolve between average size or weight per individual insect
and the total number of insects/plants so that the total insect mass will
be commensurate with the resources available (Janzen, 1968).  Size and
number especially in gall systems, depend on such basic aspects as plant
size, density, continuity or stability through space and time, and perhaps the plant defences as well.  Curiously this norm gets affected in
high resulting in the entire plant becomes galled.  The galls of
*Schedothrips orientalis* on the leaves of *Ventilago maderasapatana* is a
typical example, exceeding the available resources so that colonization
to new plants becomes difficult, particularly when distribution of other
susceptible plants is sparse.  Therefore, qualitative defenses are often
employed by herbaceous plants and quantitative defenses by woody plants.
In exceptional circumstances, high host-plant selection would favour
adults which distribute their eggs equally among host plants, so that it
is seldom necessary for the immature to redistribute themselves among
plants.

        In insect-host plant interactions both partners adapt themselves to
different ways with the changing conditions.  Other environmental press-
ures like climate and disease also have their effect in the interaction.
Insects can develop new feeding habits, and are more mobile than plants
and can move away to new host plants, and are capable of destroying de-
toxification mechanisms, leading to a position in which they no longer
act as barriers to feeding.  Within the evolving series of the cecidogenous and free-living insects, and hosts such as ferns, gymnosperms,
woody and herbaceous angiosperms, there is a trend towards higher chemical complexity.  In galls, purine based cytokinins, amono-acid based
auxins and terpenoid based gibberellins may interact with insect hormones
(McCalla et al., 1962).  Kinetins and auxins possess only limited activity and whether these substances can stimulate growth of 'preferred' galls
or can actually initiate galls is an open question.  However, it is
generally believed that the growth substances produced by insects
interact with those of plants.

        An overview of the gall-forming traits among the Thysanoptera
indicates their capacity to exploit the host plants more efficiently and
besides being host specific in terms of food requirements, the gall
systems actively function as specific breeding sites culminating in
specificity of the niche as well.  Zwolfer (1978) attributes the initiation and exploitation of plant galls to be highly developed forms of
phytophagy originating as early as late cretaceous and during the
tertiary.  However, the problem of the independent development of the
ability of the cecidogenous insects to reorient the growth mechanics of
the host is indeed significant, so that favourable nutritional and
shelter guilds develop.  For instance, the extensive channeling and
directing of the cecidogenous *Gynaikothrips* - *Liothrips* complex reflects
the patterns of isolation and restriction to specific Natural Orders of
angiosperms, throwing significant light on this aspect of the cecidogenous phytophage-host plant interrelationships.  Further, this aspect
appears to be amply supported and documented (Ananthakrishnan, 1978) in
phylogenetically old taxa (Terebrantia) with relatively few gall-

154

examples, while the younger taxa belonging to the Tubulifera display gall associations with a spectrum of host plants, and that too in diverse categories of complexities. The identicial nature of 'gall-form' irrespective of the geographical variations underlines the consistency in the behavioural patterns in gall thrips in relation to host selection and host affinity. Host synchronisation, or the temporal adaptation of the insect life-cycle in relation to the phenology of the host plant is a decisive factor for phytophages with specialised life cycles. The presence or absence of young leaves, is an important pre-requisite for the cecidogenous thrips to develop and breed by organising galls. The

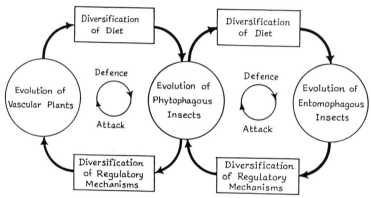

Fig.39. Evolution of phytophagous insects - A diagrammatic representation (after Zwolfer, 1978).

ability of the gravid females to locate developing foliage of the specific host species and the effective synchronisation of the biology of the gall thrips with the monthly production of the young leaves is significant, suggesting an increased behavioural sophistication. This is further confirmed by the ability of the first gall-maker thrips on a developing leaf to organise a specialised zone of nutrition for the offspring, as well as the complex interaction patterns among the diverse arthropod species within aging galls in different trophic levels. Gall insect-host plant association seems to exemplify an advanced/specialised level of 'trophic strategy'. The trait of absolute nutritional dependence ultimately functioning as an important guiding mechanism has appeared perhaps with the diversification of angiosperms. This is of special interest because many of the cecidogenous thrips are restricted to arborescent and potentially-arborescent host species of angiosperms. These possible patterns of isolation coupled with the evolution of higher plants provide a greater insight into the evolution of gall thrips supplemented by their capacity to adapt to new hosts in terms of the specialisation of mouthparts as well as the other physiological restraints. It is also equally true that the host selection of these specialised phytophages has also built-in mechanisms which permit 'minor' changes in their host range as well as loci of infections, as is evident, for instance in *Thilakothrips babuli* affecting axillary buds and florets of *Acacia leucophloea*. This is significant because in a completely inflexible host association, the phytophage relationship would become very fragile, tending to give way under any stress situation. Since this has not happened or at least not glaringly evident, it is presumed that these associations operate rather successfully. A list of possible reasons for flexibility leading to stability in the insect-host plant associations establishing a well-organised co-evolution system is provided by Zwolfer (1978), (Fig. 39). Any of these can easily be extrapolated in the present analysis of gall thrips - host plant association, although it has not been attempted here for want of established evidences.

Though, not much work has been effectively carried out to assess the chemical characteristics of host plants which would regulate the feeding, and eventually the gall-inducing behaviour of thrips, it is not impossible to assume the effective functioning of the phytochemically defined host relations, since a majority of the adaptive radiational patterns as evident in plant feeding and cecidogenous thrips are restricted within the limits of systematically related host plant groups. While on a larger scale, the species dynamics of plant feeding insects and more particularly the cecidogenous species is indeed related to the ecological bio-geography of the host species (Southwood, 1960, 61), on a smaller scale, the species richness of gall-associated arthropods could be related to the plant size as well as the population size of the single host species.

* * * * *

## EXTRACTION, SAMPLING AND REARING TECHNIQUES

Diverse methods of collection, rearing, extraction and sampling of thrips from vegetation - dead or living - have been used over the years and an understanding of at least some of the more useful methods would enable better planning and execution of bioecological studies. This is all the more important in view of the problems associated with such small insects as thrips which, with their ability to inhabit inaccessible plant parts or to get entangled in crevices of collecting apparatus, tend to excape the observer's attention.

### EXTRACTION TECHNIQUES

Dipping leaves in 70% alcohol and shaking them vigorously to dislodge thrips was advocated by le Pelley (1942). Shirck (1948) suggested a dynamic dry extraction method enabling thrips to crawl off vegetation, in particular those infesting leaf sheaths and such compact situations, using many heating funnels lined with cloth cover to prevent condensation, maintaining a temperature of around 46° for 24 hours, but varying according to species, as for instance 49-50° in case of *Thrips tabaci* on onions. Faulkner (1954) used infra red lamps to extract different species of thrips. Boyce and Miller (1954) used collecting units comprising small pots covered with a waterproof cardboard covered above by a muslin, the bottom of the pot with an opening fitted with a rubber stopper to which a small jar containing 20cc of 5% formalin was attached. The units were held in a rack in a drying oven, and with three 100 watts bulbs providing the heat for the drying of samples, thrips moved downward into the formalin. The use of repellents such as turpentine vapour has also been found to be effective. Washing of blossoms either in 70% ethyl alcohol or a detergent was used as an effective method for the extraction of thrips from flowers (Ota, 1968).

Extraction of thrips from litter involves using the Tullgren dry funnel method in which the thrips are driven down by heat applied from above by bright bulbs and the author has long been using a series of polythene funnels arranged on a rack, and collecting the material in 70% alcohol with traces of $CuSO_4$. Lewis and Navas (1962) used the turpentine vapour technique for extraction of thrips from dry litter. One end of a lamp glass was fixed to the polythene funnel and the other open end was provided with a tight lid to which a cotton wool soaked in turpentine was attached. The bottom of the funnel was led into a vial containing water and detergent.

### SAMPLING

As thrips live in different habitats, various sampling techniques need to be applied for a study of their populations. To obtain samples from vegetation, Harris (1936) selected at random ten plants as a constant number, and thrips both from the exposed surface and from the leaf axil or other parts were removed by tapping and tearing the plant on a suitable surface. Sakimura (1937) recommended a black cardboard (22.5 x 30 cm) with 5 cm$^2$ sections drawn on it as a suitable surface for *Thrips tabaci*. Bullock (1963) collected plant samples in 100 ml rectified or methylated spirit in wide-necked jars, the leaves were subsequently removed after shaking them well, and 50 ml of petrol was added to the liquid. The larger debris were removed by pouring the mixture into a dish through a coarse sieve. By adding excess water, the petrol was made to float above the spirit layer and methylene blue was added to dye the spirit bright blue so that the thrips are clearly visible and countable by the naked eye.

Irwin and Yeargan (1980) applied the Delayed Counting Method and Direct Count Method in soyabean fields for the sampling of thrips. The former involved the Dry-Count and the Wet-Count methods, the Wet-Count Method further involving what has been designated the "Lexington technique" and "Columbia techniques". In the Dry-Count technique, cut-off plant parts were placed in small tins with tight lids and subsequently, all the thrips were removed and collected in 1 ml vials containing 70% ethanol. In the "Lexington technique", plant parts were clipped and allowed to fall in 90 cm wide mouth polythene jars which were subsequently shaken vigorously and the liquid poured through a 100 x 100 mesh stainless steel sieve. Each container and plant part were thoroughly rinsed with a jet of water and the resultant liquid passed through the sieve. Thrips plus a small amount of debris remained in the sieve were washed with 70% ethanol into a 210 ml container. After settling, the excess alcohol was decanted and the thrips and remaining alcohol were poured into vials. In the "Columbia technique", aqueous 95% ethanol in a Zip-loc plastic bag was used. Plant parts were agitated in 70% ethanol to remove the thrips, and the bag was rinsed, the combined solution passed through a 200 x 200 mesh sieve. The filtrate was washed into a beaker with 50 ml of water, by vacuum filtration using a Buchner funnel. When using the Direct Count Method plant parts to be sampled were located in the field and population of thrips was assessed.

Litter thrips population could be sampled in relation to the weight or volume of the litter. The litter within a grid of 1 m$^2$ was scraped loose to soil level and collected. A metal box with a sharpened lower edge and open at either end can also be used for this sampling. Thrips were extracted from these samples by a dry funnel method of either Berlese or Tullgren (Faulkner 1954, Lewis & Navas 1964, Healy 1964).

For aerial thrips samples, Lewis (1959) used flat sticky plates 100 cm$^2$, placed against the leeward direction of the wind at different heights in horizontal and vertical positions. Cylinders with different sticky surface areas like 250 cm$^2$ and 650 cm$^2$ was also used in the place of sticky plates to collect thrips from the air-borne population in onions and cotton field (Hightower & Martin, 1956).

## REARING TECHNIQUES

In view of their varying feeding habits - Phytophagous (free living and gall-inhabiting), mycophagous (mycetophagous and sporophagous), and predatory, diverse rearing techniques have been formulated by different workers.

Bailey (1932) developed a "cage" for rearing adults which consisted of a double side open glass tube (7.5 x 2 cm) inserted upright in a wooden block. The upper end of the tube was covered with a cellophane cap and the lower end with a cotton plug through the centre of which the petiole of the leaf was inserted. The petiole was kept immersed in water in a petri dish. Sakimura (1932) employed cages made up of a thin felt piece with a circular hole, one side of which was covered by a cover glass and the other side fixed on a leaf surface of a potted plant with the help of a paper clip, to rear thrips on living plant. Host-plants were grown in small pots and young leaves of the plant were introduced into glass tubes (10 x 5 cm) open at both ends, one end was fitted with a split cork through which the branches were introduced and the other end covered with a fine muslin (Ananthakrishnan, 1973).

For rearing the immature stages of the phytophagous thrips either a small well-dish which is of 40 cm$^2$ with a cavity in the centre (30 mm diameter x 10 mm depth) or petri dishes measuring 50 mm in diameter were used by McCallan (1947). Wet blotting papers were kept inside on which 18 cm discs of the food leaves were placed. The larvae were reared on these leaf discs. A modification of the above method is the "Flotation Technique" where the cavity of the well-dish or petri dish was filled with warer or a nutrient solution and the leaf discs were floated on the surface of the liquid. Ghabn (1948) altered the former technique by using pieces of pressed wet cotton wool in the place of blotting paper.

For a study of thrips as vectors of virus diseases, wild plants infected with virus were used as initial inoculum to which thrips from non-infective colonies were allowed to feed. From this, random individuals were taken into small vials (15 x 25 cms) with 6 large cloth-covered windows (Sakimura, 1941). This technique was further elaborated in 1961.

Thrips were also reared in 4-6% sucrose solution in a feeding chamber, which consisted of a reservoir in which the nutrient medium was introduced through a long basal inlet tube. The reservoir has a raised rim into which was fitted an open glass upper chamber. A piece of stretched parafilm membrane 'B' (3x3 cms) was placed over the mouth of the reservoir. Thrips were released inside the upper chamber and the open end of the upper chamber was covered with a fine muslin to prevent the escape of thrips (Ananthakrishnan, unpublished).

For rearing mycophagous thrips, specific feeding sites of the host material were cut into bits, transferred to a 100 ml Erhenmeyer flask containing 25 ml of sterile distilled water and was shaken vigorously to bring the surface microflora into the sterile distilled water and this served as "host washing". Repeated washings in sterile distilled water were done for 8-9 times to remove any surface mycoflora. This was used as "washed host material". Guts of the sporophagous thrips were dissected and cut open, the contents were released into a sterile distilled water under aseptic condition. This was known as "gut washings". Host washing/washed host material/gut washings were plated into the medium and maintained at 34 $\pm$ 2°C for 2-3 days for the emergence of colonies. The emerging fungal colonies were isolated and transferred to the petriplates containing fresh media and this procedure was repeated until the individual pure cultures were obtained. Such fungi were then cultured in test-tubes, conical flasks and petriplates in one of the following media. (i) Potato Dextrose Agar (Agar 15 cm; potatoes 200 gm; Dextrose 20 gm; water 1000 ml), (ii) Oat Meal Agar (Agar 15 cm; Oat Meal 75 cm; water 1000ml) and (iii) Czapek's dox Agar media (Sodium nitrate 2.0 gm; Potassium chloride 0.5 gm; Ferrous sulphate 0.01 gm; Sucrose 30.0 gm; Yeast extract 1.0 gm; Agar 20 gm; Distilled water 1000 ml). These cultures were maintained at $25 \pm 2°C$. The spores/conidia obtained from the pure cultures were transferred to filter papers inside petri plates and plastic vials to feed the thrips (Ananthakrishnan et al., 1982)

* * * * *

## CROP-WISE AND WORLD DISTRIBUTION OF MAJOR THRIPS OF ECONOMIC IMPORTANCE

| Thrips species | Plant species Botanical Name | Plant species Common name | Plant Parts affected | World-wide Distribution |
|---|---|---|---|---|
| *Anaphothrips obscurus* (Muller) | *Avena sativa* | Oats | Grains | Canada, USA, UK, Scandinavia, |
| | *Triticum vulgare* | Wheat | –do– | Germany, Finland, Sweden, Australia, & |
| | *Secale cereale* | Rye | | USSR |
| | *Hordeum vulgare* | Barley | | |
| *Anaphothrips sudanensis* Trybom | *Saccharum officinarum* | Sugarcane | Leaf sheaths & young leaves | India |
| | *Oryza sativa* | Paddy | Leaf sheaths | |
| | *Triticum vulgare* | Wheat | Leaf sheaths & leaves | |
| | *Pennisetum typhoideum* | Cumbu | Leaves | |
| | *Zea mays* | Maize | Leaf sheaths & leaves | |
| | *Eleusine coracana* | Ragi | –do– | |
| *Asprothrips indicus* (Bagnall) | *Curcuma longa* | Turmeric | Leaves | India |
| *Astrothrips tumiceps* Karney | *Ricinus communis* | Castor | Leaves | India |
| *Astrothrips parvilimbus* Stannard | *Ricinus communis* | Castor | Leaves | India |
| | *Gossypium* | Cotton | Leaves | |
| | *Musa pardisiaca* | Banana | Fruit peel | |

| | | | | |
|---|---|---|---|---|
| *Ayyaria chaetophora* Karny | *Ricinus communis* | Castor | Leaves | India |
| | *Dolichos lablab* | Countrybean | -do- | |
| | *Dolichos biflorus* | Horse gram | -do- | |
| | *Corchorus capusulapi* | Jute | -do- | |
| | *Vigna catang* | Cowpea | -do- | |
| | *Cajanus cajan* | Dhall | -do- | |
| *Bregmatothrips binervis* (Kobus) | *Saccharum officinarum* | Sugarcane | Leaf sheaths & leaves | India |
| *Caliothrips fasciatius* (Pergande) | *Lactuca scariola* | Wild lettuce | -do- | Western USA, Hawaii, N.Mexico, California, Texas,Mexico, Hawaii,UK, S.America |
| *Caliothrips graminicola* Bagnall & Cameron | *Cannabis sativa* | Ganja | Leaves | India, Sudan, Rhodesia, & S.Africa |
| *Caliothrips impurus* (Priesner) | *Gossypium hirsutum* | Cotton | Leaves | Nigeria, Sudan, Gambia, Rhodesia |
| | *Allium cepa* | Onion | -do- | |
| | *Arachis hypogaea* | Groundnut | Leaves | |
| | *Dolichos lablab* | Countrybean | -do- | |
| *Caliothrips indicus* (Bagnall) | *Arachis hypogea* | Groundnut | -do- | India |
| | *Dolichos lablab* | Countrybean | -do- | |
| | *Medicago sativa* | Alfalfa | -do- | |
| | *Pisum sativum* | Pea | -do- | |
| | *Vigna catang* | Cowpea | -do- | |
| | *Sesbania aegyptiaca* | Agathi | | |
| | *Solanum melongena* | Brinjal | Leaves | |
| | *Lycopersicum esculentum* | Tomato | -do- | |
| | *Solanum tuberosum* | Potato | -do- | |

|  |  |  |  |  |
|---|---|---|---|---|
| | *Cannabis sativus* | Ganja | -do- | |
| | *Carthamus tinctoricus* | Sawflower | -do- | |
| | *Brassica oleracea* | Cabbage | Leaves | |
| | *Musa paradisiaca* | Banana | -do- | |
| | *Allium cepa* | Onion | -do- | |
| | *Gossypium hirsutum* | Cotton | -do- | |
| | *Triticum vulgare* | Wheat | -do- | |
| | *Cajanus cajan* | Dhall | -do- | |
| | *Cicer arietinum* | Bengal gram | -do- | |
| | *Phaseolus aureus* | Green gram | -do- | |
| | *Linum usitatissiumum* | Linseed | -do- | |
| | *Crotalaria juncea* | Sunnhemp | -do- | |
| | *Sesbania speciosa* | Agathi | -do- | |
| | *Colocasia antiquorum* | Taro | -do- | |
| | *Faeniculum vulgare* | Fennel | -do- | |
| *Caliothrips luckmani* Wilson | *Sesbania aegyptiaca* | Agathi | Leaves | India |
| *Caliothrips phaseoli* Hood | *Gossypium hirsutum* | Cotton | Leaves | Brazil, Panama, Mexico, Peru, West Indies, South Wales, USA (Florida-Georgia), & Colombia |
| | *Phaseolus vulgaris* | Broad bean | -do- | |
| *Caliothrips sudanensis* (Bagnall & Cameron) | *Gossypium hirsutum* | Cotton | Leaves | S.Africa, Sudan South Rhodesia |
| | *Phaseolus vulgaris* | Broad beans | -do- | |
| | *Dolichos lablab* | Country beans | -do- | |
| | *Citrus medica* | Orange | -do- | |
| *Chaetanaphothrips orchidii* (Moulton) | *Citrus* sp. | Citrus | -do- | India |
| | *Musa paradisiaca* | Banana | -do- | Dominican Rep. |

| | | | | |
|---|---|---|---|---|
| Chaetanaphothrips singipennis (Bagnall) | Musa paradisiaca | Banana | Fruit rust | India,Fiji, Australia, Central & South America, Africa |
| Chirothrips manicatus Haliday | Avena sativa | Oats | Grains | USSR, Europe, Sweden,North America, Central Asia Transcarpathia |
| | Hordeum vulgare | Barley | Grains | |
| | Triticum vulgare | Wheat | Young seedlings | |
| Chirothrips mexicanus Crawford | Pennisetum typhoides | cumbu | leaves | India |
| Corynothrips stenoapterus | Manihot esculenta | Cassava | Leaves & buds | Central & South America |
| Diarthrothrips coffeae Williams | Coffea arabica | Coffee | Leaves | Kenya, India |
| Drepanothrips reuteri Uzel | Vitis vinifera | Grapevine | Leaves | Transcaucasus, Italy,Europe, California, Switzerland, USSR |
| Dolichothrips indicus Hood | Nepileum litchi | Litchi | Leaves | India |
| Dinurothrips hookeri Hood | Lycopersicum esculentum | Tomato | Leaves | Neotropics, Brazil,Cuba, Jamaica,Panama Puerto Rico, Florida,Peru, Trinidad |
| | Ipomea | Sweet potato | -do- | |
| Eurhynchothrips ordinarius (Hood) | Sesbania aegyptiaca | Agathi | Shoot tip | India |
| Exothrips hemavarna (Ramk & Marg) | Mangifera indica | Mango | Leaves | India |
| | Sorghum vulgare | Cholum | -do- | |
| Exothrips sacchari (Shumsher) | Saccharum officinarum | Sugarcane | Young seedlings | India |

| | | | | |
|---|---|---|---|---|
| *Florithrips traegardhi* Trybom | *Sorghum vulgare* | Cholam | Very young leaves | India |
| | *Saccharum officinarum* | Sugarcane | Leaf sheaths & leaves | |
| *Frankliniella fusca* (Hinds) | *Gossypium hirsutum* | Cotton | Young plants | India |
| *Frankliniella intonsa* Schmutz | *Trifolium repens* | White clover | Inflorescence | England, North Germany, Central Bohemia Sweden, USSR, Africa, India |
| | *Trifolium pratense* | Red clover | -do- | |
| | *Melilotus officinalis* | Sweet clover | -do- & sheath | |
| | *Medicago* | Alfalfa | Inflorescence | |
| | *Melilotus alba* | Sweet clover | Sheath | |
| *Frankliniella moultoni* Hood | *Vitis vinifera* | Grape vine | Flower | Canada, Oregon, USA |
| *Frankliniella musaeperda* Hood | *Musa pardisiaca* | Banana | Fingers & Flowers | Dominican Rep. |
| *Frankliniella occidentalis* | *Pyrus communis* | Pear | Fruit | Canada, USA |
| | *Allium cepa* | Onion | Seed & flower | |
| | *Medicago sativa* | Alfalfa | Flower | |
| | *Gossypium hirsutum* | Cotton | Seedlings | |
| | *Phaseolus vulgaris* | Broad bean | Pod | |
| *Frankliniella parvula* Hood | *Musa paradisiaca* | Banana | Flowers | Trinidad |
| | *Theobroma cacao* | Cocoa | -do- | |
| *Frankliniella schultzei* (Trybom) | *Dolichos lablab* | Countrybean | Flowers | S. Africa, India, Argentina, Egypt |
| | *Glycine max* | Soy bean | Flowers | |
| | *Arachis hypogaea* | Groundnut | -do- | |
| | *Carthamus tinctorious* | Safflower | -do- | |
| | *Sesamum indicum* | Gingely | -do- | |

| | | | | |
|---|---|---|---|---|
| | *Gossypium arboreum* | Cotton | -do- | |
| | *Abelomoschus esculentus* | Bhendi | -do- | |
| | *Brassica oleracea* | Cabbage | -do- | |
| | *Benincasa cerifera* | Ash Pumpkin | -do- | |
| | *Cucurbita maxima* | Pumpkin | -do- | |
| | *Lycopersicum esculentum* | Tomato | -do- | |
| | *Solanum melongena* | Brinjal | -do- | |
| | *Achras sapota* | Sapota | -do- | |
| | *Punica granatum* | Pomegranate | -do- | |
| | *Papaya somniferum* | Poppy | Flowers | |
| | *Medicago sativa* | Alfalfa | -do- | |
| | *Vigna catang* | Cow pea | -do- | |
| | *Phaseolus mungo* | Black gram | -do- | |
| | *Phaseolus radiatus* | Green gram | -do- | |
| *Frankiniella williamsi* Hood | *Manihot esculenta* | Cassava | Leaves & Young buds | Central & S. America |
| *Frankliniella tenuicornis* Uzel | *Triticum vulgare* | Wheat | -do- | England, Germany, Scandinavia, Finland |
| | *Secale cereale* | Rye | -do- | Sewden |
| *Frankliniella tritici* (Fitch) | *Gossypium hirsutum* | Cotton | Leaves | Carolina, Illinois, USA |
| | *Prunus avium* | Cherry | Blossoms | |
| | *Prunus domestica* | Plum | -do- | |
| | *Arachis hypogaea* | Groundnut | Flowers | |
| *Haplothrips bagrolis* Bhatti | *Triticum vulgare* | Wheat | Leaves | India |
| *Haplothrips ceylonicus* Schmutz | *Cocos nucifera* | Coconut | Flowers | India |
| | *Coffea arabica* | Coffee | -do- | |

| | | | | |
|---|---|---|---|---|
| Haplothrips faurei Hood | Pyrus malus | Apple | Leaves | Europe |
| Haplothrips ganglbaueri Schmutz | Oryza sativa | Paddy | Inflorescence | India |
| | Mangifera indica | Mango | Inflorescence | |
| | Eleusine coracana | Ragi | Ear head | |
| | Pennisetum typhoideum | Cumbu | –do– | |
| | Triticum vulgare | Wheat | –do– | |
| | Zea mays | Maize | Inflorescence | |
| Haplothrips gowdeyi (Franklin) | Zea mays | Maize | Inflorescence | Tropics |
| Haplothrips tenuipennis | Camellia thea | Tea | Leaves | India |
| Haplothrips tritici (Kurdjumov) | Triticum vulgare | Wheat | Ear-head & young plants | N. Khazakhstan, Europe, Central Asia, Bulgaria USSR, Louisiana, France |
| Haplothrips tolerabilis Priesner | Saccharum officinarum | Sugarcane | Inflorescence | India |
| Heliothrips haemorrhorid- alis (Bouche) | Camellia thea | Tea | Leaves | Trinidad, California, Palestine, E. Africa, |
| | Coffea arabica | Coffee | Shoot | New Zealand, Great Britain, Java, Hawaii |
| | Anona squamosa | Custard apple | Leaves | Italy, Israel, USA, India, Egypt, S. of Central Asia, Spain, |
| | Achras sapota | Sapota | Leaves | Caucasus |
| Helionothrips kadaliphilus (Ramk. & Marg) | Musa paradisiaca | Banana | Leaves | India |
| Hercinothrips bicinctus (Bagnall) | Musa paradisiaca | Banana | Leaves | S. Africa, Kenya, Canary Islands, India |

| | | | | |
|---|---|---|---|---|
| *Hercinothrips femoralis* (Reuter) | *Beta vulgaris* | Sugarbeet | Leaves | U.S.A., Brazil, Japan |
| *Hydatothrips ramaswamiahi* Karny | *Arachis hypogaea* | Groundnut | Leaves | India |
| | *Ricinus communis* | Castor | –do– | |
| *Isothrips orientalis* Bagnall | *Jasminum indicum* | Jasmine | Flowers | India |
| *Lefroyothrips lefroyi* (Bagnall) | *Camellia thea* | Tea | Flowers | India |
| *Lefroyothrips obscurus* (Ananth. & Jaga.) | *Coffea arabica* | Coffee | Leaves | India |
| *Limothrips cerealium* Haliday | *Triticum vulgare* | Wheat | Inflorescence | Western Europe, Germany,Canada, Israel |
| | *Avena sativa* | Oats | Leaf sheaths & stem | Scotland, Seychelles, Transcaucasus, Central Asia |
| | *Secale cereal* | Rye | Inflorescence | |
| *Limothrips denticornis* Haliday | *Hordeum vulgare* | Barley | Leaf sheath | USA, Asia, Western Europe, N. America, USSR |
| *Liothrips karnyi* (Bagnall) | *Piper nigrum* | Pepper | Leaf (Gall) | India |
| *Megalurothrips distalis* Karny | *Cajanus cajan* | Dhall | Flowers | India |
| | *Dolichos lablab* | Country bean | –do– | |
| | *Arachis hypogaea* | Groundnut | –do– | |
| | *Vigna catang* | Cowpea | –do– | |
| | *Phaseolus mungo* | Black gram | –do– | |
| *Megalurothrips sjostedti* (Trybom) | *Vigna catang* | Cowpea | Flowers | Nigeria |

| | | | | |
|---|---|---|---|---|
| *Megaphysothrips subramanii* Ramk. & Marg. | *Coffea arabica* | Coffee | Leaf | India |
| *Neoheegeria mangiferae* Priesner | *Mangifera indica* | Mango | Inflorescence | India |
| *Odontothrips confusus* Priesner | *Medicago sativa* | Alfalfa | Flowers | Hungary, France, USSR |
| *Odontothrips loti* (Haliday) | *Trifolium pratense* | Red clover | -do- | Central Bohemia, Sweden, USSR USA, |
| *Panchaetothrips indicus* (Bagnall) | *Curcuma longa* | Turmeric | Leaves | India |
| | *Gossypium herbaceum* | Cotton | -do- | |
| | *Musa paradisiaca* | Banana | -do- | |
| | *Musa sapientum* | Banana | -do- | |
| *Parthenothrips dracaenae* (Herger.) | *Citrus aurantium* | Loos-jacke | Leaves | India |
| *Prosopothrips cognatus* Hood | *Triticum vulgare* | Wheat | | Kansas, Oklahoma Missouri, Nebraska (U.S.A.) |
| *Pseudodendrothrips dwivarna* Ramk. & Marg. | *Artocarpus heterophyllus* | Jak | Young Leaves | India |
| *Ramaswamiahiella subnudula* Karny | *Citrus medica* | Orange | Flowers | India |
| | *Glycine max* | Soybean | -do- | |
| | *Sesamum indicum* | Gingelly | -do- | |
| | *Tamerindus indicus* | Tamerind | -do- | |
| | *Mangifera indica* | Mango | Leaves | |
| | *Santalum album* | Sandal | Shoots | |
| *Retithrips syriacus* (Mayet) | *Ricinus communis* | Castor | Leaves | India, Israel |
| | *Gossypium herbaceum* | Cotton | -do- | |

| | | | | |
|---|---|---|---|---|
| | *Anacardium occidentale* | Cashew | Young Leaves | |
| | *Punica granatum* | Pomagranate | Leaves | |
| | *Vitis vinifera* | Grape vine | –do– | |
| | *Arachis hypogaea* | Groundnut | –do– | |
| | *Manihot utilissima* | Cassava | –do– | |
| *Rhipiphoro-thrips cruentatus* Hood | *Vitis vinifera* | Grapevine | –do– | India |
| | *Areca catechu* | Betelnut | Young Leaves | |
| | *Ricinus communis* | Castor | Leaves | |
| | *Anacardium occidentale* | Cashew | –do– | |
| | *Anona squamosa* | Custard apple | –do– | |
| | *Mangifera indica* | Mango | Young leaves | |
| | *Punica granatum* | Pomgranate | leaves | |
| *Rhipidothrips elegans* Priesner | *Triticum vulgare* | Wheat | | England & Kahazaklastan |
| | *Secale cereale* | Rye | | |
| *Sciothrips cardamomi* (Ramk.) | *Elettaria cardamomum* | Cardamom | Inflorescence Young leaves Spindles and Shoot tip | India |
| *Scirtothrips aurantii* Faure | *Citrus* sp. | Citrus | Leaves | S. Africa, S. Rhodesia,Transvaal |
| *Scirtothrips bispinosus* Bagnall | *Camellia thea* | Tea | Flowers | India |
| | *Coffea arabica* | Coffee | Young leaves | |
| *Scirtothrips citri* Moulton | *Citrus* sp. | Citrus | Leaves | USA |
| *Scirtothrips dorsalis* Hood | *Capsicum fruitescens* | Chillies | Leaves | India |
| | *Capsicum minima* | Chillies | Leaves | |
| | *Lycopersicum esculentum* | Tomato | Flowers | |

| | | | | |
|---|---|---|---|---|
| | *Anacardium occidentale* | Cashew | Young leaves and Flowers | |
| | *Mangifera indica* | Mango | Inflorescence | |
| | *Vitis vinifera* | Grapevine | Leaves | |
| | *Ricinus communis* | Castor | Young leaves and inflorescence | |
| | *Camellia thea* | Tea | Flowers | |
| | *Gossypium herbaceum* | Cotton | Flowers, leaves Fruits | |
| | *Tamerindus indicus* | Tamerind | Flowers | |
| | *Sauropus androgynus* | Chekurmanis | Leaves | |
| *Scirtothrips manihoti* Bondar | *Manihot utilissima* | Cassava | Young leaves | Brazil |
| *Selenothrips rubrocintus* Giard | *Anacardium occidentale* | Cashew | Leaves | India, Trinidad, Puerto Rico, Ghana, |
| | *Theobroma cacao* | Cocoa | Leaves | Brazil and Surinam |
| *Sericothrips ramaswamiahi* Karny | *Canavalia gladiata* | Sword bean | Leaves | India |
| *Sericothrips variabilis* (Beach) | *Glycine max* | Soyabean | Leaves | U.S.A. |
| *Sorghothrips jonnaphilus* (Ramk.) | *Saccharum officinarum* | Sugarcane | Leaf sheaths & Leaves | India |
| | *Sorghum vulgare* | Cholam or Jowar | Leaf sheaths | |
| | *Sorghum nitidum* | Cholam | -do- | |
| *Stenothrips graminum* Uzel | *Triticum vulgare* | Wheat | Ears | England, Sweden, N. Germany, USSR, Asia, Khazakhastan |
| | *Avena sativa* | Oats | -do- | |
| | *Hordeum vulgare* | Barley | -do- | |
| *Taeniothrips alliorum* Priesner | *Allium cepa* | Onion | Flower | Japan |

| | | | | |
|---|---|---|---|---|
| *Taeniothrips atratus* (Haliday) | *Avena sativa* | Oats | Flower | England, N. Germany, Sweden, Asia, USSR |
| *Taeniothrips inconsequens* Uzel | *Pyrus malus* | Pear | Flower | Canada, England, USA, |
| | | Apple | –do– | Columbia and Sweden |
| *Florithrips traegardhi* Trybom | *Sorghum vulgare* | Cholam | very young leaves | India |
| | *Saccharum officinarum* | Sugarcane | Leaf sheaths & leaves | |
| *Thrips angusticeps* Uzel. | *Linum usitatissmum* | Flax | Young seedlings | Holland, Germany, Sweden, Khazakhstan and Finland |
| *Thrips flavus* Schrank | *Pyrus malus* | Apple | Flowers | England, Switzerland India |
| | *Citrus medica* | Orange | –do– | |
| | *Gossypium herbaceum* | Cotton | Leaves | |
| | *Brassica campestris* | Mustard | –do– | |
| *Thrips hawaiiensis* (Morgan) | *Pennisetum typhoideus* | Cumbu or bajara | Inflorescence | India, Hawaii |
| | *Cajanus cajan* | Dhall | | |
| | *Cicer arietinum* | Bengal gram | –do– | |
| | *Brassica juncea* | Mustard | –do– | |
| | *Brassica campestris* | –do– | –do– | |
| | *Helianthus annus* | Sunflower | Inflorescence | |
| | *Anacardium occidentale* | Cashew | Flowers | |
| | *Citrus* sp. | Citrus | –do– | |
| | *Musa paradisiaca* | Banana | –do– | |
| | *Pyrus malus* | Apple | –do– | |
| | *Areca catechu* | Betelenut | –do– | |

| *Thrips*<br>*linarius*<br>Uzel | *Linum*<br>*usitatissimum* | Flax | Flowers and<br>Leaves | Europe, Russia |
|---|---|---|---|---|
| *Thrips*<br>*nigripilosus*<br><br>Uzel | *Linum*<br>*usitattissimum*<br><br>*Triticum*<br>*vulgare*<br>*Allium cepa* | Flax<br><br><br>Wheat<br><br>Onion | | England, Holland,<br>Great Britian<br>Khazakhastan,<br>USA, Kenya |
| *Thrips tabaci*<br>Lindeman | *Allium cepa*<br><br>*Gossypium*<br>*herbaceum*<br>*Brassica*<br>*oleracea*<br>*Papaver*<br>*somnifernum* | Cotton<br><br>Cotton<br><br>Cabbage<br><br>Poppy<br>Cauliflower | Young plants<br><br>Leaves<br><br>-do-<br><br>-do-<br>-do- | India, Europe, Iowa,<br>Queensland, Sweden,<br>Hawaii, USA, Japan,<br>Java, Trinidad,<br>Puerto Rico, San<br>Domingo |
| *Zaniothrips*<br>*ricini*<br>Bhatti | *Ricinus*<br>*communis* | Castor | Leaves | India |
| *Xylaplothrips*<br>*pellucidus*<br>Anan. | *Sorghum*<br>*nitidum* | Cholam | Very young<br>leaves | India |

* * * * *

## INDEX TO GENERA REFERRED TO IN THIS WORK

*Diarthrothrips* Williams, 1915
*Diceratothrips* Hood, 1908
*Dimorphothrips* Bagnall, 1928
*Dinothrips* Bagnall, 1908
*Dinurothrips* Hood, 1913
*Dixothrips* Ananthakrishnan, 1969
*Dolicholepta* Priesner, 1932
*Dolichothrips* Karny, 1920
*Drepanothrips* Uzel, 1895
*Ecacanthothrips* Bagnall, 1908
*Elaphrothrips* Buffa, 1909
*Empresmothrips* Karny, 1920
*Emprosthiothrips* Moulton, 1942
*Enneothrips* Hood, 1935
*Eothrips* Hood, 1915
*Erotidothrips* Priesner, 1939
*Erythrothrips* Moulton, 1911
*Eugynothrips* Priesner, 1926
*Euoplothrips* Hood, 1918
*Euphysothrips* Bagnall, 1928
*Eurhyncothrips* Bagnall, 1918
*Exopthalmothrips* Moulton, 1923
*Exothrips* Priesner, 1939
*Frankliniella* Karny, 1910
*Franklinothrips* Back, 1912
*Gynaikothrips* Zimmerman, 1900
*Halmathrips* Stannard, 1936
*Haplothrips* Amyot and Serville, 1843
*Hartwigia* Faure, 1949
*Heligmothrips* Mound, 1970
*Helionothrips* Bagnall, 1982
*Heliothrips* Bagnall, 1936
*Hercinothrips* Bagnall, 1932
*Holopothrips* Hood, 1914
*Holurothrips* Bagnall, 1914
*Hoplandrothrips* Hood, 1912
*Hoplothrips* Amyot and Serville, 1843
*Hydatothrips* Karny, 1913
*Hyidiothrips* Hood, 1938
*Indusiothrips* Priesner, 1953
*Iridothrips* Priesner, 1940
*Isoneurothrips* Bagnall, 1915
*Kakothrips* Williams, 1914
*Karaotohrips* Sharov, 1972
*Karnyothrips* Watson, 1923
*Kladothrips* Froggatt, 1906
*Kleothrips* Schmutz, 1913
*Leeuwenia* Karny, 1912
*Lefroyothrips* Priesner, 1938
*Leptogastrothrips* Hood, 1912
*Leptothrips* Hood, 1909
*Leucothrips* Reuter, 1904
*Limothrips* Haliday, 1938
*Liophlaeothrips* Priesner, 1919

*Loyolaia* Ananthakrishnan, 1964
*Liothrips* uzel, 1895
*Machatothrips* Bagnall, 1908
*Macrophthalmothrips* Karny, 1924
*Mallothrips* Ramakrishna, 1928
*Matilethrips* Bournier, 1978
*Mecynothrips* Bagnall, 1908
*Megalurothrips* Bagnall, 1895
*Megaphysothrips* Ramakrishna & Margabandhu, 1939
*Meiothrips* Priesner, 1929
*Mesicothrips* Priesner & Seshadri, 1953
*Merothrips* Hood, 1912
*Mesandrothrips* Stannard & Mitri, 1962
*Mesothrips* Zimmerman, 1900
*Microcephalothrips* Bagnall, 1926
*Monilothrips* Moulton, 1929
*Mycterothrips* Trybom, 1910
*Mymarothrips* Bagnall, 1928
*Nanothrips* Faure, 1938
*Neolimothrips* Shumsher, 1942
*Nesothrips* Kirkaldy, 1907
*Neurothrips* Hood, 1924
*Odontothrips* Serville, 1843
*Oedaleothrips* Hood, 1916
*Oncothrips* Karny, 1911
*Organothrips* Hood, 1940
*Oxythrips* Uzel, 1895
*Palmiothrips* Bhatti, 1978
*Panchaetothrips* Bagnall, 1912
*Parascolothrips* Mound, 1967
*Parthenothrips* Uzel, 1895
*Perissothrips* Hood, 1919
*Phibalothrips* Hood, 1918
*Phlaeothrips* Haliday, 1836
*Physothrips* Karny, 1912
*Plectrothrips* Hood, 1908
*Plesiothrips* Hood, 1915
*Podothrips* Hood, 1919
*Poecilothrips* Uzel, 1895
*Polyphemothrips* Schmutz, 1909
*Praepodothrips* Priesner and Seshadri
*Preeriella* Hood, 1939
*Prosopothrips* Uzel, 1895
*Psalidothrips* Priesner, 1932
*Pseudodendrothrips* Schmutz, 1913
*Pseudothrips* Hands, 1902
*Pygothrips* Hood, 1915
*Ramaswamiahiella* Karny, 1926
*Retithrips* Marchal, 1910
*Rhabdothrips* Hood, 1933
*Rhamphothrips* Karny, 1912
*Rhinothripiella* Zur Strassen
*Rhinothrips* Faure, 1933
*Rhipidothrips* Uzel, 1895
*Rhipiphorothrips* Morgan, 1913

*Rhopalandrothrips* Priesner, 1922
*Rhynchothrips* Hood, 1912
*Sciothrips* Bhatti, 1969
*Scirtothrips* Shull, 1909
*Scolothrips* Hinds, 1902
*Segnothrips* Ananthakrishnan, 1965
*Selenothrips* Karny, 1911
*Sericothrips* Haliday, 1936
*Smilothrips* Bhatti, 1976
*Sophiothrips* Hood, 1933
*Sophikothrips* Mound,
*Sorghothrips* Priesner, 1936
*Sphingothrips* Ananthakrishnan, 1971
*Stenchaetothrips* Bagnall, 1926
*Stenothrips* Uzel, 1895
*Stephanothrips* Trybom, 1912
*Stepterothrips* Hood, 1933
*Stictothrips* Hood, 1924
*Stigmothrips* Ananthakrishnan, 1964
*Taeniothrips* Amyot and Serville, 1843
*Terthrothrips* Karny, 1925
*Teuchothrips* Hood, 1919
*Thilakothrips* Ramk, 1928
*Thrips* Linnaeus, 1761
*Tiarothrips* Priesner, 1935
*Tolmetothrips* Mound,
*Toxothrips* Bhatti, 1967
*Trichinothrips* Bagnall, 1929
*Tryphactothrips* Bagnall, 1921
*Tusothrips* Bhatti, 1967
*Uzelothrips* Hood, 1953
*Veerabahuthrips* Ramakrishnan, 1932
*Williamsiella* Hood, 1925
*Zaniothrips* Bhatti, 1967

\* \* \* \* \*

# INDEX TO SPECIES REFERRED TO IN THIS WORK

*Choleothrips percnus* Mound
*Corycidothrips inquilinus* Ananthakrishnan
*Crotonothrips dantahasta* (Ramkrishna)
*Crotonothrips davidi* Ananthakrishnan
*Crotonothrips dhirgavadana* (Ramakrishna)
*Cryptothrips latus* Uzel
*Cryptothrips rectangularis* Hood
*Dactylothrips priscus* (Girault)
*Damerothrips gemmatus* Hood
*Diarthrothrips coffeae* Williams
*Dimorphothrips idoliceps* (Karny)
*Dimorphothrips microchaetus* Bagnall
*Dimorphothrips solitus* Bagnall
*Dinothrips longicaudus* (Ananthakrishnan)
*Dixothrips onerosus* Ananthakrishnan
*Dolicholepta inquilinus* Ananthakrishnan
*Elaphrothrips procer* Bagnall
*Empresmothrips fallax* (Bagnall)
*Erythrothrips asiaticus* Ramakrishna & Margabandhu
*Eugynothrips adulator* Priesner
*Euopothrips buxtoni* Bagnall
*Euoplothrips incognatus* Bagnall
*Euphysothrips minozzi* Bagnall
*Exothrips hamavarna* (Ramakrishna and Margabandhu)
*Frankliniella fusca* (Hinds)
*Frankliniella intonsa* (Trybom)
*Frankliniella lilivora* Takahashi
*Frankliniella moultoni* Hood
*Frankliniella parvula* Hood
*Frankliniella schultzei* (Trybom)
*Frankliniella tenuicornis* (Uzel)
*Frankliniella tritici* (Fitch)
*Frankliniella williamsi* Hood
*Franklinothrips vespiformis* (Crawford)
*Gastrothrips anolis* Hood
*Gastrothrips falcatus* (Ananthakrishnan)
*Gynaikothrips flaviantennatus* Moulton
*Gynaikothrips hopkinsoni* Bagnall
*Gynaikothrips hystrix* Bagnall
*Gynaikothrips schefflericola* Ananthakrishnan
*Gynaikothrips uzeli* (Zimmerman)
*Haplothrips acanthoscelis* (Karny)
*Haplothrips apicalis* Bagnall
*Haplothrips bagnalli* (Trybom)
*Haplothrips chinensis* Priesner
*Haplothrips ganglbaueri* Schmutz
*Haplothrips hukkineni* Priesner
*Haplothrips nigricornis* (Bagnall)
*Haplothrips pini* (Watson)
*Haplothrips statices* Haliday
*Haplothrips talpa* (Priesner)
*Hoplothrips angusticeps* (Hood)
*Hoplothrips bradleyi* Hood
*Hoplothrips fungosus* Moulton
*Hoplothrips orientalis* (Ananthakrishnan)

*Hoplothrips pedicularius* (Haliday)
*Hoplothrips propinquus* Bagnall
*Hoplothrips semicaecus* Uzel
*Hoplothrips ulmi* (Fabricius)
*Hydatothrips ramaswamiahi* Karny
*Indusiothrips seshadrii* Priesner
*Iridothrips mariae* Pelikan
*Isoneurothrips australis* Bagnall
*Isothrips orientalis* Bagnall
*Kakothrips pisivorus* (Westwood)
*Kakothrips robustus* (Uzel)
*Karnyothrips flavipes* (Jones)
*Kladothrips augonsaxxos* Moulton
*Leptothrips mali* (Fitch)
*Limothrips cerealium* Haliday
*Limothrips denticornis* Haliday
*Limothrips schmutzi* Priesner
*Liophlaeothrips vichitravarna* (Ramakrishna)
*Liothrips associatus* Ananthakrishnan & Jagadish
*Liothrips bosei* Moulton
*Liothrips brevitubus* Karny
*Liothrips chaviceae* (Zimmerman)
*Liothrips confusus* Priesner
*Liothrips emulatus* Ananthakrishnan
*Liothrips flavitibia* (Moulton)
*Liothrips fragilis* Ananthakrishnan
*Liothrips fumipennis* (Karny)
*Liothrips kannani* (Moulton)
*Liothrips karnyi* (Bagnall)
*Liothrips loranthi* Priesner
*Liothrips mucronis* Ananthakrishnan
*Liothrips nigripes* (Karny)
*Liothrips oleae* (Costa)
*Liothrips ramakrishnai* Ananthakrishnan & Jagadish
*Liothrips retusus* Ananthakrishnan
*Liothrips setinodis* (Reuter)
*Liothrips taurus* (Karny)
*Liothrips tersus* Ananthakrishnan & Jagadish
*Liothrips urichi* Karny
*Liothrips vaneckeei* Priesner
*Lygothrips jambuvasi* (Ramakrishna)
*Mallothrips indicus* Ramakrishna
*Mecynothrips simplex* (Bagnall)
*Mecynothrips wallacei* (Priesner)
*Megalurothrips distalis* (Karny)
*Megalurothrips Sjastedti* (Trybom)
*Megaphysothrips subramanii* Ramakrishna
*Melanthrips affluens* Ananthakrishnan
*Melanthrips baileyi* Ananthakrishnan
*Melanthrips indicus* Bhatti
*Mesothrips apatelus* Karny
*Mesothrips bhimabahu* Ramakrishna
*Mesothrips extensivus* Ananthakrishnan & Jagadish
*Mesandrothrips inquilinus* Priesner

*Mesothrips claripennis* Moulton
*Mesothrips melinocnemis* Karny
*Microcephalothrips abdominalis* (Crawford)
*Moultonoides geijerae* (Moulton)
*Monilothrips kempi* Moulton
*Nesidoothrips alius* Ananthakrishnan
*Nesothrips diversus* Ananthakrishnan
*Nesothrips robustus* Ananthakrishnan
*Neurothrips indicus* Ananthakrishnan
*Odontothrips loti* (Haliday)
*Odontothrips phaleratus* Haliday
*Onychothrips hakeae* Bagnall
*Organothrips bianchi* Hood
*Parascolothrips priesneri* Mound
*Parthenothrips dracaenae* Heeger
*Peeriella jacotia* Hartwig
*Permothrips longipennis* Martynov
*Phibalothrips peringueyi* (Faure)
*Phlaeothrips coriaceus* Haliday
*Phlaeothrips albovittatus* Schille
*Phlaeothrips minor* Uzel
*Podothrips aegyptiacus* Priesner
*Podothrips graminum* Priesner
*Podothrips moultoni* Ananthakrishnan
*Podothrips placitus* Ananthakrishnan
*Podothrips scitulus* Ananthakrishnan
*Praepodothrips nigrocephalus* Ananthakrishnan
*Prosopothrips cognatus* Hood
*Psectrothrips delostomae* Hood
*Pseudothrips inequalis* (Beach)
*Pteridothrips pteridicola* (Karny)
*Ramaswamiahiella subnudula* Karny
*Retithrips syriacus* (Mayet)
*Rhiphidothrips longistylosus* Uzel
*Rhipidothrips elegans* Pelikan
*Rhipidothrips gratiosus* Uzel
*Rhipiphorothrips cruentatus* Hood
*Rhynchothrips hungaricus* Priesner
*Sacothrips galbus* Moulton
*Sacothrips ingens* Mound
*Sacothrips milvus* Mound
*Sciothrips cardamomi* (Ramakrishna)
*Scirtothrips bispinosus* (Bagnall)
*Scirtothrips citri* Moulton
*Scirtothrips pteridicola* Ananthakrishnan
*Scolothrips acariphagus* Yakhontov
*Scolothrips indicus* Priesner
*Scolothrips longicornis* Priesner
*Scolothrips sexmaculatus* (Pergande)
*Segnothrips trivandrensis* Ananthakrishnan
*Selenothrips rubrocinctus* (Giard)
*Sericothrips variabilis* (Beach)
*Schedothrips orientalis* Ananthakrishnan
*Sorghothrips jonnaphilus* (Ramakrishna)

*Sphingothrips trachypogon* Ananthakrishnan
*Stenchaetothrips bambusae* (Shumsher)
*Stenchaetothrips biformis* (Bagnall)
*Stenchaetothrips bicolor* (Ananthakrishnan & Jagadish)
*Stenchaeththrips graminis* (Ananthakrishnan & Jagadish)
*Stenchaetothrips indicus* (Ramakrishna & Margabandhu)
*Stannardiana variegata* Ananthakrishnan
*Stenothrips graminum* Uzel
*Stigmothrips limpidus* Ananthakrishnan
*Taeniothrips aethiops* Priesner
*Taeniothrips alliorum* Priesner
*Taeniothrips atratus* (Haliday)
*Taeniothrips dianthi* Priesner
*Taeniothrips inconsequens* (Uzel)
*Taeniothrips laricivorus* Kratochvil
*Taeniothrips simplex* (Morrison)
*Thilakothrips babuli* (Ramakrishna)
*Thrips angusticeps* Uzel
*Thrips discolor* Haliday
*Thrips flavus* Schrank
*Thrips fulvipes* Bagnall
*Thrips fuscipennis* Haliday
*Thrips hawaiiensis* (Morgan)
*Thrips imaginis* Bagnall
*Thrips linarius* Uzel
*Thrips nigropilosus* Uzel
*Thrips physapus* Linnaeus
*Thrips tabaci* Lindemann
*Tiarothrips subramanii* (Ramakrishna)
*Thaumatothrips froggatti* Karny
*Toxothrips ricinus* Bhatti
*Trichinothrips brviceps* Bagnall
*Veerabahuthrips bambusae* Ramakrishna
*Zaniothrips ricini* Bhatti

\* \* \* \* \*

REFERENCES

Ahmad, M. (1977). Studies on the host range of the pea thrips (*Caliothrips indicus*) (Thys:Thripidae). *FAO Pl.Protection Bull*, 24(3):83-85.

Altieri, M.A., A. Van Schoonhoven and J.D. Doull. (1977), The ecological role of weeds in insect pest management systems: a review illustrated with bean (*Phaseolus vulgaris* L.) cropping systems. *PANS*, 23(2):195-206.

Altieri, M.A. and W.H. Whitecomb (1978/79). Manipulation of insect populations through seasonal disturbance of weed communities. *Protection Ecology*, 1:185-202.

Amin, P.N. (1979). Leaf curl disease of chilli peppers in Maharashtra. *PANS*, 25(2):131-134.

Anand, P.N. (1926). Thysanoptera and the pollination of flowers. *Amer.Nat.*, 60:177-182.

Ananthakrishnan, T.N. (1955). Host preferences in *Retithrips syriacus* (Mayet). *Agra Univ.J.Res.(Science)*, 4(1):283-288.

Ananthakrishnan, T.N. (1969). Indian Thysanoptera. CSIR, Zoological Monograph, 1:1-171 pp.

Ananthakrishnan, T.N. (1971). Thrips in Agriculture, Horticulture and Forestry - Diagnosis, Bionomics and Control. *J.Scient.& Ind.Res.*, 30(3):113-146.

Ananthakrishnan, T.N. (1973). Thrips, biology and control. *Macmillan India*, 120 pp.

Ananthakrishnan, T.N. (1974). *Aleurodothrips fasciapennis* (Franklin) predatory on coccids and aleyrodids. *J.Bombay.Nat.Hist.Soc.*, 71(1):157-160.

Ananthakrishnan, T.N. (1974). The distribution and host range of predatory thrips. *Indian J.Pl.Prot.*, 4(1):67-78.

Ananthakrishnan, T.N. (1978). Thrips galls and gall thrips. Zoological Survey of India, Technical Monograph 1:1-69.

Ananthakrishnan, T.N. (1979). Diversity indices in relation to intrapopulation variation in two species of Mycophagous tubuliferan Thysanoptera. *Proc.Symp.Zool.Surv.India* 1:19-26.

Ananthakrishnan, T.N. (1979). Biosystematics of Thysanoptera. *Ann.Rev.Entomol.*, 24:159-183

Ananthakrishnan, T.N. (1980). On some aspects of thrips galls. In 'Colloque International de Cecidologie et de Morphogenese Pathologique', Strasbourg, France: *Bull. Soc. bot.Fr.*, 127:31-34.

Ananthakrishnan, T.N. (1980). Thrips and Agroecosystems. *Proc.Symp.Environ.Biol.Trivandrum*: 82-85

Ananthakrishnan, T.N. (1980). Thrips. *In Vectors of Plant pathogens*. (Academic Press, Inc.):149-164.

Ananthakrishnan, T.N. (1981). Thrips-Plant gall association with special reference to patterns of gall diversity in relation to varying thrips populations. *Proc.Indian Natn.Sci.Acad.*, B47(1):41-46.

Ananthakrishnan, T.N. (1982). Thrips and Pollination Biology. *Curr.Sci.*, 51(4):168-172.

186

Ananthakrishnan, T.N., A. Daniel and N. Suresh Kumar (1982). Spatial and
seasonal distribution patterns of some phytophagous thrips
(Thysanoptera:Insecta) infesting *Ricinus communis* Linn.
(Euphorbiaceae) and *Achyranthes aspera* Linn. (Amarantaceae).
*Proc.Indian natn.Sci.Acad.*, B48(2):183-189.
Ananthakrishnan, T.N. and A. Jagadish (1968). On the seasonal
fluctuation and biology of *Anaphothrips flavicinctus* (Karny) on
*Panicus maximum* in Madras. *J.Bombay.Nat.Hist.Soc.*, 65(1):243-248.
Ananthakrishnan, T.N. and C.Kandaswamy (1977). On the trends of
infestation of two species of *Baliothrips* Uzel on paddy, maize and
their weed hosts. *Curr.Sci.*, 46(10):344-45.
Ananthakrishnan, T.N. and N. Muraleedharan (1972). Free amino acids in
relation to host plant preferences in the polyphagous heliothripines
*Rhipiphorothrips cruentatus* Hood and Retithrips syriacus (Mayet).
*Curr.Sci.*, 23(1):846-847.
Ananthakrishnan, T.N. and N.Muraleedharan (1974). On the incidence and
effects of infestation of *Selenothrips rubrocinctus* (Giard)
(Thysanoptera:Heliothripinae) on the free amino acids of some
susceptible host plants. *Curr.Sci.*, 43(7):216-218.
Ananthakrishnan, T. N., B. Padmanabhan and K. Dhileepan (1983) Gut spore
composition and influence of fungal host on the rate of mortality
and post-embryonic development in *Tiarothrips subramanii* (Ranmk).
*Proc. Indian Acad. Sci.*, (B) 92:11-17.
Ananthakrishnan, T.N. and A.Raman (1977). In *Insects and Host-specificity*,
ed.T .N. Ananthakrishnan (New Delhi:MacMillan India).
Ananthakrishnan, T.N. and S.Sen (1980). Taxonomy of Indian Thysanoptera.
*Zool.Sur.India.Calcutta*, Handbook Series, 1:1-234.
Ananthakrishnan, T.N. and G.Suresh (1983). Patterns of fungal resource
utilization and feeding range in some mycophagous Tubulifera
(Insecta:Thysanoptera). *Proc.Indian Acad.Sci.*, (B) 92:285-291.
Ananthakrishnan, T.N. and S. Swaminathan (1977). Host-parasite and
host-predator interactions in the gall thrips *Schedothrips
orientalis* Anan. (Insecta:Thysanoptera) Entomon, 2(2):247-251.
Ananthakrishnan, T.N. and S. Swaminathan (1977). Host parasite /Host
predator interactions in the gall thrips *Schedothrips orientalis*
Anan. (Insecta:Thysanoptera). *Entomon*,2(2):247-251.
Ananthakrishnan, T.N. and S. Swaminathan (1979). On the population trends
on *Aneurothrips priesneri* Bhatti (Insecta:Thysanoptera) from the
leaf galls of *Cordia obliqua*. *Bull.Zool.Sur.India*, 2(1):91-94.
Ananthakrishnan, T.N. and K. Thangavelu (1976). The cereal thrips
*Haplothrips ganglbaueri* Schmutz with particular reference to the
trends of infestation on *Oryza sativa* and the weed *Echinochloa
crusgalli*. *Proc.Ind.Acad.Sci.*, (B) 83(5):196-201.
Ananthakrishnan, T.N. and G. Thirumalai (1977). The grass seed infesting
thrips *Chirothrips mexicanus* Crawford on *Pennisetum typhoides* and
its principal alternate host *Chloris barbata*. *Cur.Sci.*,
46(6):193-194.
Ananthakrishnan, T.N. and G. Thirumalai (1978). Population fluctuations
of three species of anthophilous Thysanoptera with notes on the
biology of the seed feeding species *Chirothrips mexicanus* Crawford.
*Bull.Zool.Sur.India*,1(2):197-201.
Ananthakrishnan, T.N. and S. Varadarasan (1977). *Androthrips flavipes*
Schmutz (Insecta:Thysanoptera), a predatory inquiline in thrips
galls. *Entomon*, 2(1):105-107.

Ananthakrishnan, T.N., R. Varatharajan and K. Gopinathan (1981).
Pollination in *Wedelia chinensis* (Osbeck) Merr and *Tridax procumbens*
L. by thrips. *Proc.Indian natn.Sci.Acad.*, B47:159-165.

Ananthakrishnan, T.N., R. Varatharajan and K. Gopinathan (1981). Seasonal
periodicity of thrips infesting some Compositae in relation to
pollination. *Proc.Indian natn.Sci.Acad.*, B47:811-815.

Ananthakrishnan, T.N. and T.R. Viswanathan (1973). On partial
ovoviviparity in *Tiarothrips subramanii* (Ramakrishna)
(Thysanoptera:Insects). *Curr.Sci.*, 42(18):649-650.

Ananthakrishnan, T.N. and T.R. Viswanathan (1973). Observations on the
biology, ecology and behaviour of *Ecacanthothrips sanguineus* Bagnall
(Tubulifera:Thysanoptera). *Curr.Sci.*, 42(20):727-728.

Ananthakrishnan, T.N. and T.R. Viswanathan (1974). Population
fluctuations of 3 species of anthophilous Thysanoptera in relation
to the numerical response of their predator *Orius minutus* L.
(Anthocoridae:Hemiptera). *Curr.Sci.*, 43(1):19-20.

Ananthakrishnan, T.N. and T.R. Viswanathan (1976). Aspects of host
preference and succession in thrips infesting *Ruellia tuberosa.*
*Entomon*, 1(1):71-77.

Andrewartha, H.G. (1971). *Introduction to the study of animal
population.* The University of Chicago Press, Chicago, 282 pp.

Annappan, R.S. and D.S. Aaron (1965). Incidence of thrips (*Thrips tabaci*
Lind.) on Desi cotton (*Gossypium arboreum* L.). *Indian Cotton J.*,
19:329-330.

Anonymous. (1976). Studies on the rice thrips *Thrips oryzae* Williams in
Tungtai area, Kiangsu Province. *Acta Ent.Sinica*, 19(1):13.

Back, E.A. (1912). Notes on Florida Thysanoptera, with description of a
new genus. *Ent.News.*, 23:73-77.

Bagnall, R.S. (1912). Some considerations in regard to the
classification of the order Thysanoptera. *Ann.Mag.Nat.Hist.*,
8(10):220.

Bagnall, R.S. (1931). On the Aelothripid-complex and the classification
of the order Terebrantia. *Bull.Soc.Nat.Luxemb.*, 7:115.

Bailey, S.F. (1932). A method employed in rearing thrips. *J.econ.Ent.*,
25:1194-96.

Bailey, S.F. (1933). The biology of the bean thrips. *Hilgardia*
7:467-522.

Bailey, S.F. (1935). Thrips as Vectors of plant diseases.
*J.econ.Ent.*, 28:95-98.

Bailey, S.F. (1937). The bean thrips. *Mon.Bull.Calif.Dep.Agric.*,
609:1-36.

Bailey, S.F. (1939). The six-spotted thrips, *Scolothrips sexmaculatus*
Perg. *J.econ.Ent.*, 32:43-47.

Bailey, S.F. (1940). The black hunter. *Leptothrips mali* Fitch.
*J.econ.Ent.*, 33:539-44.

Bailey, S.F. (1940). Cocoon-spinning Thysanoptera. *Pan.Pacif.Ent.*,
16:77-79.

Bailey, S.F. (1942). The grapevine thrips. *Drepanothrips reuteri*
*J.Econ.Ent.*, 35(3):382-86.

Bailey, S.F. (1948). Grain and grass infesting thrips. *J.econ.ent.*,
41:701-705.

Bardner, R. and K.E. Fletcher (1974). Insect infestation and their
effects on the growth and yield of field crops: a review.
*Bull,Ent.Res.*, 64:141-160.

188

Barnes, H.F. (1930). A new thrips eating gall midge *Thripsobremia liothrips*. gen et sp.n. (Cecidomyidae). *Bull.Ent.Res.*, 21:331-332.

Beck, S.D. (1965). Resistance of plants to insects. *Ann.Rev. Entomol.*, 10:206-232.

Beckham, C.M. (1969). Color preference and flight habits of thrips associated with cotton. *Jour.Econ.Ent.*, 62(3):591-92.

Bennett, F.D. (1965). Observations on the natural enemies of *Gynaikothrips ficorum* Marchal in Brazil *Tech.Bull.Commonw. Inst.biol.control*, 5:117-125.

Beshear, R. (1974). A chalcidoid planidium on Thrips larvae in Georgia. *J.Georgia Entomol.Soc.*, 9(4):255-256.

Billes, D.J. (1941). Pollination of *Theobroma Cacao* L. in Trinidad, B.W.I. *Tropical Agric.*, *Trinidad*, 18:151-156.

Boucek, Z. (1976). Taxonomic studies on some Eulophidae (Hym) of economic interest, mainly from Africa. *Entomophaga*, 21(4):401-141.

Boucek, Z. and R.R. Askew (1979). Index of Palaerctic Eulophidae: 137-138.

Bournier, A. (1956)*. Contribution a l'etude de la parthenogenise des thysanopteres et de sa cytologie. *Arch.Zool. exp.gen.*, 93:135-141.

Bournier, A. (1957). Un deuxieme cas d'ovoviviparite' chez les Thysanoptera *Caudothrips buffai* Karny (Tubulifera: Megathripidae) *c.r.habd.Seane.Acad.Sci.*, Paris, 244:506-508.

Bournier, A. (1966). L'embryogenese de *Caudothrips buffai* Karny (Thysanoptera:Tubulifera). *Ann.Soc.ent.Fr.(N.S.)*, 2:415-435.

Bournier, A., A. Lacasa and Y. Pirot (1978). Biologie D'un Thrips predator *Aelothrips intermedium* (Thys:Aeolothripidae), *Entomophaga*, 23(4):403-410.

Boyce, K.E. and Miller L.A. (1954). Overwintering habitats of the onion thrips, *Thrips tabaci* Lind. (Thysanoptera: Thripidae), in Southwestern Ontario. *Rep.Ent.Soc.Ontario*, 84:82-86.

Bryan, D.E. and R.F. Smith (1956). The *Frankliniella occidentalis* complex in California (Thysanoptera:Thripidae). *Univ.Calif. Publ.Ent.*, 10(6):359-410.

Bullock, J.A. (1963). Extraction of Thysanoptera from samples of foliage. *J.Econ.Ent.*, 56:612.

Bullock, J.A. (1965). The assessment of population of *Thrips nigripilosus* Uzel in pyrethrum. *Ann.appl.Biol.*, 55:1-12.

Carlson, E.C. (1964). Damage to safflower plants by thrips and lygus bugs and a study of their control. *J.Econ.Ent.*, 57:140-145.

Carlson, E.C. (1964). Effect of flower thrips on onion seed plants and a study of their control. *J.Econ.Ent.*, 57:735-741.

Callan, E.McC. (1943). Natural enemies of the cacao thrips. *Bull.Ent. Res.*, 34:313-321.

Cary, L.R. (1902). The grass thrips (*Anaphothrips striata* Osborn). *Maine Agr.Expt.Sta.Bull.*, 83:97-128.

Carayon, J. and J.R. Steffan (1959). Observations sur le regime alimentaire des Orius et particulierement d'*Orius pallidicornis* (Reuter) (Heteroptera:Anthocoridae). *Cah.nat.Paris n.s.*, 15:53-63.

Cederholm, L. (1963). Ecology of Thysanoptera. *Opuscula Ent. Suppl.*, 22:215 pp.

Chapman, R.F. (1977). The role of the leaf surface in food selection by Acridids and other insects. Colloque Internationaux du C.N.R.S., Comportment des Insectes at Milieu Trophique. 265:134-149.

*Bournier (1983) has since published "Les Thrips - Biologie Importance Agronomique: 128 pages.

Clausen, C.P. (1978). *Introduced parasites and predators of arthropod pests and weeds: A world review.* U.S. Dept. Agriculture Handbook 480. U.S. Govt.Printing Office, 545 pp.

Cody, M.L. and J.M. Diamond (1975). *Ecology and evolution of communities.* Belknap Press of Harvard University Press, 534 pp.

Coulibary, N. (1979) Some aspects of the damage caused by *Selenothrips rubrocinctus* (Giard) and the biology of this cocoa tree thysanopterous pest. *Cacao, 23:* 283-290.

David, B.V. and P. Thangavel (1973). On the host range of the Mycophagous thrips *Euphysothrips minozzi* Bagnall. *Madras agric.J., 60:*337.

Davidson, J. and C.G. Andrewartha (1948). The influence of rainfall, evaporation and atmospheric temperature on fluctuation in size of a natural population of *Thrips imaginis* Bagnall (Thysanoptera). *J.Animal Ecol., 17:*200-222.

Davies, R.G. (1961). The post-embryonic development of the female reproductive system in *Limothrips cerealium* Haliday (Thysanoptera:Thripidae). *Proc.Zool.Soc.Lond., 136:*411-437.

Davies, R.G. (1969). The skeletal musculature and its metamorphosis in *Limothrips cerealium* haliday (Thys:Thripidae). *Trans.R.ent.Soc. Lond., 121:*167-233.

Delattre, P. and J.P. Torregrossa (1975). Comparison de quatre methodes d'echantillonnage applicables a L'etude du thrips de la rouille de la banane *Chaetanaphothrips signipennis* (Thysanoptera:Thripidae). Estimation rapide des oscillations de population. *Nouv.Agron.Ant. Guy., 1:*186-198.

Delattre, P. and J.P. Torregrossa (1978). Seasonal abundance, distribution and population movements of the *Chaetanaphothrips orchidii* (Moulton) (Thsanoptera:Thripidae) in the french Antilles. (in French with English summary). *Ann.Zool.Ecol.anim., 10:*149-169.

Derbeneva, N.N. (1967). New data on the biology and structure of preimaginal phases and stages of the predatory thrips *Aeolothrips intermedius* Bagnall (Thysanoptera:Aeolothripdae). *Ent.Rev., 46:*626-646.

Dethier, V.G. (1954). Evolution of feeding preferences in phytophagous insects. *Evolution, 8:*33-54.

Dethier, V.G. (1966). Feeding behaviour. *Symp.R.ent.Soc.Lond., 3:*46-58.

Dev, H.N. (1964). Preliminary studies on the biology of the Assam thrips *Scirtothrips dorsalis* Hood on tea. *Indian J.Ent., 26:*184-194.

Doesberg, P.H. (1964). *Termatophylidea opaca* Carvalho, a predator of thrips (*Selenothrips rubrocinctus* Giard). *Ent.Ber.Amst., 24:*248-253.

Doul, K.F. (1956). Thrips infesting Cocksfoot in New Zealand, II. The Biology and economic importance of the *Cocksfoot* thrips *Chirothrips manicatus* Haliday. *N.Z.J.Sci.Technol.,* (A)*38:*56-65.

Dyadechko, N.P. (1977). *Thrips or Fringe winged Insects (Thysanoptera) of the European part of USSR.* Amerind Publishing Co.Pvt.Ltd., New Delhi 344 pp.

Eddy, C.O. and W.H. Clarke (1930). The onion thrips on seedling cotton with a season's record of parthenogenetic development *J.Econ.Ent., 23:*704-708.

El Badry, E.A. and M.S.F. Tawfik (1966). Life-cycle of the mite *Adactylidium* (Acarina:Pyemotidae) a predator of thrips eggs in United Arab Republic. *Ann.Ent.Soc.Amer., 59:*458-461.

Emden, H.F. van. (1965). The effect of uncultivated land on the distribution of the cabbage aphid (*Brevicoryne brassicae*) on an adjacent crop. *J.appl.Ecol.*, 2:171-196.

Emden, H.F. van. (1966). Plant resistance to insects induced by environment. *Scient.Hort.*, 18:94-102.

Emden, H.F. van. (1966a). Plant insect relationship and pest control. *Wld.Rev.Pest Control*, 5:115-123.

Emden, H.F. van. (1972). Aphids as phytochemists. In Harbourne of B. (ed.), *Phytochemical ecology*. Academic Press, London and New York. 25-43.

Entwhistle, P.F. (1972). *Thysanoptera in Pests of Cocoa*. Tropical Science Series, Longmans. 331-362.

Evans, J.N. (1935). Further observations on the seasonal fluctuations in number of *Thrips imaginis* by associated blossom thrips. *J.Coun.Sci.Ind.Res.(Aust.).*, 46:86-92.

Faulkner, L.R. (1954). Economic thrips of Southern New Mexico. *Bull.New Mex. Agric.Expt.sra.* :387.

Fennah, R.G. (1955). The epidemiology of cacao-thrips on Cacao in Trinidad. *Rep.Cacao Res.Trinidad*, 24:7-26.

Fennah, R.G. (1963). Nutritional factors associated with seasonal populations increase of cacao-thrips *Selenothrips rubrocinctus* (Giard) (Thysanoptera) on Cashew, *Anacardium* occidentale. *Bull.Ent.Res.*, 53:681-713.

Fennah, R.G. (1965). The influence of environmental stress on the cacao tree in predetermining the feeding sites of cacao thrips *Selenothrips rubrocinctus* (Giard), on leaves and pods. *Bull.Ent.Res.*, 56:333-349.

Ferriere, C.H. (1958). Un nouveau parasite de Thrips en Europe centrale (Hym.Euloph.). *Mitt.Schweiz.Entomol.Geselh.*, 31:320-324.

Fletcher, R.K. and J.C. Gaines (1939). The effect of thrips injury on production of cotton. *J.Econ.Ent.*, 32:78-80.

Fox, C.J.S. and R.W. Delbridge (1977). Onion thrips injuring stored cabbage in Nova Scotia and Prince Island. *Phytoprotection*, 58:57-58.

Franssen, C.J.H. (1958). Biology and control of the pea thrips (*Kakothrips robustus* Uzel). *Landbouwvoorl.*, 15:271-279.

Franssen, C.J.H. (1960). Biology and control of the pea thrips. *Versl.Land.bouwk.Onderz.*, 66:1-15.

Franssen, C.J.H. and P.E. Huisman (1958). The biology and control of *Thrips angusticeps* Uzel. *Versl.Landbouwk.Onderz. RijkslandbProefstn*, 64:1-104.

Franssen, C.J.H. and W.P. Mantel (1960). The flax thrips: *Thrips Lini* Lad. or *Thrips linarius* Uzel. *Entom.Ber.*, 20:30-33.

Franssen, C.J.H. and W.P. Mantel (1961). Preventing damage by thrips in flax. *T.Pl.Ziekton.* 67:39-51.

Franssen, C.J.H. and W.P. Mantel (1962). *Thrips in flax and their importance in flax cultivation.* Versl.Landbouk.Onderz. NR.68.17 Wageniugen, 77 pp.

Franssen, C.J.H. and W.P. Mantel (1963). The prediction of damage by brachypterous *Thrips angusticeps* Uzel in spring. *Landbouwkundig Tijd schr.*, 75:121-132.

Franssen, C.J.H. and W.P. Mantel (1965). Thrips in cereal crops (Biology, economic importance and control). *Biology.Versl. Landbouwk.Onderz.Rijkslandb.Proefetn.* 662:1-97.

Fritzsche, R. (1958). Zur Kenntnis der Raubinsekten van *Tetranychus urticae* Koch (Thysanoptera:Heteroptera). *Beitr.Ent.* 8:716-724.

Futuyma, D.J. (1973). Community structure and stability in constant environments. *Amer.Nat.* 107:443-446.

Gadgil, M. (1972). Male dimorphism as a consequence of sexual selection. *Amer.Nat.*, 106:574-580.

Gagne, W.C. (1979). Canopy-associated arthropods in *Acacia koa* and *Metrosideros* tree communities along an altitudinal transect on Hawaii island. *Pacific Insects.* 21:56-82.

Gaines, J.C. (1934). A preliminary study of thrips of seedling cotton with special reference to the population, migration and injury. *J.Econ.Ent.*, 27:740-743.

Ghanekar, A.M., D.V.R. Reddy, N. Tizuka, P.W. Amin, and R.W. Gibbons (1979). Bud necrosis of groundnut in India caused by tomato spotted wilt virus. *Ann.Appl.Biol.*, 93:173-179.

Ghesquiere, J. (1939). Contributions a l'etude des Hymenopteres du Congo Belge. VI Description d'un nouveau et remarques sur leg. *Megaphragma Timb.Rev.Zool.Bot.Afr.*, 33:33-41.

Gilstrap, F.E. and Oatman (1976). The bionomics of *Scolothrips sexmaculatus* (Perg.) (Thys:Thripidae), an insect predator of spider mites (Acari:Tetranychidae) *Hilgardia*, 44:27-59.

Goncalues, C.R. and A.J.L. Goncalues (1976). Observations on syrphid flies as predators of homopterous insects. *Ann.Soc.Entomol.Bras.*, 5:3-10.

Gopinathan, K. and R. Varatharajan (1983). On the topography of floral nectaries of some Compositae. *Indian Bot.J.(In press)*.

Graves, R.C. (1960). Ecological observations on the insects and other inhabitants of woody shelf fungi (Basidiomycetes: Polyporaceae) in the Chicago area. *Ann.Entomol.Soc.Amer.*, 53:61-78.

Graves, R.C. and A.C.F. Graves (1970). The insects and other inhabitants of shelf fungi in the southern Blue ridge region of Western North Carolina. IV. The Thysanoptera. *Ann.Ent.Soc.America.*, 63:96-98.

Grinfel'd, E.K. (1959). The feeding of thrips (Thysanoptera) on pollen of flowers and the origin of asymmetry in their mouth parts (in Russian). *Ent.Obozr.*, 38:798-804.

Grist, H.D. and R.J.A.W. Lever (1969). *Pests of Rice.* Tropical Science Series, Longmans Green Co. Ltd. Lond, 520 pp.

Gromadska, M. (1954). Thysanoptera flower-fauna of sandune biotype (An essay on ecological characteristics). *ekol.Pol.* 2:93-137.

Gromadska, M. (1977). Adaptive forms in Thysanoptera. *Przeglad Zoologicyny*, 21:298-301.

Haga, K. (1974). Post-embryonic development of Megathripine species, *Bactridothrips brevitubus* Takahashi (Thysanoptera). *Bull.Sugadaira Biol.Lab.* of *Tokyo Kyoiku Univ.*, 6:1-11.

Haga, K. (1975). Female reproductive system of Megathripine species, *Bactridothrips brevitubus* (Thysanoptera:Insecta). *Bull.Sugadaira Biol.Lab.* of *Tokoyo Kyoiku Univ.*, 7:13-24.

Hagerup, O. (1950). Thrips pollination in *Calluna*. *D.Kgl.Danske* Vidensk.Selsk. *Biol.Medd.*, 18:1-116.

Hagerup, E. and O. Hagerup (1953). Thrips pollination of *Erica tetralix* New phytol, 52:1-7.

Hamilton, W.D. (1978). Evolution and diversity under bark. In *'Diversity of Insect Faunas'* Ed.L.A.Mound & N.Waloff, Blackwell Scientific Publication, 154-175.

Hamilton, W.D. (1978a). Wingless and fighting males in fig wasps and other insects. In 'Reproductive competition and selection in Insects'. Ed. M.S. Blum and N.A. Blum, Academic Press, New York.

Harding, J.A. (1961). Effect of migration, temperature and precipitation on thrips infestation in South Texas. J.Econ.Ent., 54(1):77-79.

Harris, H.M. C.J. Drake and H.D. Tate (1936). Observations on the Onion thrips (Thrips tabaci Lind.) Iowa State Coll. J.Sci., 10:155-171.

Harrison, J.O. (1963). Notes on the biology of the banana flower thrips Frankliniella paravula in the Dominion republic (Thysanoptera:Thripidae). Ann.Ent.Soc.AMerica, 56:644-666.

Hartwig, E.K. (1964). Termitophilous Thysanoptera from South Africa. Ent.Soc.S.Africa, 29:44-47.

Hartwig, E.K. (1978). Two new species of Hydiothripini (Thysanoptera: Phaeothripidae) from South Africa, with notes on two species. J.ent.Soc.South Africa, 41:149-158.

Hartwig, E.K. (1978a). A new species of Preeiella (Thysanoptera: Phlaeothripidae) from South Africa with comments on Hydiothripini characters. J.Ent.Soc.South Africa, 41:259-264.

Hassel, M.P. (1978). The dynamics of arthropod predator-prey systems. Princeton University Press, Princeton, N.J., 237 pp.

Heeger, E. (1852). Beitrage Zur Insekten-Fauna Osterricks, V. Naturw.Sitz.Wien., 9:473.

Heinrich, B. and P.H. Raven (1972). Energetics and Pollination ecology. Science, 176:597-602.

Heming, B.S. (1970). Post-embryonic development of the female reproductive system in Frankliniella fusca (Thripidae) and Haplothrips verbasci (Phlaeothripidae) (Thysanoptera). Misc.Publ.Ent.Soc.Amer., 7:197-234.

Heming, B.S. (1970a). Post-embryonic development of the male reproductive system in Frankliniella fusca (Thripidae) and Haplothrips verbasci (Phlaeothripidae:Thysanoptera). Misc.Publ.Ent.Soc.Amer., 7:235-272.

Heming, B.S. (1971). Functional Morphology of the thysanopteran pretarsus. Can.J.Zool., 49:91-108.

Heming, B.S. (1978). Structure and function of the mouth parts in larvae of Haplothrips verbasci (Osborn) (Thysanoptera, Tubulifera, Phlaeothripidae). J.Morph., 156:1-38.

Heming, B.S. (1979). Origin and fate of germ cells in male and female embryos of Haplothrips verbasci (Osborn) (Insecta, Thysanoptera, Phlaeothripidae). J.Morph., 160(3):323-334.

Heming, B.S. (1980). Development of the mouthparts in embryos of Haplothrips verbasci (Osborn) (Insecta, Thysanoptera, Phlaeothripidae). J.Morph., 164:235-263.

Hendrix, S.D. (1980). Insect fauna of ferns. Amer.Nat., 15:171-196.

Hightower, B.G. and D.F. Martin (1956). Ecological Studies of thrips found on cotton in Central Texas. J.Econ.Ent., 40:423-424.

Hill, M.O. (1973). Diversity and evenness: a unifying notation and its consequences. Ecology, 54:427-32.

Hodson, W.E.H. (1935). The lily thrips (Liothrips vaneeckei Pr.) Bull.Ent.Res., 26:469-74.

Holtman, H. (1962). Untersuchungen Zur Biologie der Getreide - Thysanopteran. Teii.I.Zeit.Angew.Entomol., 51:1-41.

Holtman, H. (1963). Untersuchungen zur Biologie der Getreide - Thysanopteran. Teii.II, 51:285-299.

Hood, J.D. (1915). An outline of the subfamilies and higher groups of the insect order Thysanoptera. *Proc.Bull.Soc.Wash.*, *28*:53.

Hood, J.D. (1934). New Thysanoptera from Panama. *J.New York Ent.Soc.*, *41*:407-434.

Hood, J.D. (1936). Studies in Neotropical Thysanoptera-I. *Rev.de.Ent.*, *6*:248-279.

Hood, J.D. (1938). Studies in Neotropical Thysanoptera-VI. *Rev.de.Ent.*, *8*(1-2):175-187.

Hood, J.D. (1939). The cause and significance of macropterism and brachypterism in certain Thysanoptera with descriptions of a new Mexican species. *Esc.Nac.Cien.Bio.*, *1*:497-505.

Hood, J.D. (1955). A new *Hoplothrips* from Florida. *Fla.Entomol.*, *38*:27-32.

Huffaker, C.B. (1974). Some implications of plant-Arthropod and higher level Arthropod-Arthropod Food links. *Environ.Ent.*, *1*:1-9.

Irwin, M.E. and D.E. Kuhlman (1979). Relationships among *Sericothrips variabilis*, systemic insecticides and soyabean field. *J.Georgia Entomol.Soc.*, *14*:148-154.

Irwin, M.E. and P.W. Price (1976). Entomophagous insects in a soyabean pest control strategy, in *'Expanding the use of soybeans'*. Ed. R.M. Goodman. *Proc.Conf.Asia and Oceania.* College of Agriculture, University of Illinois, 108-113 pp.

Irwin, M.E. and K.V. Yeargan (1980). Sampling phytophagous thrips on soyabean in *'Sampling procedures in Soyabean Entomology'* Eds. M. Kogan and D. Herzog, Springer Verlag, New York, 283-303 pp.

Irwin, M.E., K.V. Yeargan and N.L. Marston (1979). Spatial and seasonal patterns of phytophagous thrips in soyabean fields with comments on sampling techniques. *Environ.Entomol.*, *8*:131-140.

Isenhour, D.J. and N.L. Marston (1981). Seasonal cycles of *Orius insidiosus* (Hemiptera:Anthocoridae) in Missouri soyabeans. *J.Kansas Ent.Soc.*, *54*:129-142.

Isenhour, D.J. and K.V. Yeargan (1981). Interactive behaviour of *Orius insidiosus* (Hem:Anthocoridae) and *Sericothrips variabilis* (Thys:Thripidae) predator searching strategies and prey escape tactics. *Entomophaga*, *26*:213-220.

Ishi, T. (1933). Notes on two Hymenopterous parasites in Japan. Tokyo, *7*:13-16.

Jacot-Guillarmod, C.F. (1974). Catalogue of the Thysanoptera of the world (Part 3). *Ann.Cape.Prov.Mus.* (Nat.Hist.), *7*:518-976.

Janzen, D.H. (1968). Host plants as islands in evolutionary and contemporary time. *Amer. Nat.*,*102*:592-595.

Janzen, D.H. (1977). Why are there so many species of insects? *Proc.XVth Int.Cong.Ent.Washington*, 84-96.

Jenser, G. (1974). Observations on the autumn mass flight of *Frankliniella intonsa* Trybom (Thysanoptera: Thripidae) *Acta Phytopath.Acad.Scient.Hung.*, *8*:227-230.

Johansen, R.M. (1976). Algunos aspects sobre is conducts mimetica de *Franklinothrips vespiformis* (Crawford) (Insecta: Thysanoptera). *An.Inst.Biol.Univ.Nal.Auto'n.* Mexico *Ser.Zoologia*, *1*:25-50.

Johansen, R.M. (1980). A revision of the North American Thysanopteran genus *Torvothrips* inhabiting *Olliffiella* galls in *Quercus Foliaa*. *Ent.Mexicana*, *44*:19-38.

John, O. (1923). Fakultative Viviparitat bei Thysanopteren *Ent.Mitt.*, *12*:227-232.

194

Johnson, C.G. (1969). *Migration and dispersal of insects by flight*.
Methuen, London, 763 pp.
Jones, H.A., S.F. Bailey and S.L. Emsweller (1934). Thrips resistance in
the Onion. *Hilgardia*, *8*:215-232.
Jordan, K. (1888). Anatomie und Biologie der Physopoda. *Z.wiss.Zool.*,
*47*:541-620.
Joshi, G.P. (1974). The biology of *Stictothrips fimbriata*, Anan.,a
mycophagous Thysanopteran on different meals. *Z.angew.Ent.*, *76*:146-149.
Kamm, J.A. (1971). Silver top of Bluegrass and Bentgrass produced by
*Anaphothrips obscurus*. *J.Econ.Ent.*, *64*:1383-1387.
Kamm, J.A. (1972). Environmental influence on reproduction, diapause and
morph determination in *Anaphothrips obscurus*
(Thysanoptera:Thripidae). *Envir.Ent.*, *1*:16-19.
Kamm, J.A. (1972). Thrips that effect production of grass seed in
Oregon. *J.Econ.Ent.*, *65*:1050-1055.
Karny, H. (1921). Zur Systematik der Orthopteroiden Insekten. III.
Thysanoptera. *Treubia*, *1*:211-261.
Karny, H. (1922). Zur Phylogenia der Thysanopteran. *Treubia*, *3*:29-37.
Kennedy, J.S. (1958). Physiological condition of the host-plant and
susceptibility to aphid attack. *Entomologia.exp.appl.*, *1*:50-65.
Kennedy, J.S. (1965). Mechanism of host plant selection.
*Ann.Appl.Biol.*, *56*:317-322.
Kennedy, J.S. (1974). Changes of responsiveness in the patterning of
behavioural sequences:1-6, In *Experimental analysis of Insect
behaviour* (ed. L. Barton-Browne)Springer-Verlag, Berlin.
Khalil, F.M., A.H. El Sebae and G.A. Karaman (1973). Some ecological
studies in *Thrips tabaci* L. *Bull.Soc.Ent.Egypte*, *LVII*:33-40.
Kisha, J.S.A. (1977). Cultural and insecticidal control of *Thrips tabaci*
on onions in the Sudan. *Ann.appl.Biol.*, *86(2)*:219-228.
Kjellsen, E.K. (1975). Dynamics of Thysanoptera populations on
Hardangervidda. *Ecol.Studies.*, *17*:80-83.
Kogan, M. (1977). The role of chemical factors in Insect/plant
relationships. *Proc.IV.Int.Congr.Ent.Washington*:211-226.
Kontakkannen, P. (1950). Quantitative and seasonal studies on the
leafhopper fauna of the field stratum in open areas in North
Karelia. *Ann.Zool.Soc.Zool.Bot.Vanamo.*, *13*:1-91.
Koppa, P. (1976). The composition of the thrips species in cereals in
Finland. *Ann.Agric.Fenn.*, *6*:30-45.
Koppa, P. (1969). The sex index of some species of thrips living on
cereal plants. *Ann.Ent.Fenn.*, *35*:66-73.
Koppa, P. (1969). Studies on the hibernation of certain species of
thrips on cereal plants. *Ann.Agricult.Fenn.*, *8*:1-8.
Koppa, P. (1970). Studies on the Thrips (Thysanoptera) species most
commonly occurring on cereals in Finland. *Ann.Agric.Fenn.*,
*9*:191-265.
Korting, A. (1931). Beobachtung uber die Fluggerwohuherton der Frifliege
und einiger Getreidethysanopteren. *Z.angew.ent.*, *18*:154-160.
Kosztarab, M. (1982). Observation on *Torvothrips kosztarabi*
(Thysanoptera:Phlaeothripidae) inhabiting coccid galls. *Florida
Ent.* *65(1)*:159-164.
Krishnamurthy, K.V., A. Raman and T.N. Ananthakrishnan (1977). Studies
on plant galls from India. 2.Leaf galls of *Cordia obliqua* Willd. (=
Cordia myxa L.) (Boraginaceae). *Ceylon J.Sci. (Biol.Sci.)*,
*12*:110-116.

Krombein, K.V. (1956). Biological and taxonomic notes on the wasps of lost river state park, West Virginia, with additions to the faunal list (Hymenoptera:Aculeata). *Ent.Soc.Wash.*, *58*:153-161.

Krombein, K.V. (1958). Additions during 1956 and 1957 to the wasp fauna of lost river State park, West Virginia, with biological notes and dimorphism of new species (Hymenoptera,Aculeata). *Proc.Ent.Soc.Wash.*, *60*:49-64.

Krombein, K.V. (1958). Miscellaneous prey records of solitary wasps-III (Hymenoptera,Aculeata). *Proc.Biol.Soc.Wash.*, *71*:21-26.

Krombein, K.V. (1962). Natural History of Plummers island, Maryland XIII. Descriptions of new wasps from plummers island, Maryland (Hymenoptera,Aculeata). *Proc.Biol.Soc.Wash.*, *75*:1-18.

Kryger, J.P. (1932). One new genus and species and three new species of Trichogrammatidae from Egypt. *Bull.Soc.Ent.Egypte*, *16*:38-44.

Kudo, I. (1971). Observations on relative abundance, phenology and flower preference of Thysanoptera in Sapporo and the vincinity. *Jour.Fac.Hokkaido Univ.Ser VI.Zool.*, *17*:610-627.

Kurdjumov, N.V. (1913). The more important insects injurious to grain crops in Middle and South Russia (in Russian). *Dept.agric.Ent.*, *Rev.appl.Ent.*, *2*:170-173.

Kurkina, L.A. (1979). Biology of robber-fly *Machimus annulipes* Br. (Diptera:Asilidae) *Entomol.Oboyr.*, *58*:57-63.

Labeyrie, V. (1978). Insect reproduction and coevolution with plants. *Ent.exp.and appl.*, *24*:296-304.

Laughlin, R. (1970). The gum tree thrips, *Isoneurothrips australis* Bagn. Survival at different temperatures and humidities and its relation to capacity for survival. *Aust.J.Ecol.*, *2*:391-398.

Leeuwen, van (1956). The aetiology of some thrips galls found on leaves of Malaysian *Schefflera* sp. *Acta Bot.Neerland.*, *5*:80-89.

Le Pelley, R.H. (1942). A method of sampling thrips population. *Bull.ent.Res.*, *33*:147-148.

Le Pelley, R.H. (1968). Thysanoptera in Pests of Coffee. Longmans, Tropical Science Series, 381-388 pp.

Lewis, H.C. (1965). Factors influencing citrus thrips damage. *J.Econ.Ent.*, *28*:1011-1015.

Lewis, T. (1959). The annual cycle of *Limothrips cerealium* Haliday (Thysanoptera) and its distribution in a wheat field. *Entomologia exp.appl.*, *2*:187-203.

Lewis, T. (1961). Factors affecting primary patterns of infestation. *Ann.appl.Biol.*, *63*:315-317.

Lewis, T. (1962). The effect of temperature and relative humidity on mortality in *Limothrips cerealium* Haliday (Thysanoptera) overwintering in bark. *Ann.appl.Biol.*, *50*:313-326.

Lewis, T. (1963). The effect of weather on emergence and take-off of overwintering *Limothrips cerealium* Haliday (Thysanoptera). *Ann.appl.Biol.*, *51*:489-502.

Lewis, T. (1965). The effects of shelter on the distribution of insect pests. *Scient.Hort.*, *17*:74-84.

Lewis, T. (1959). Comparison of water traps, cylindrical sticky traps and suction traps for sampling thysanopteran population at different levels. *Ent.Exp.Appl.*, *2*:204-215.

Lewis, T. (1969). The distribution of flying insects near a low hedgerow. *J.appl.Ecol.*, *6*:443-452.

Lewis, T. (1970). Patterns of distribution of insects near a windbreak of tall trees. *Ann.appl.Biol*, *65*:213-220.

Lewis, T. (1973). *Thrips: their biology, ecology and economic importance*. Academic Press, London. 349 pp.

Lewis, T. (1980). Applied Entomology and world crop production, 1930-2000. In CAB Jubilee Volume 'Perspectives in World Agriculture', *Commonwealth.Agric.Bureaux*, 237-258.

Lewis, T. and G.W. Hurst (1966). Take-off thresholds in Thysanoptera and the forecasting of migratory flight. *Biometeorology*, II:576-578.

Lewis, T. and E. Navas (1962). Thysanopteran population overwintering in hedge bottom, from litter and bark. *Ann.appl.Biol.*, 50:299-311.

Lincoln, C., F.J. Williams and G. Barnes (1953). Importance of thrips in red spider control. *J.Econ.Ent.*, 46:899-900.

Loan, C. and F.G. Holdaway (1955). Biology of the red clover thrips *Haplothrips niger* (Osborn) (Thysanoptera:Phlaeothripidae), *Canad.Ent.*, 87:210-219.

Lord, E.T. (1949). The influence of spray programmes on the fauna of apple orchards in Nova Scotia.III. Mites and their predators. *Can.Ent.*, 81:202-14 and 217-30.

Lord, F.T., H.J. Hubert and A.W. Macphee (1958). The natural control of phytophagous mites on apple trees in Nova Scotia. *Proc.Intern.Congr.Entomol.*, 10th, Montreal, 4:617-622.

Lysaght, A.M. (1936). A note on the adult female of *Anguillulina aptini* (Sharga), a nematode parasitising *Aptnothrips rufus* Gmelin, *Parasitology*, 28:290-292.

Lysaght, A.M. (1936a). A note on an unidentified fungus in the body cavity of two Thysanopterous insects. *Parasitology*, 28:293-294.

Lysaght, A.M. (1938). An ecological study of a thrips *(Aptinothrips rufus)* and its nematode parasite *(Anguillulina aptini)*. *J.Anim.Ecol.*, 6:169-192.

MacGill, E.I. (1939). A gamasid mite *(Typhlodromus thripsi* n.sp.) a predator of *Thrips tabaci* Lind. *Ann.appl.Biol.*, 26:309-317.

Macphee, A.W. (1953). The influence of spray programmes on the fauna of apple orchards in Nova Scotia. v. The predacious thrips *Haplothrips faueri* Hood. *Canad.Ent.*, 85:32-40.

MacArthur, R.H. (1965). Patterns of species diversity. *Bot.Rev.*, 40:510-533.

MacArthur, R.H. (1965a). Fluctuations of animal populations and a measure of community stability. *Ecology*, 36:533-536.

Maddox, D.M. (1973). *Amynothrips andersoni* (Thysanoptera:Phlaeothripidae), a thrips for the biological control of Alligator weed 1. Host specific studies. *Environ.Ent.*, 2(1):31-37.

Maddox, D.M. and A. Mayfield (1979). Biology and life history of *Amynothrips andersoni*, a thrips for biological control of alligator weed. *Anns.Ent.Soc.America*, 72:136-140.

Maksymov, J.K. (1976). The soil as a pupation site of *Taeniothrips laricivorus* Krat.et.far. (Thys:Thripidae) *Anz.Schadlingskde.Pflanz.-Umweltschutz.*, 49(8):117-122.

Mani, M.S. (1964). *Ecology of Plant galls*. W.Junk Publ., The Hague. 434 pp.

Mantel, W.P. (1969). Thrips in oats - (On the degree of infestation of oats by thrips species). *Landbouw voorl.*, 26:35-41.

Mathur, G. and H.Y. Mohan Ram (1978). Significance of petal colour in thrips pollinated *Lantana camera* L.*Ann.Bot.*, 42:1473-1476.

Mathews, R.W. (1970).  A new thrips-hunting *Microstigmus* from Costa Rica (Hymenoptera:Sphecidae: Pemphredoninae).  *Psyche*, ;*77*:120-126.

Mattson, W.J. (1977).  Size and abundance of forest Lepidoptera in relation to host plant resources.  *Colloque Internationaux du C.N.R.S., Comportment des Insectes et Milieu Trophique.* *265*:429-442.

McCallan, D.R., M.K. Gentle and W. Hovanitz (1962).  Chemical nature of the Insect Gall growth-factor.  *Plant Physiol.*, *37*:98-103.

Melis, A. (1935).  Tisanotter italiani.  Studio anatomo-morphologico et biologico de Liothripidae dell olivo (*Liothrips oleae* Costa).  Redia, *21*:1-188.

Mori, H. (1967).  A review of the biology of spider mites and their predators in Japan.  *Mushi*, *40*:47-65.

Morison, G.D. (1957).  A Review of British Glass House Thysanoptera.  *Trans.R.ent.Soc.Lond.*, *109*:467-534.

Mound, L.A. (1967).  A new genus and species of Thysanoptera predatory on mites in Iraq.  *Bull.ent.Res.*, *57*:315-319.

Mound, L.A. (1968).  A review of R.S. Bagnall's Thysanoptera collections.  *Bull.Brit.Mus.Nat.Hist.Entomol.Suppl.*, *11*:1-181.

Mound, L.A. (1970).  Sex intergrades in Thysanoptera.  *Ent.Mon.Mag.*, *105*:186-189.

Mound, L.A. (1970).  Convoluted maxillary stylets and the systematics of some phlaeothripine Thysanoptera from *Casuarina* trees in Australia.  *Aust.J.Zool.*, *18*:439-463.

Mound, L.A. (1971).  Gall-forming thrips and allied species (Thysanoptera:Phlaeothripinae) from *Acacia* trees in Australia.  *Bull.Br.Mus. (Nat.Hist.)*, *25*:387-466.

Mound, L.A. (1971a).  The feeding apparatus of thrips.  *Bull.Ent.Res.*, *60*:547-548.

Mound, L.A. (1972).  Grass-flower infesting thrips of the genus Chirothrips Haliday in Australia.  *J.Aust.Ent.Soc.*, *11*:332-339.

Mound, L.A. (1973).  Thrips and white flies.  In '*Viruses and Invertebrates*.  Ed. A.J. Gibbs, North Holland Publ. Co., Amsterdam & London.  *31*:232-242.

Mound, L.A. (1974).  Spore-feeding Thrips (Phlaeothripidae) from leaf litter and dead wood in Australia.  *Aust.J.Zool.*, *27*:1-106.

Mound, L.A. (1974a).  The *Nesothrips* complex of spore feeding Thysanoptera.  (Phlaeothripidae:Idolothripinae).  *Bull.Br.Mus.(Nat. Hist.).Ent.*, *31*;109-188.

Mound, L.A. (1976).  American leaf-litter Thysanoptera of the genera *Erkosothrips, Eurythrips*, and *Terthrothrips* (Phlaeothripidae: Phlaeothripinae).  *Bull.Br.Mus.(Nat.Hist.).Ent.Jr.*, *35*:27-64.

Mound, L.A. (1977).  Species diversity and the systematics of some New World leaf litter Thysanoptera (Phlaeothripidae:Glyptothripini).  *Syst.Ent.*, *2*:225-244.

Mound, L.A. (1977a).  Leaf-litter Thysanoptera of the subtribe Williamsiellina (Phlaeothripidae).  *Bull.Br.Mus.(Nat.Hist.).Ent.Ser.*, *36*:171-192.

Mound, L.A. (1977b).  The complex of Thysanoptera in rolled leaf galls on Geijera.  *J.Aust.Entomol.Soc.*, *10*:83-97.

Mound, L.A., Heming B.S. and J.M. Palmer (1980).  Phylogenetic relationship between the families of recent Thysanoptera (Insecta).  *Zool.Linn.Soc.*, *69*:111-141.

198

Mound, L.A. and K. O'Neill (1974). Taxonomy of the Merothripidae, with ecological and phylogenetic considerations (Thysanoptera). *J.nat.Hist.*, *8*:481-509.

Mound, L.A., G.D. Morison, B.R. Pitkin and J.M. Palmer (1976). Thysanoptera. *Handbook for the identification of British Insects Royal Entomological Society of London*, 79 pp.

Mound, L.A. and J.M. Palmer (1981). Identification, distribution and host plants of the pest species of the genus Scirtothrips Shull (Thys:Thripidae). *Bull.Ent.Res.*, *71*:467-479.

Mound, L.A. and J.M. Palmer (1982). The generic and tribal classification of spore feeding Thysanoptera (Phlaeothripidae:Idolothripinae). *Bull.Br.Mus.(Nat.Hist.).Ent.*, (in press).

Mound, L.A. and A.K. Walker (1982). Evolutionary significance and generic classification of the Williamsiellina (Thysanoptera: Phlaeothripidae). *Syst.Ent.*, *7*:347-355.

Muma, M.H. (1955). Three thrips predatory on citrus insects and mites in Florida. *Citrus Mag.*, *17*(9):11-13.

Muraleedharan, N. and T.N. Ananthakrishnan (1971). Bionomics of *Montandoniola moraguesi* (Puton) (Heteroptera:Anthocoridae) a predator on gall thrips. *Bull.Ent.*, *12*:4-10.

Muraleedharan, N. and T.N. Ananthakrishnan (1977). Bioecology of Anthocorids predatory on thrips. *Occ.Publ.Zool.Sur.India.*

Muryer, F. (1942). A method of rearing citrus thrips in the laboratory. *J.Econ.Entomol.*, *35*:373-5.

Mushtaq Ahmed. (1976). Studies on the host range of pea thrips *Caliothrips indicus*. *FAO.Pl.Pr.Bull.*, 24(3):83-85.

Natarajan, K. and N. Sundaram (1977). Control of cotton leaf hopper and thrips with dust formulation of certain insecticides. *Pesticides* (Bombay), *11*(8):57.

Newsom, L.D., J.S. Russel and C. E. Smith (1953). The tobacco thrips - its seasonal histroy and status as a cotton pests. *Louisiana Tech.Bull.*, *474*, 36 pp.

Nowakowski, J.T. (1962). Introduction to a systematic revision of the family Agromyzidae (Diptera) with some remarks on host plant selection by these flies. *Ann.Zool.Warszawa*, *20*(8):67-183.

Obertel, R. (1963). Subterranean phase of metamorphosis in *Odontothrips loti* Hall. *Zool.Listy.*, *12*:139-48.

Oettingen, H. von (1942). Die Thysanopteren de Norddeuteschen Graslandes *Entomologische Beihefte*, *9*:80-141.

Oettingen, H. von (1951). Geographische und okologische Analyse der Thysanopteren fauna der ostlichen Gebiete Mitteleuropan. *Beit. zur Ent.*, *1*(1):43-59.

Oettingen, H. von (1951). Die Thysanopteran fauna des Harzes, *Beit. zur Ent.*, *1*(2):140-186.

Oetting, R.D. and R.J. Beshear (1980). Host selection and control of the banded greenhouse thrips on Ornamentals. *J.Georgia Entomol.Soc.*, 15(4):475-479.

Ostmark, H.E. (1974). Economic insect pests of bananas. *Ann.Rev.Ent.*, 19:168.

Ota, A.K. (1968). Comparison of three methods of extracting the flower thrips from rose flowers. *J.econ.Ent.*, *G1*:754-55.

Painter, R.H. (1941). The economic value and biological significance of insect resistance in plants. *J.Econ.Ent.*, *34*:358-367.

Painter, R.H. (1951). Insect resistance in crop plants. Macmillan Co., New York.

Paliwal, Y.C. (1979). Occurrence and localization of spherical virus-like particles in tissues of apparently healthy tobacco thrips, *Frankliniella fusca*, a vector of tomato spotted wilt virus. *J.Invert.Pathol.*, 33(3):307-315.

Palmer, J.M. and L.A. Mound (1975). Nine genera of fungus-feeding Phlaeothripidae (Thysanoptera) from the Oriental region. *Bull.Br.Mus.(Nat.His.).Ent.Ser.*, 37(3):153-215.

Parencia (Jr.), C.R. (1978). One hundred twenty years of Research on cotton insects in the United States. *Thrips Agri. Handbook*, 515, USDA, Washington:37-38.

Parrella, M.P., J.P. McCaffrey and R.L. Horsburgh (1980). Compatibility of *Leptothrips mali* with *Stethorus punetum* and *Orius insidiosus:* predators of *Panonychus ulmi*. *Environ.Ent.*, 9(5):694-696.

Patel, N.G. and G.A. Patel (1953). The bonomics of the Wheat thrips *Anaphothrips flavicinctus*. *Indian J.Ent.*, 15(3):251-261.

Pelikan, J. (1954). Remarks on the orchid thrips *Chaetanaphothrips orchidii*. *Zool.Ent.Listy.*, 3(7):3-12.

Pelikan, J. (1961). New species of Thysanoptera from Czechoslovakia-IV. *Cesk.Spol.Ent.*, 58(1):60-70.

Perrin, R.M. and M.L. Phillips (1978). Some effects of mixed cropping on the population dynamics of insects. *Ent.exp. and appl.*, 24:385-93.

Pimm, S.L. (1979). The structure of food webs. *Theoretical population Biology*, Academic Press, New York, and London, 16(2):144-158.

Pitkin, B.R. (1977). A revision of the genus *Chaetanaphothrips* Priesner. *Bull.Entomol.Res.*, 67:599-605.

Poole, R.W. (1974). *An introduction to quantitative Ecology.* McGraw Hill Kogakusha Ltd., Tokyo, 532 pp.

Poos, F.W. (1941). On the cause of peanut 'pouts'. *J.Econ.Ent.*, 34(5):727-728.

Post, R.L. (1957). The barley thrips in North Dakota. *North Dakota Seed Journal*, (March):4.

Post, R.L. and W.J. Colberg (1958). Barley thrips in North Dakota, *Circ.N.Dak.agric.Coll.Extn.Serv.*, A 292.

Price, P.W. (1975). *Insect Ecology.* John Wiley & Sons, New York, 514 pp.

Price, P.W. (1976). Colonization by Arthropods: non-equal communities in soyabean pulses. *Environ.Ent.*, 5(4):605-611.

Priesner, H. (1925). Die winterquartiere der Thysanoptera, *Ent.Jb.*, 33-4:152.

Priesner, H. (1949). Genera Thysanopterorum. *Bull.Soc.Fouad. ter.Ento.*, 83:31-157.

Priesner, H. (1960). A monograph of the Thysanoptera of Egyptian deserts. *Publ.Inst.Desert Egypte.*, 13:549 pp.

Priesner, H. (1964). Ordnung Thysanoptera. Bestimm. Buch. Bodenfauna Europas, 2:1-242, Akademie-Verlag, Berlin.

Putman, W.L. (1942). Notes on the predacious thrips *Haplothrips subtilissimus* Haliday and *Aeolothrips melaleucas* Hal. *Canad.Ent.*, 74:37-43.

Putman, W.L. (1965). The predacious thrips *Haplothrips faurei* Hood (Thysanoptera:Phlaeothripidae) in Ontario peach orcaards. *Canad.Ent.*, 97:1208-1221.

Putman, W.L. and D.H.C. Herne (1966). The role of predators and other biotic agents in regulating the population density of phytophagous mites in Ontario peach orchards. *Canad.Ent.*, 98:808-819.

Quissenberry, J.E. and D.R. Rummel (1979). Natural resistance to thrips injury in cotton as measured by differential leaf area reduction. *Crop.Sci.*, *19*(6):879-881.

Race, S.R. (1965). Predicting Thrips population on seedling cotton. *J.Econ.Ent.*, *58*(5):1013-1014.

Rahman, K.A. and N.K. Bharadaraj (1937). The grapevine thrips *Rhipiphorothrips cruentatus* Hood (Thripidae:Terebrantia:Thysanoptera). Indian J.agri.sci, 7:633-651.

Raizada, U. (1976). A preliminary report on the fungi infesting thrips (Thysanoptera, Thripidae). *Entomon*, *1*(2):155-157.

Raizada, U. (1976). On the occurrence of *Mrazekia* sp., a microsporidian parasite infecting some thrips larvae. *Curr.Sci.*, *45*(17):627-628.

Rajasekharan, K. S. Chatterji and M.G. Ramdas Menon (1964). Biological notes on *Psallus* sp. (Miridae) a predator of *Taeniothrips nigricornis* Schmutz., *Indian.J.Ent.*, 26:62-66.

Ramakers, P.M.J. (1978). Possibilities for biological control of *Thrips tabaci* Lind. (Thysanoptera:Thripidae) in glasshouses. *Med.Fac.Landbouwk. Rijksunir.Gent.*, 43:463-469.

Ramakers, P.M.J. (1980). Biological control of *Thrips tabaci* (Thysanoptera:Thripidae) with *Amblyseias* spp. (Acari:Phytoseidae). *Bull.S.R.O.P./W.P.R.S.III/3*:203-208.

Raman, A. (1981). Morphological studies on some Galls induced by Thrips (Thysanoptera:Insecta) from South India. Ph.D. Thesis, Madras University.

Raman, A., T.N. Ananthakrishnan and S. Swaminathan (1978). On the simple leaf galls of *Casearia tomentosa* Roxb., (Samydaceae) induced by *Gynaikothrips flaviantennatus* Moulton (Thysanoptera:Phlaeothripidae). *Proc.Indian Acad.Sci.*, *B87*:231-242.

Reyne, A. (1920). A cocoon spinning thrips. *Tijd schr.Ent.*, *63*:40-45.

Reyne, A. (1921). De cacaothrips (*Heliothrips rubrocinctus*, Giard), *Bull.Landh.Suriname*, No.44, 214 pp.

Richards, O.W. (1959). The study of natural population of insects. *Proc.R.Ent.Soc.Lond.*, (C):75-79.

Richards, O.W. (1961). An introduction to the study of polymorphism in insects. *Symp.R.ent.Soc.Lond.*, *1*:1-10.

Riherd, P.T. (1954). Thrips, a limiting factor in Grass-seed production. *J.Econ.Ent.*, *47*(4):709-710.

Risler, H. and E. Kempter (1962). Die Haploidie der Mannchenund die Endopolypolidie in einigen Geweben von *Haplothrips*. *Chromosoma*. *12*:351-61.

Robinson, A.G., L.J. Stannard and E.J. Armstrong (1972). Observations on predators of *Sericothrips variabilis* Beach (Thysanoptera). *Entomol.News.*, *83*:107-11.

Roff, D. (1981). On being the right size. *Amer.Nat.*, *118*:405-422.

Rosenthal, G.A. and D.H. Janzen (1979). *Herbivores: Their Interactions with secondary plant metabolites.* New York: Academic Press, 718 pp.

Rosenzweig, M.L. (1978). Competitive speciation. *Biol.J.Linn.Soc.*, *10*:275-289.

Rummel, D.R. and J.E. Quisenberry (1979). Influence of thrips injury on leaf development and yield of various cotton genotypes. *J.Econ.Ent.*, *72*:706-709.

Rust, R.W. (1980). Pollen movement and reproduction in *Arisaema triphyllum*. *Bull.Torrye.Bot.Club.*, *107*(4):539-42.

201

Sakimura, K. (1932). Life history of *Thrips tabaci* on *Emilia sagitata* and its host plant range in Hawaii. *J.econ.Ent.*, 25:884-891.

Sakimura, K. (1932). Life history of *Thrips tabaci* in *Emilia Sagitata* and its host plant range in Hawaii. *J.econ.Ent.*, 75:884-891.

Sakimura, K. (1937a). The life and seasonal histories of *Thrips tabaci* Lind. in the icinity of Tokyo, Japan. *Oyo Dobuts.-Zasshi*, 9:1-24.

Sakimura, K. (1937b). On the bionomics of *Thripoctenus brui* Vuillet, a parasite of *Thrips tabaci* Lind. in Japan. (I) *Kontyu*, 11:370-390.

Sakimura, K. (1937c). On the bionomics of *Thripoctenus brui* Vuillet, a parasite of *Thrips tabaci* Lind. in Japan. (II) *Kontyu*, 11:410-424.

Sakimura, K. (1937d). Introduction of *Thripoctenus brui* Vuillet, a parasite of *Thrips tabaci* Lind. from Japan to Hawaii. *J.econ.Ent.*, 30:799-802.

Sakimura, K. (1940). Evidence for the identity of the yellow-spot virus with the spotted-wilt virus: Experiments with the vector, *Thrips tabaci*, Phytopathol., 30:281-299.

Sakimura, K. (1960). The present status of thrips-borne viruses. In *Biological transmission of desease agents*. (Maramorosch K., ed.), 192 pp. Academic Press, New York and London, 30-40.

Sakimura, K. (1961). Techniques for handling thrips in transmission experiments with the Tomato spotted wilt virus. *Pl.Dis.Reptr.*, 45:766-777.

Sakimura, K. (1969). A comment on the color forms of *Frankliniella schultzei* (Thysanoptera:Thripidae) in relation to transmission of the tomato-spotted wilt virus. *Pacif.Inscets*, 11:761-762.

Sakimura, K. and N.L.H. Krauss (1944). Thrips from Maui and Molokai. *Proc.Hawaii.ent.Soc.*, 12:113-122.

Sakimura, K. and N.L.H. Krauss (1945). Collections of thrips from Kauai and hawaii. *Proc.Hawaii.ent.Soc.*, 12:319-331.

Samson, R.A., P.M.J. Ramakers and T.Oswald (1979). *Entomophthora thripidum* a new fungal pathogen of *Thrips tabaci*. *Can.J.Bot.*, 57(12):1317-1323.

Sathpathy, J.M., M.S. Das and K. Naik (1977). Effect of multiple and mixed cropping on the incidence of some important pests. *J.Entomol.Res.*, 1(1):78-85.

Saxena, R.C. (1971). Some observations on *Ceranisus* sp. (Hymenoptera: Eulophidae) parasitising *Thrips tabaci* Lind. (Thysanoptera: Thripidae). *Indian J.Ent.*, 33:91-92.

Schliephake, G. (1961). Beitrage Zur Biologi Thysanopteren der Luzerne (Medicago sativa). *Beit.Zur.Ent.*, 11(5-6):577-593.

Schiephake, G. (1979). Thysanoptera, Fransenfluger Die Tierwelt Deutichlands. 66, Teil Veb Gustav Fischer Verkag, Jena. 477 pp.

Schoonhoven, A. van (1974). Resistance to Thrips damage in Cassava. *J.Econ.Ent.*, 67(6):728-730.

Schoonhoven, A. van and J.E. Pena (1976). Estimation of yield lossess in Cassava following attack from Thrips. *J.Econ.Ent.*, 69(4):514-516.

Schoonhoven, A. van (1978). Thrips on Cassava: economic importance, sources and mechanisms of resistance. *Proc.Cassava Protection Workshop*, *CIAT (COLUMBIA)*:177-180.

Sekhar, P.S. and S. Sekhar (1964). Investigations on thrips occurring on arabica coffee, 1.Bionomics. *Indian Coffee, Bangalore*, 28(8):173-179.

Sekar, P.S. et al., (1965). 'Investigation on thrips of arabica coffee. Coffee arabica L II. Ecological relationships and control of *Scirtothrips sweetmani* Bianchi', *Turrialba*, 15:14.

Selhime, A.C., M.H. Muma and D.W. Clancy (1963). Biological, Chemical and Ecological studies on the predatory thrips *Aleurodothrips fasciapennis* in florida citrus grooves. *Ann.ent.Soc.America,* 56:709-712.

Seshadri, A.R. (1953). Observations on *Trichinothrips brevicops* (Bagnall) a little known predatory thrips from South India. *Indian J.agric.Sci.,* 23:27-39.

Sharga, U.S. (1932). A new nematode. *Tylenchus aptini* n.sp. parasite of Thysanoptera (Insecta: *Aptinothrips rufus* Gmelin). *Parasitology* 24(2):268-79.

Sharga, U.S. (1933). Biology and life history of *Limothrips cerealium* Haliday and *Aptinothrips rufus* Gmelin, feeding on Gramineae. *Ann.Appl.Biol.,* 20:308.

Sharov, A.G. (1972). 'On Phylogenetic relations of the order of Thrips (Thysanoptera). *Rev.d'Ent.URSS.,* 51(4):854.

Simberloff, D.S. (1978). Colonization of islands by insects: Immigration, extinction and diversity. *Roy.Ent.Soc.Symp.,* 9:139-153.

Smith, F.E. (1953). Density dependence in Australian thrips. *Ecology,* 42:403-407.

Smith, J.W. Jr. and R.L. Sams (1977). Economics of thrips-control on peanuts in Texas. *Southwest.Entomol.,* 2(3):149-154.

Sondhi, K.C. (1962). The evolution of a pattern. *Evolution,* 16:186-191.

Soumalaines, E. (1962). Significance of parthenogenesis in the evolution of insects. *Ann.Rev.Ent.,* 7:349-366.

Soute, M. (1971). The variation problem: The gene flow variation hypothesis. *Taxon.,* 20(1):37-50.

Sogawa, K. J(1971). Effects of feeding of brown plant hopper on components of leaf blade of rice plants. *Jap.J.appl.Ent.Zool.,* 15:175-179.

Southwood, T.R.E. (1960). The evolution of insect-tree relationship - a new approach. *XIth Int.Kong.Entomol.Wien.,* 1:651-655.

Southwood, T.R.E. (1961). The number of species of insects associated with various trees. *J.Anim.Ecol.,* 30:7-8.

Southwood, T.R.E. (1962). Migration of terrestrial arthropods in relation to habitat. *Biol.Rev.,* 37:171-214.

Southwood, T.R.E. (1973). *The insect/plant relationships.* John Wiley & Sons, New York.

Southwood, T.R.E. (1975). The dynamics of insect populations in *Insects, Science and Society* (Ed.D.Pimental):151-99, Academic Press, New York.

Southwood, T.R.E. (1967). Bionomic strategies and population parameters. In R.M.May (ed) *Theoretical Ecology,* Blackwell Scientific Publication, Oxford.

Southwood, T.R.E. (1977). The relevance of population dynamics theory to pest status. The Origins of pest, parasite, disease and weed problems (Ed. by J.M.Cherett and G.R.Sagar): 35-54., *Br.Ecol.Soc.Symp.,* No. 18.

Southwood, T.R.E. (1977). Habitat, the templet for ecological strategies, *J.Anim.Ecol.,* 46:337-365.

Southwood, T.R.E., R.M. May, R.M. Russel and G.R. Conway (1974). Ecological strategies and population parameters. *Amer.Natur.,* 108:791-804.

Stannard, L.J. (1957). The phylogeny and classification of the North American genera of the suborder Tubulifera. *Ill.Biol.Monogr.*, 25:1-200.

Stannard, L.J. (1968). The thrips or Thysanoptera of Illinois. *Ill.Nat.His.Surv.Bull.*, 29(4):215-552.

Stannard, L.J. and T.J. Mitri (1962). Preliminary studies on the *Tryphactothrips* complex in which *Anisopilothrips*, *Mesostenothrips* and *Elixothrips* are erected as new genera. *Trans.Am.Entomol.Soc.*, 88:183-224.

Staub, P.F. (1979). Post-embryonic development of the nervous system of *Parthenothrips dracaenae* Heagr. *Rev.Suisse.Zool.*, 86(2):367-394.

Stefanov, D., A. Dimitrov and D. V'zharov (1979). Furadan granules - a soil insecticide against thrips and virus on tobacco. *Rastitelna Zashcita*, 27(3):11-13.

Stiling, P.D. (1980). Host plant specificity, oviposition behaviour and egg parasitism in some leaf hoppers of the genus *Eupteryx* (Hemiptera:Cicadellidae). *Ecol.Ent.*, 5:79-85.

Stoltz, R.L. and V.M. Stern (1978). The longevity and fecundity of *Orius tristicolor* (Het.Anthocoridae) when introduced to increasing numbers of the prey *Frankliniella occidentalis* (Thys:Thripidae). *Environ.Entomol.*, 7(2):197-198.

Stradling, D.I. (1968). Investigations on the natural enemies of the Onion thrips (*Thrips tabaci* Lind.). *Rept.Commonw.Inst.Biol.Control.*

Subba Rao, B.R. (1969). A new species of *Megaphragma* (Hymenoptera: Trichogrammatidae) from India. *Proc.R.ent.Soc.Lond.*, (B) 38(7-8):114-116.

Suman, C.L., S.D. Wahi and N.J. Mohan (1979). Distribution pattern of Onion thrips. *Curr.Sci.*, 49(1):28-29.

Syed, R.A. (1978). Thrips pollination of Oil palm in West Malaysia Rept.10 pp., *Rept.Commonw.Inst.Biol.Control.*

Syed, R.A. (1979). Studies on oil palm pollination by insects. *Bull.Ent.Res.*, 60:213-224.

Takagi, S. (1980). An interpretation of second instar male characters in the systematics of the Diaspididae. *Israel J.Ent.*, 14:99-104.

Takahashi, R. (1938). Monophagy and polyphagy among phytophagous insects: an evolutionary consideration. *Kontyu*, 12:130-39.

Tallamy, D.W. and R.F. Denno (1979). Responses of sap-feeding insects (Homoptera:Hemiptera) to simplification of host plant structure. *Ent.Soc.America*, 8(6):1021-28.

Tanagoshi, L.K., J.Y. Nishio, D.S. Moreno and J. Fargerlund (1980). Effect of temperature on development and survival of *Scirtothrips citri* on citrus foliage. *Anns.Ent.Soc.Amer.*, 73(4):378-281.

Tansky, V.I. (1958). The biology of wheat thrips *Haplothrips tritici* Kurd. (Thysanoptera:Phlaeothripidae) in Northern Kazakhastan and the proposed cultural methods of its control. (in Russian) *Rev.d'ent U.R.S.S.*, 37:785-797.

Taylor, T.A. (1969). On the population dynamics and flight activity of *Taeniothrips sjostedti* (Tryb.). *Bull.Ent.Soc.Nigeria*, 2(1):60-71.

Taylor, T.A. (1974). On the population dynamics of *Taeniothrips sjostedti* (Tryb.) (Thysanoptera:Thripidae) on cowpea and an alternative host *Centrosoma pubescens* Benth, in Nigeria. *Rev.Zool.Afr.*, 88(4):689-701.

Taylor, R.A.J. and L.R. Taylor (1979). A behavioural model for the evolution of spatial dynamics. In *Population dynamics*. Blackwell Scientific Publications, Oxford:1-27.

Thompson, W.R. and F.J. Simmonds (1965). A catalogue of the parasities and predators of insects. *C'wealth Inst.Biol. Control, London,* 183-185.

Titschack, E. (1969). Der *Tarothrips*, ein neues Schadinsekt in Deutschland. *Sonderdr.Anz.Schadlingsk.Pflschutz.,* 42:1-6.

Uzel, H. (1895). *Monographie der Ordnung Thysanoptera.* Koniggratz, 472 pp.

Varadarasan, S. and T.N. Ananthakrishnan (1981). Biological Studies on some Gall-Thrips. *Proc.Indian natn.Sci.Acad.,* B48(1):35-43.

Varadarasan, S. and T.N. Ananthakrishnan (1981). Population dynamics and prey predator/parasite relationships of gall-forming thrips. *Proc.Indian natn.Sci.Acad.,* B47:321-340.

Varley, G.C. (1963). The interpretation of change and stability in insect population. *Proc.R.Ent.Soc.Lond.,* (C):52-57.

Varley, G.C. and G.R. Gradwell (1960). Key factor in population studies. *J.Anim.Ecol.,* 29:399-401.

Vasiliu L. (1976). Biology of Thysanoptera *Bagnalliella yuccae* Hinds 1902 (Thys). *Rev.Roum.biol.Ser.Bio.Anim.,* 21(2):151-154.

Viswanathan, T.R. and T.N. Ananthakrishnan (1974). Population fluctuations of 3 species of anthophilous Thysanoptera in relation to the numerical response of their predator, *Orius minutus* L. (Anthocoridae:Heteroptera). *Curr.Sci.,* 43(1):19-20.

Viswanathan, T.R. and T.N. Ananthakrishnan (1976). Aspects of host preference and succession in thrips infesting *Ruellia tuberosa,* Entomon, 1:71-77.

Vite, J.P. (1956). Populatistudien an larchublasewfuz *Taeniothrips laricivorus* Krat. *Zeit.angew.Entomol.,* 38(4):417-448.

Vuillet, A. (1914). Note sur un Chalcidien parasite du Thrips des pois. *C.R. Soc.Biol.Paris,* 76:552-554.

Walker, W.F. (1974). Responses of selected Thysanoptera to colored surfaces. *Environ.Ent.,* 3(2):295-304.

Ward, L.K. (1966). The biology of Thysanoptera. Ph.D. thesis, London University.

Wardle, R.A. and R. Simpson (1927). The biology of Thysanoptera with reference to the cotton plant. 3. The relation between feeding habits and plant lesions. *Ann.appl.Biol.,* 14:513-528.

Waterston, J. (1923). On an internal parasite of a thrips from Trinidad. *Bull.Ent.Res.,* 13:453-55.

Watson, T.F. (1965). Influence of thrips on cotton yields in Alabama. *J.Econ.Ent.H.,* 58(6):1118-1122.

Watts, J.G. (1936). A study of the biology of the flower thrips *Frankliniella tritici* (Fitch) with special reference to cotton. *Bull.S.Carol.agric.Exp.Stn.,* 306:1-46.

Watts, J.G. (1937). Reduction of cotton yields by thrips. *J.econ.Ent.,* 30(6):860-863.

Watts, J.G. (1965). *Chirothrips falsus* on Black Gamma grass. *Agr.Exp. Sta.Bull.,* 499. New Mexico State Univ. 20 pp.

Weitmeier, H. (1956). Zur Oekologie der Thysanopteren Frankens. *Dt.ent.Z.,* 3:285-330.

Wetzel, T. (1963). Zur Frage der Uberwinterung der Graser-Thysanopteren. *Z.angew.Ent.,* 51:429-441.

Wetzel, T. (1964). Untersuchungen zum Auftreten, zur Schadwirkung und zur Bekampfung von Thysanopteren in Grassamenbestanden. *Beitr.Ent.,* 14:427-500.

Whitham, T.G. (1980). The theory of habitat selection: Examined and extended using *Pemphigus* aphids. *Amer.Nat.*, 115(4):450-466.

Whittaker, R.H. (1962). Classifications of natural communities. *Bot.Rev.*, 28:1-239.

Whittaker, R.H. (1965). Dominance and diversity in land plant communities. *Science*, 147:250-260.

Whittaker, R.H. (1967). Gradient analysis of vegetation. *Biol.Rev.*, 42:207-264.

Wien, H.C. and C. Roesingh (1980). Ethlene evolution by thrips-infested cowpea provides a basis for thrips resistance screening with ethephon sprays. *Nature*, 283(5743):192-914.

Wilde, W.H.A. (1962). A note on colour preferences of some Homoptera and Thysanoptera in British Columbia. *Can.Ent.*, 94:107.

Willaims, C.B. (1944). The index of diversity as applied to ecological problems. *Nature Lond.*, 155:390-1.

Wilson, T.H. (1975). A monograph of the subfamily Panchaetothripinae (Thysanoptera:Thripidae). *Mem.Amer.Ent.Inst.*, 23:1-354.

Wilson, T.H. and T.A. Cooley (1972). A chalcidoid planidium and an entomophilic nematode associated with the western flower thrips. Annals of the Entomological Society of America. 65(2):414-418.

Yakhontov, V.V. (1935). An ally of the cotton grower, the acariphagous thrips (*Scolothrips acariphagus*)Yakh.). *Sots.Nauka Tekh.*, 12:96-98.

Yarwood, C.E. (1943). Association of thrips with powdery mildews. *Mycologia* 35:189-191.

Yokoyama, V.Y. (1977). *Drepanothrips reuteri* on Thompson grapes. *Environ.Ent.*, 6(1):21-24.

Yokoyama, V.Y. (1977). *Frankliniella occidentalis* and scars on table grapes. *Envir.Ent.*, 6(1):25-30.

Zenther-Moller, O. (1965). *Taeniothrips laricivorus* (Krat.) (Thripidae, Thysanoptera) in Danish stands of *Larix decidua* (Mill). *Oikos*, 16:58-69.

Zenther-Moller, O. (1966). Investigations of the biology, geographical distribution and forestry importance of *Taeniothrips laricivorus* Krat. in Denmark 1961-1963. *Det.forst.Forsqsvoesen*, 30:101-166.

Zwolfer, H. (1978). Mechanismen und Ergebnisse der Co-Evolution von rhytophagen und entomophagen Insekten und hoheren Planzen. *Sonderbd.Naturwiss.Ver Hamburg* 2:7-50.

Zur Strassen, R. (1976). Hochmontane *Arisaema*-Asten (Araceae) in Nepal als Wirtspflanzen floricoler fransenfluger. *Senckenbergiana biol.*, 57(1-3):55-59.

---

G. Suresh and Ananthakrishnan, T.N. (1983) have since published "Association of some sporophagous thrips in forest communities with plant pathogenic fungi, with some observations on their natural control agents. *Indian J. For.*, 6(3):196-201.

\* \* \* \* \*

# SUBJECT INDEX

* * * * *

## AUTHOR INDEX

\* \* \* \* \*